FATHERS' FAIR SHARE

FATHERS' FAIR SHARE

Helping Poor Men Manage Child Support and Fatherhood

Earl S. Johnson, Ann Levine, and Fred C. Doolittle

A Manpower Demonstration Research Corporation Study

RUSSELL SAGE FOUNDATION / NEW YORK

362.71
T66f

The Russell Sage Foundation

The Russell Sage Foundation, one of the oldest of America's general purpose foundations, was established in 1907 by Mrs. Margaret Olivia Sage for the "improvement of social and living conditions in the United States." The Foundation seeks to fulfill this mandate by fostering the development and dissemination of knowledge about the country's political, social, and economic problems. While the Foundation endeavors to assure the accuracy and objectivity of each book it publishes, the conclusions and interpretations in Russell Sage Foundation publications are those of the authors and not of the Foundation, its Trustees, or its staff. Publication by Russell Sage, therefore, does not imply Foundation endorsement.

Library of Congress Cataloging-in-Publication Data

Johnson, Earl (Earl S.)
    Fathers' Fair Share: helping poor men manage child support and fatherhood /
    Earl S. Johnson, Ann Levine, and Fred C. Doolittle.
        p.   cm.
    Includes bibliographical references and index.
    ISBN 0-87154-411-3
    1. Child welfare—Government policy—United States.   2. Child support—Government
    policy—United States.   3. Fathers—Services for—United States.   4. Fathers—
    Employment for—United States.   5. Poor men—Services for—United States.
    6. Poor men—employment for—United States.   7. Children of single parents.—United
    States—Economic conditions.   I. Levine, Ann.
    II. Doolittle, Fred C.   III. Title.
    HV741.J63   1999   98-47551
    3627'1—dc21   CIP

The Manpower Demonstration Research Corporation's preparation of this volume was supported by the U.S. Department of Health and Human Services, Pew Charitable Trusts, W. K. Kellogg Foundation, Charles Stewart Mott Foundation, U.S. Department of Agriculture, Annie E. Casey Foundation, U.S. Department of Labor, Smith Richardson Foundation, Ford Foundation, McKnight Foundation, and Northwest Area Foundation. The findings and conclusions presented herein do not necessarily represent the official positions or policies of the funders or the states participating in the Parents' Fair Share Demonstration, which are listed in this document. Interested readers may wish to contact the states for more information on the program.

RUSSELL SAGE FOUNDATION
112 East 64th Street, New York, New York 10021

To our parents

CONTENTS

FOREWORD

This book is about unknown men. More than forty years after Ralph Ellison's (1952) great imaginative evocation of the invisibility of all African Americans and more than thirty years after Elliot Liebow's (1968) classic ethnography of streetcorner men, men like those portrayed here are still seen by most people, if they are noticed at all, through the distorting lenses of stereotyping, scapegoating, and, at best, condescension.

To say that is not to deny that many children with noncustodial fathers could be lifted out of poverty if their fathers provided adequate financial support or that this lack of paternal financial support is not a major social problem. Effective and reasonable child support policies need to be devised and implemented. Despite considerable recent attention by policymakers to this issue, however, we are a long way from having such policies. There are many reasons for this failure. One of the most important is that policy is so poorly informed about the men it seeks to change, especially men like these who have the least ability to provide support. When the policy alternatives are defined on a spectrum that runs from patronizing neglect to tough love to just plain tough, as they have been, it should not be surprising that efforts to force men who have trouble supporting themselves to bail their children out of poverty are not very productive.

A few years ago, Fred Doolittle called me from the Manpower Demonstration Research Corporation (MDRC) to invite me to a meeting with a young researcher named Earl Johnson who had just been hired to do ethnographic research with participants in the Parents' Fair Share program (PFS). Having done qualitative studies with noncustodial fathers and having been involved with MDRC's early efforts to design the program, I looked forward to the meeting with interest and curiosity. Subsequently, I have had many conversations with Earl about his efforts to engage and build rapport with PFS participants and to craft a report on that experience within the context of MDRC. This is not a piece of cookie cutter research, and the results may challenge readers accustomed to program evaluations that follow more standardized formats. Ann Levine, an experienced freelance writer, has helped shape the sometimes sprawling qualitative data. The results are important, though, for reasons that have everything to do with the significance of the problem addressed and the difficulties involved.

The men Earl Johnson followed around for two years play a symbolic role in national policy debates about poverty and social welfare that often has very little to do with the actual fabric of their daily lives. These men are not even typical of nonsupporting fathers. They are the ones at the bottom of the heap: the unemployed, the sporadically employed, the unskilled—some of them saddled with substance abuse problems and criminal records. At a time when many fathers never even make themselves liable to child support orders by establishing paternity, they are the ones hapless enough to establish paternity and then get caught by the child support system for their inability to pay. Yet these men, with their multiple problems, have been the fulcrum of a national debate about personal responsibility that has erased the debate of an earlier era about social responsibility. As the war on the poor has replaced the war on poverty, the truly disadvantaged have become the truly demonized. The discipline of the marketplace seems to be the only panacea taken seriously now, never mind if children are still poor and their fathers even more desperate than before.

For anyone like Earl or myself who has worked with these stigmatized men, there is often a temptation to react to stereotypes of individual personal irresponsibility in the other direction—to delve into the real complexity of these lives and accentuate the positive. Let people know that many of them really care about their children, that being a father is an important, albeit painful, part of their image of themselves. We do frequently find that and it is terribly important to let that be known. If we go too far in that direction, however, we distort it another way. We romanticize. We invite pity, condescension, and neglect. That will not do either because it is just another way of keeping people invisible.

The hard job undertaken in this study is that of the unblinking gaze. It is difficult to look straight at poverty. It is difficult intellectually, morally, and emotionally. The things that you see do not conform to the conceptions of human motivation or capability you start with, no matter how hard you have studied the literature on poverty, no matter how much toughness or compassion you think you bring to the task. The things you see surprise you. You see degradation and defeat. You see humor, resilience, tenderness, and critical awareness. They are all mixed up together, in the most unsettling combinations.

The experience of dealing with such mixed feelings and then trying to produce an orderly account of that experience can be wrenching. People you talk about it with and discuss your drafts with, often friends and colleagues with whom you share a great deal, get upset with your portrayals because they too have difficulty looking at the complexity. People who are sympathetic to what you are trying to accomplish want "clear policy implications," and you want that too, but you paint such an intricate picture. If only clear policy implications were more readily available, from various sources!

The sources of poverty are many, though, and the conditions of poverty genuinely complex. Brisk, crisp policymaking that cannot deal with the myriad of issues is unlikely to get very far. This book is a needed, if sometimes bitter, tonic. Like old-fashioned remedies, it is not laced with sugar. It is certainly not a modern wonder drug, but it provides a perspective that has been missing—reality. Poverty, crime, and out-of-wedlock births have been declining. That is wonderful news, but it is much too early to celebrate the triumph of the dismantling of the welfare state or the perfection of social control. Many people are still struggling. The dangers currently held in abeyance by prosperity may well be poised to crash down on the vulnerable at the turn of a business cycle. Problems that have been long in the making have not disappeared.

There is some credible good news associated with this study. The formal evaluation of the Parents' Fair Share program found that programmatic intervention can increase child support payments. That finding is entirely consistent with the qualitative findings here about program engagement, especially through the peer support groups. Appeals to paternal feeling apparently can work. Surely no one will be saddened to learn that personal responsibility can be propped up by the exercise of social responsibility through creative, painstaking program development and evaluation.

The bad news is that the program did not improve employment. Once again the complementarity of qualitative and quantitative research methods is evident, in the ethnographic documentation of the disappointments of those fathers who took the program at its word but missed the payoff. The sobering message we are left with is that it is becoming an increasingly uphill struggle in the labor market for those without skills and education. Until we devote enough attention to that problem, the sometimes bewildering complexities recounted here will remain.

Recent public policy debates have frequently invoked lack of child support as a cause of poverty. While the limited but solid achievements of PFS are admirable, the problems that are left over should prompt us to realize that poverty is also a cause of lack of child support. Poverty remains concentrated in certain communities, particularly those suffering from a combination of residential and occupational discrimination and a rapidly changing labor market. Fixing child support is not going to fix that situation until child support reform is linked to some larger strategy for addressing this broader context of poverty.

I believe there are social movements to redefine manhood and fatherhood within these communities and that part of PFS's success in engaging participants is linked to this awareness at the community level. I also think further progress is most likely to come from efforts to link social support from the wider society to these strivings at the community level. I cannot as yet point to definitive proof of those propositions, but, if they are ever to be tested, it will require the kind of fine-grained, unblinking scrutiny to be found in this book.

MERCER L. SULLIVAN
Rutgers University
December, 1998

References

Ellison, Ralph. 1952. *Invisible Man*. New York: Random House.

Liebow, Elliott. 1968. *Tally's Corner: A Study of Negro Streetcorner Men*. Boston: Little, Brown, and Co.

ACKNOWLEDGMENTS

This book owes a great deal to those who saw value in its mission and to the individuals who inhabit its pages. We would like to thank the Manpower Demonstration Research Corporation (MDRC) and especially Gordon Berlin, a senior vice-president, for their continued institutional support for conducting qualitative research to improve the knowledge base on low-income individuals. There were many funders who contributed both intellectually and financially to this portion of the Parents' Fair Share (PFS), including Robert Harris of the Office of Child Support Enforcement at the U.S. Department of Health and Human Services (HHS), Linda Mellgren at the Office of the Assistant Secretary for Planning and Evaluation at HHS, Howard Rolston and Mark Fucello at the Administration for Children and Families at HHS, and Ray Uhalde and Roxie Nicholson of the Employment and Training Administration at the U.S. Department of Labor. A very special thank you also goes to Ronald Mincy of the Ford Foundation, whose passionate concern for and interest in low-income noncustodial parents and the fragile families of which they are a part has served as a continuing source of inspiration.

We also wish to recognize those involved in the earlier stages of the Parents' Fair Share demonstration, when support for programs and research on poor noncustodial parents was rare. An initial grant from the Pew Charitable Trusts and the support of Drew Altman (then at Pew) were vital in launching the initiative. Over the course of the demonstration, MDRC and its staff benefited greatly from the assistance of all the funders listed at the end of these acknowledgments. Their farsighted support of this research allowed us to conduct the unusual, in-depth qualitative research on which this book is based.

At MDRC, our thanks in particular go to Judith M. Gueron, president, and to Sharon Rowser, Marilyn Price, Virginia Knox, Maxine Bailey, and the other members of the PFS team who reviewed versions of this document and provided thoughtful comments. We would also like to thank a few people who were at MDRC at the start of this project and whose insights, comments, and encouragement were invaluable to the completion of this book: Dudley Benoit, for his exceptional work in the field and his sharp insights, and Paula LeePoy, Jackie Peters, Joan Johnson, and Cate Taylor for their dogged support and care in providing technical and research assistance. Stephanie Cowell meticulously transcribed many of the early interview tapes. Thanks are also owed to Tamar Perla, a friend, transcriber, and ray of hope when times were gray.

Many thanks go to the Russell Sage Foundation, specifically Eric Wanner, the foundation's president, and David Haproff, its director of publications, and their fine editorial and production staff for their support and effort in publishing this book.

There are other persons who were important in helping this book become a reality. We are deeply grateful for the encouragement and intellectual support unselfishly given by professors Mercer Sullivan, Thomas Weisner, Carol Stack, and Waldo Johnson. There were also people in the field who not only made this project a reality but also created safe places for noncustodial parents. Their contribution to the book and to the PFS effort cannot go unrecognized: Larry Jackson, Ray Jackson, Vernon Washington, Antoine Voss, Geraldo Rodriguez, Chuck Adams, Derrick Smith, Linda Jenkins, Paul Bryant, Nussan Mohamad, and the many other staff members who opened their programs and hearts to us.

There is also a special group of people to whom this project owes everything: the noncustodial parents who allowed us into their lives. It is a great regret that this forum does not allow for a personal thanks to each and every one of you, your friends, and your families. Due to the promise of anonymity, it is necessary to thank you as a group, but your individual contributions to this project are greatly appreciated and we wish you and your families well.

Finally, we would like to thank our families. Without constant support, love, and belief in us and the value of the project during the days in the field and in front of the computer, this book would never have been completed.

The Parents' Fair Share demonstration was supported by the U.S. Department of Health and Human Services, Pew Charitable Trusts, W. K. Kellogg Foundation, Charles Stewart Mott Foundation, U.S. Department of Agriculture, Annie E. Casey Foundation, U.S. Department of Labor, Smith Richardson Foundation, Ford Foundation, McKnight Foundation, and Northwest Area Foundation.

The findings and conclusions presented in this book do not necessarily represent the official positions or policies of the funders, the participating parties, or MDRC.

EARL S. JOHNSON
ANN LEVINE
FRED C. DOOLITTLE

Chapter 1

INTRODUCTION

To walk in another person's shoes is to experience life as one would never experience it otherwise. This book introduces readers to men who, for various reasons, were unable to meet their child support obligations and consequently agreed to participate in a program called Parents' Fair Share (PFS). The book introduces men like Geraldo and Jah, who looked to the program as an opportunity to enter a labor market that seemed ominous and impenetrable, and like Mack, whose guarded and suspicious approach toward the child support system masked an underlying fear—based on his experience with other public agencies—of being turned away or treated with disrespect. Young and old men of color discuss how they were looking for a chance to change and expand their options and, by becoming more involved in their children's lives, for a chance to improve the next generation's prospects. The book also introduces men whose greatest concern was to survive another day and who saw child support and PFS as two more obstacles to success.

This book seeks to provide insights into the lives, experiences, and perspectives of thirty-two men who participated in Parents' Fair Share, a national research and demonstration project organized by the Manpower Demonstration Research Corporation. All of these men were low-income, noncustodial fathers who had not been paying court-mandated child support and whose children were (or had been) receiving Aid to Families with Dependent Children (AFDC, commonly known as welfare). Most were African American or Latino and lived in inner city, low-income neighborhoods. When they entered PFS, they were unemployed, underemployed, or "hustling," a concept examined in this book. Parents' Fair Share was designed to help such men get a better job than they could get on their own, pay child support, and become more involved with their children.

As noncustodial parents of poor children, these men found themselves enmeshed in two public programs that were, and still are, under great stress and in the midst of major reform: welfare and child support enforcement. For more than sixty years, AFDC gave cash assistance to poor mothers with underage children, forming the cornerstone of U.S. poverty programs. Until the mid-1970s, when federal involvement increased, child support enforcement was largely a concern of state and local government, governed by state statutes and case law and varying widely in procedures and the attention it received.

By the 1970s, AFDC had lost broad public support, and major reforms were frequently proposed (for a review of these criticisms and reform efforts, see Murray 1984 and Blank 1997). AFDC was blamed for undermining the work ethic of mothers because it provided cash assistance (albeit at low levels in most states) and in-kind support (health insurance, food stamps) and its program rules created a strong financial disincentive to work. AFDC was also held responsible for the breakup of families (and family values). Because access to the program was more difficult (or, in some states, impossible) for families with both parents living in the home, welfare allegedly acted as a disincentive for couples to get married and/or stay married. Further, some critics of the program charged that the provision of assistance shifted the responsibility for supporting children from parents to taxpayers and that the existing level of enforcement was not sufficient to force noncustodial parents to contribute financially to their children. Finally, at various times during the past twenty-five years, critics focused on "welfare dependency" or welfare as an alleged "way of life," especially for minority women and children living in inner-city ghettos. Although these criticisms were not supported by strong research evidence, they formed a central part of the public debate about poor families and the reform of welfare and child support.

Pressure for welfare reform intensified during the past three decades. Congress enacted into law major increases in federal involvement in child support in the 1970s and 1980s and passed the Family Support Act of 1988, which—most relevant for noncustodial parents—required states to add new enforcement tools to their child support repertoire and to meet federal standards of enforcement. In

1996, these pressures culminated in passage of new federal welfare and child support legislation (the Personal Responsibility and Work Reconciliation Act of 1996, P.L. 104-193), which replaced AFDC with Temporary Aid to Needy Families (TANF), imposed time limits on the period of time families can receive federal income support, and called for stricter child support enforcement. The goal of these new policies was to get *families* off welfare by encouraging or requiring both parents to support their children. If states strictly implement the federal time limits on aid, the payment of benefits eventually will stop. Dramatically increasing support from fathers is more difficult to achieve, leading to efforts like PFS, which sought to find new ways to increase child support payments by poor men.

As the number of never-married, separated, or divorced mothers has grown—at all socioeconomic levels and in many racial groups—so has recognition that many noncustodial fathers do not meet their socially and legally defined parental obligations (financial and otherwise). Enforcing child support, which usually means collecting money from fathers, thus has strong bipartisan support. In the public mind, this need for child support enforcement is often linked to the notion that noncustodial fathers have "dropped out" of their parental roles and the lives of their children. Thus at a 1995 hearing, Eleanor Holmes Norton, a liberal African American female, and Pete Wilson, a conservative white male, both stood up and said that "Fatherlessness is the [number] one problem in the United States of America" (from Blankenhorn 1995, quoted in Tamar Lewin, "Creating Fathers Out of Men with Children," *New York Times*, June 18, 1995; Johnson and Doolittle 1996). In the public debate, this focus on "father failure" has led to use of the term "deadbeat dad" to describe a class of men who are not meeting their parental obligations. As this book shows, the reality is much more complex.

Although the need for better child support enforcement has often formed part of the welfare reform debate, little of the research on "absent fathers" has focused on the full range of topics relevant to low-income children. Much of the research has looked at fathers who are *able but unwilling* to pay child support regularly, either at all or at the level ordered in family court or agreed to by the parents. Very little is known about the significant subset of noncustodial fathers whose children are receiving welfare. These fathers are chronically unemployed or underemployed, have unstable housing and possibly no real permanent residence, possess few or no assets, yet nevertheless have little contact with the public institutions intended to serve as a social safety net—the employment training, welfare, and social insurance systems. For these parents, the issue is often inability—not unwillingness—to pay court-mandated child support.

A second gap in the literature is research linking information on child support for children receiving welfare to information on the labor market prospects and the persistence of racial discrimination in the labor market for low-income men with few educational credentials or marketable skills. Much has been written about the striking decline in the earnings of men without high school credentials over the past three decades (especially relevant here is work by Wilson 1987, 1996; Holzer 1996; Levy and Murnane 1992; and Sullivan 1993). Other work documents the perpetuation of employment discrimination, especially against men of color (see Kirschenman and Neckerman 1991). This body of work makes the important argument that these dismal labor market prospects have important social implications in low-income neighborhoods, including discouraging the formation or undermining the stability of two-parent families (Wilson's work is especially important here). But there is little research exploring the implications of these trends for child support (and the research that does exist focuses largely on young, unwed fathers; see, for example, Lerman and Ooms 1993; Sullivan 1993; and Furstenburg, Sherwood, and Sullivan 1992).

Low-income noncustodial fathers have long been ignored by both social policymakers and social scientists. The very structure of welfare was based on their *absence;* in the vast literature on welfare, they appear only as background statistics. Much has been written about "fatherless children," but all children have fathers somewhere, fathers who call and visit regularly, occasionally, or not at all; fathers who appear in the conversations of other adults and the imaginations of children. Likewise, children form part of their father's identity, even during long separations with no contact. Yet virtually nothing has been written about "fathers without children" (in Liebow's phrase; Liebow 1968). Until recently in the social policy world, low-income noncustodial fathers were largely written off as unreachable (Watson 1992).

Not only are fathers of children on welfare missing from research and poverty programs, they also are almost universally stigmatized. Widely viewed as uncaring and irresponsible (as well as possibly dangerous and predatory), they come to public attention only when they commit crimes (confirming the stereotype) or when they become visibly homeless (evoking mixed emotions). Almost by definition, they rank among the "undeserving" poor who are outside the coverage of most income support programs. The one cash assistance program available to men living apart from their children—general assistance—is gradually disappearing from the national scene. Although not direct beneficiaries of AFDC or TANF, these men are cast as villains in the welfare drama. Ironically, poor men who manage to scrape by, who do not live on the streets, and who do not get arrested, receive the least attention.

In real life, many low-income noncustodial parents inhabit the social and economic margins of society. For most purposes, their identity as fathers is largely invisible. But given the changing world of public assistance, the time has come to hear their stories—how they manage, with varying degrees of success, to cope with poverty and fatherhood. Their stories should be listened to with equal interest as is given to those of the custodial parent, for they are the other side of the world of poverty and the other half of the welfare equation. If we are to confront poverty, especially in the context of time limits on public assistance, it is a mistake to dismiss half the population of poor adults.

One possible explanation for social scientists' lack of attention to poor noncustodial fathers is that the men themselves avoid anyone associated with authority and officialdom, are difficult to identify or locate, and, when contacted, are reluctant to talk about their personal lives. This last point is one of a number of preconceptions about low-income noncustodial parents that this book challenges. All of the fathers interviewed participated in the Parents' Fair Share program and agreed to discuss their experiences, on their own volition.

BACKGROUND AND PURPOSE OF THE PARENTS' FAIR SHARE DEMONSTRATION

The purposes of PFS are complex and fraught with potential contradictions, as illustrated by the effort by one noncustodial parent to describe the goals of the program:

> What I think the purpose of the program is? The purpose of the program is to find you a job so you can be a better father to your kid, so you can be able to pay this child support. I figure it like that because

you can come into this program through the courts, right? And when the courts allow you, when you get into this program, the courts are trying to say they want you to pay this support, they don't care how much money you make, and to take care of your family or nothing, that's irrelevant. What they're trying to do is get you a better job so you can pay this child support. That's the big main factor. The main job ain't to find you a better job to take care of your family and children. That ain't it. The main objective is to pay child support. So that's what I think this program is based on, is to help you find a better job for you to pay child support and they say have a little extra for yourself.

[Jah, Nov. 11, 1994]

The Parents' Fair Share demonstration grew out of the Family Support Act of 1988, which added two initiatives to the then existing AFDC agenda: the Job Opportunities and Basic Skills Training (JOBS) Program for AFDC recipients and a mandate for stronger child support enforcement. In addition, the act authorized five states (later increased to seven) to create pilot programs offering unemployed noncustodial parents (NCPs) the same employment and job training opportunities offered AFDC recipients through JOBS.[1] The demonstration services were limited to NCPs whose children were receiving or had received welfare and who were "unemployed or underemployed and unable to meet their child support obligation."[2] The legislation further stated that any services for NCPs must be evaluated. The Parents' Fair Share program was conceived and implemented by the Manpower Demonstration Research Corporation as a response to this legislative provision.

After a series of focus groups and small-scale tests, in 1992 PFS pilot programs were opened at Grand Rapids, Michigan; Jacksonville, Florida; Memphis, Tennessee; Springfield, Massachusetts; Dayton, Ohio; and Trenton, New Jersey.[3] Los Angeles, California, joined the project in late 1994 (for details of the pilot phase of the project, see Bloom and Sherwood 1994). The agencies involved at the local level included county child support agencies, local employment and training organizations, and providers of mediation and peer support services. In late 1994, the project moved to a full-scale demonstration, with analyses of program implementation, impacts on key outcomes, and benefits and costs.

PFS was designed to increase low-income NCPs' employment, earnings, and ability to pay child support and possibly to help them establish or reestablish contact with their children.[4] In general, NCPs were referred to the program by the courts and were required to participate through a process described in the next section of this chapter. Program services can be grouped into four main components:

- Peer support groups, scheduled meetings in which the NCPs and trained facilitators discussed issues related to parenting, relationships, communication, racism, and other themes (see appendix C for a description of the sessions);

- A menu of employment and training services including job search assistance, on-the-job training, education, and skills training;

- Enhanced child support enforcement, including a temporary reduction or adjustment of the NCP's child support order so that he could participate in the program, plus closer monitoring of his status so that the order could be rescinded when he found a job or stopped meeting program requirements;

- An offer of voluntary formal mediation of disputes between custodial and noncustodial parents.

Other goals emerged as potential participants in Parents' Fair Share voiced their expectations of the program. It is important to lay these very real hopes and expectations side-by-side with the objectives of the program to see if the administrators of PFS understood or shared the vision of the persons the intervention was designed to assist. The four objectives voiced most often by participants were:

- Finding meaningful and stable work,

- Getting some stability in their lives so that they could start living as opposed to just surviving (finding work so that they could get their own apartments and gain some independence),

- Understanding how the child support system worked,

- Keeping the child support system from further interfering in their lives.

This book explores the challenge of meeting these expectations by the program, the participant, or a combination of both working together. It also shows that, although some of the program's expectations of participants and participants' expectations of the

program and of themselves coincided, in fact they were often interpreted as dissimilar or even opposing (chapter 6 takes a closer look
at this issue).

THE PROCESS OF REFERRAL TO PFS AND THE NATURE
OF THE SAMPLE

The qualitative data in this book came from a sample of thirty-two
noncustodial parents who participated in at least one PFS service.
Participants in PFS were *not* a random sample of the target population, which consisted of all unemployed or underemployed noncustodial fathers in the research areas whose children were receiving
AFDC benefits and who were not paying formal child support.[5]
Rather they were funneled toward the program through a selection
process that was part coercion (in the form of court orders) and part
individual choice (see figure 1.1). Although legally required to cooperate with the child support enforcement system, most low-income
NCPs can evade this system at least some of the time if they wish.

The process of enforcing child support and of selecting participants
for PFS began with AFDC. A 1975 amendment to the Social Security
Act requires applicants for AFDC to assign their rights to child support to the AFDC system and to cooperate in identifying and locating
the noncustodial parent, establishing paternity, and enforcing child
support obligations. When an NCP of a child receiving welfare makes
formal child support payments, only the first $50 paid each month
goes to his children; the remainder goes to the state and federal
government as partial or full reimbursement for public assistance
provided the family.[6] This disbursement of child support payments
poses serious dilemmas for parents, as discussed in more detail in
chapter 4. In theory, the NCP can provide more support for his children outside the formal system. However, to the extent that he avoids
formal child support, he is incurring a growing legal obligation.

The custodial parent, usually the mother, also faces a dilemma.
Mothers are required to cooperate with child support enforcement
(CSE) as a condition for receiving AFDC benefits.[7] Within the families in the sample for this book, however, some mothers were reluctant to cooperate in enforcing formal child support, especially if they
were receiving informal assistance from the father (which he might
discontinue if she cooperated) or were secretly living with the father
(in which case AFDC benefits might be terminated). The penalty for

Figure 1.1   The PFS Qualitative Participant's Funnel

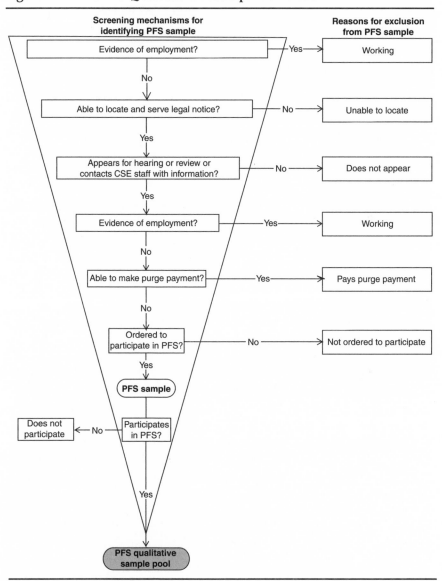

not cooperating is substantial: if caught, she stands to lose all or part of her AFDC grant. But this is a risk many AFDC recipients linked to the NCPs apparently take by providing incomplete or outdated information to the child support agency.

NCPs can accumulate "past due" child support (usually known as arrearages) in two ways. Prior to the establishment of a formal child support order, NCPs can be obligated to repay all public assistance and Medicaid expenditures for the children and custodial parent. For example, if paternity is established after a birth where medical expenses were covered by Medicaid, the NCP can be hundreds of dollars in arrears on his payments at the point when an initial child support order is issued. Once a child support order is in place (which caps the NCP's monthly obligation), the NCP must begin meeting his monthly obligation or fall further behind. For the fathers referred to PFS, these arrearages often amounted to several thousands and, in extreme cases, tens of thousands of dollars.

Tables 1.1 and 1.2 offer an inside view of the range of income and expenditures for NCPs in this study. Table 1.1 highlights the reported aggregate incomes and expenses of NCPs. These participants were not earning large amounts of money on a monthly basis; in fact, during the course of this study, most claimed to make less than $1,000 a month, with rent and food alone consuming a substantial portion of their limited income.

In addition, other expenses were important to the participants' general health, well-being, and survival. NCPs in this study could not always make consistent payments toward utility bills, transportation, and other expenses, and it was not unusual for a participant to lose access to the telephone or have his gas and electricity turned off because he fell a few months behind in his bills. The additional fees that utility companies require in order to reinstate such services often contributed to the seemingly insurmountable financial burdens of participants. Even so, for some NCPs, paying these expenses often took precedence over paying child support. Table 1.1 also shows the amount of modified/PFS-adjusted child support that participants were required to pay each month, and this information can be contrasted with the estimated range of arrearages that NCPs were expected to pay in full to the state (in table 1.2).

State and local child support agencies seek to locate and enforce the obligation of NCPs who fall behind in their payments. Typically, the child support agency initiates a search to locate the father or his

Table 1.1 Range of Monthly Income and Expenditures of Participants in the Parents' Fair Share Program from the Qualitative Research Sample (U.S. Dollars)

Site	Income			Expenses			
	Reported Income from Work[a]	Income from Other Sources	Public Assistance[b]	Rent	Food	Child Support	Other Expenses[c]
Memphis	390[d]–1,000	0	0–119	0–450	90–400	50	100–320
Dayton	500	100	0–119	0–400	100–350	100	100–250
Grand Rapids	360–760	100–500	0–119	200–450	150–500	56	300–400
Trenton	50–800	150	0–338	0–450	300–400	0	300–500
Los Angeles	150–1,000	100	0–338	100–650	100–400	50	100–400

Source: Data based on reported income and expenditures from the month of November 1995.

[a] From employment where income is reported.

[b] Includes food stamps and general assistance or general relief, depending on the location of the participant.

[c] Includes personal items such as toiletries, support for relatives and other family members, utilities, transportation costs (public transit and personal car expenses when there is a car involved), expenses for children outside the realm of child support (if they have contact with them), fines, personally accrued debts, recreation (cigarettes, alcohol, movies, video), and medical and emergency expenditures.

[d] Based on an hourly wage of $6.50 working part time at fifteen hours a week in warehouse, maintenance, general work, and convenience store work. Men often have to work part time for anywhere from a month to four months before they become eligible for a full-time position.

Table 1.2 One Month Income, Expenditure, and Debt for Four PFS Participants (U.S. Dollars)

| Name | Site | Income | | | | | | Expense | | | |
| | | Assistance | | | | | | | | | |
		Reported and Unreported Income	General Relief or General Assistance	Food Stamps	Unemploy-ment Insurance	Housing	Other Sources	Rent	Food and Other Expenses	Child Support Owed	Long-term Debt (Arrearages)
Viceroy	Grand Rapids	760	0	0	425	Yes	Some from father	300	420	250	500–1,000
Fila-G	Memphis	200–400	0	119	0	No	None	0[a]	600	600	35,000
Jah	Trenton	0	100	119	0	Yes	Small amount	450	0[b]	50	10,000
Arron	Los Angeles	220[c]	0	0	0	No	None	350	450–500	100	5,000

Source: MDRC calculations from the Parents' Fair Share qualitative research sample.
[a] Living rent free.
[b] No reported food or other expenses for this particular month due to incarceration.
[c] Amount received when working as a temporary employee.

employer and to secure payment of the order. With limited budgets and caseloads of 500 or more, child support staff typically work at their desks, looking for NCPs in computer databases (for details on CSE procedures, see Doolittle and Lynn 1998). Fathers with regular income and financial assets are usually easier to locate than their low-income counterparts through income and tax records, banks, credit bureaus, motor vehicle departments, and the like. If an NCP with children on welfare is working regularly at a legitimate job and his name appears in official records, CSE staff issue an income deduction order and support payments are garnished from his paycheck.

When there is no evidence that an NCP is employed, CSE staff attempt to serve a legal notice requiring him to appear in court or at the administrative agency for a hearing or review on nonpayment of support. Locating low-income NCPs can be difficult because they are relatively mobile and not always available to be "on call." Often, they work off and on, stay with friends or family, move frequently, do not have phone numbers or bank accounts, and do not leave a clear paper (or electronic) trail. Due to time lags in reporting and recording, by the time information appears in official records, many poor NCPs have moved on. Estimates from two PFS sites suggest that about one-fifth of NCPs who otherwise were eligible for participation in PFS could not be located by the CSE agency (this and subsequent figures on appearance rates are from Doolittle and Lynn 1998).

Of those who are served hearing notices, only some respond.[8] In the PFS sites, the appearance rate ranged from 10 to 70 percent depending on factors such as the nature of the notice and efforts made to encourage NCPs to appear. A substantial proportion of those who did appear or who contacted the child support agency—in some PFS sites as many as one-fourth—admitted to previously unreported employment, and an income deduction order was issued. A smaller percentage provided evidence that they were disabled, reunited with the other parent, or otherwise did not meet the criteria for PFS. Some were able to pay all or most of their arrearage through "purge payments."[9] Only those who were unemployed and unable to reduce or eliminate their accumulated support arrearage were eligible for PFS.

Through a lottery-type process, members of this pool of NCPs were randomly assigned to either a program or a control group. NCPs in the control group were subject to normal enforcement practices. NCPs in the program group went before a judge or hearing officer and, in most cases, were ordered into the PFS program. About one-third of these NCPs never appeared at the PFS site (possibly because they had an unreported job during program hours). The remaining two-thirds participated in some PFS activities. The sample for this study was drawn from program participants.

In comparing the findings of this book to other work on noncustodial parents, it is important to keep this selection process in mind. On the one hand, the child support enforcement system locates fathers who are working but not reporting their income. This means that the sample was likely to be *more disadvantaged* than the average NCP whose children were on welfare. On the other hand, many NCPs elude the CSE system—and the PFS program—by moving farther outside the mainstream economy. Not anchored to a steady job or permanent address, a low-income NCP who wants to disappear usually can. This suggests that participants were *more highly motivated* than some other noncustodial parents to find ways to improve their earnings and pay support. For various reasons, they wanted to change their current circumstances. They chose to appear in court, and when ordered into PFS, they chose to participate, even if briefly. Although there is no single explanation for their motivation, the threat of jail or the hope of employment are two reasons why these individuals appeared at the court's child support review.

Despite the substantial drop-off on the continuum from the overall child support caseload to referral to PFS, the attitudes, behavior, and experiences of the sample for this book and the larger PFS study are of clear policy relevance. These men represent the type of noncustodial parent who apparently is unable to pay child support for lack of income. Programs emerging now to serve low-income noncustodial parents can use the insights from this book to understand the needs of these parents and the challenges of serving them in a program like Parents' Fair Share.

THIS RESEARCH

This book is based on semistructured interviews, informal conversations, and observations made between February 1994 and August 1996 with thirty-two noncustodial parents who participated in the Parents' Fair Share program. These men were selected because they met the requirements of the program and were present when the researcher was either at court or at a peer support or job club/job search session or were recommended by a friend, administrator, or program staff member. Many more NCPs were interviewed and observed; however, the thirty-two men included in this book had at least three or more contacts and observations either in a program component or through outside interviews (see appendix A on methodology).

Also, it should be kept in mind that these individuals made their own choices and decided and will continue to decide for themselves how to live their lives. The reader may not understand, like, or empathize with the individuals or experiences presented in the following pages. Yet their experiences offer insight into issues of child support, welfare, parenting, and the social and economic conditions faced by low-income noncustodial parents, as these relate to their personal life experiences.

OTHER PFS FINDINGS

This research constitutes part of a larger analysis of PFS that includes a study of the effect of the program on the employment, child support payments, and parenting behavior of a large sample of noncustodial parents. Interim findings from other parts of the research suggest that PFS increased the payments to the child support agency but had limited effects on parents' employment in mainstream jobs covered under the unemployment insurance system. Findings on parenting behavior and based on longer follow-up were not available at the time of this writing. This research—in addition to offering an important piece of research on low-income families—complements the other PFS findings. Much of the other PFS research rests on interviews with program staff, observation of activities, or examination of administrative records. This aspect of the research is designed to provide a view—from the perspective of the noncustodial parents—of the program and how it relates to the larger world in which they live.

THE GOALS AND STRUCTURE OF THIS BOOK

In the next six chapters, participants offer their opinions of and reactions to Parents' Fair Share and discuss whether the program helped them to become consistent child support–paying fathers. They also talk about their lives outside of PFS. They try to articulate the obstacles they encountered in becoming active parents while being "absent fathers." They describe the world in which they live and how that world looks to them, and they talk about their desires and efforts to "get their act together" and be connected parents. Their stories—in their words—offer a glimpse into a corner of society that has long been in the shadows, challenging many stereotypes about low-income men.

This picture is complicated by the situations and life stories of the men themselves, the viewpoints and emotions of the general public concerning the issues of welfare and child support, and the challenge of helping poor men to meet substantial, long-term financial obligations that appear, and are, daunting. This book attempts to shed light on three particular areas that have received scant attention in order to understand how a social intervention like PFS can better assist poor men in meeting their child support obligations and becoming active fathers, when possible.

Three questions guided this research:

1. Who are the men who chose to participate in Parents' Fair Share, and what do they tell us about the lives of low-income noncustodial parents and the challenges of designing and operating programs to serve them?

2. Why was participation in the program important to these men, and what did the program offer them?

3. What were the accomplishments and setbacks of NCPs throughout their involvement in PFS, and what expectations should public policymakers and administrators have about the types of change that can occur in a program such as PFS?

The answers to these questions highlight the challenges ahead for policymakers as they try to develop policies and programs that address the issues of poverty in the United States.

Chapter 2 introduces the men in this book by recounting the major themes in their lives, their views of the world, and some of their thoughts about child support. Chapter 3 places the research and the sample within an environmental context and details the NCPs' economic situations, social positions, and relationships. It attempts to show how the opportunities and resources available to these men, filtered through their personal perceptions of possibilities, shape the choices they make regarding themselves and their children. Chapter 4 presents their views of the child support enforcement system. Chapters 5 and 6 present their observations of the strengths and weaknesses of the PFS program and introduce the programmatic portion of PFS. Chapter 5 discusses the peer support component, while chapter 6 describes the employment training and mediation components. Chapter 7 examines the types of changes made by men in the sample and presents qualitative outcomes grouped into four categories of experience. It closes with a discussion of recommendations that may be of assistance to both this and similar programs and their participants.

Chapter 2

THE PARTICIPANTS

Noncustodial fathers of children who receive welfare have long been neglected in studies of poverty and debates over public assistance. This qualitative study was designed to help fill that gap, not to prove or disprove specific hypotheses or to test a set of assumptions. Rather, the goal was to learn about thirty-two men, a small sample of the more than 5,500 noncustodial parents who participated in the Parents' Fair Share demonstration. By listening to, observing, and interacting with these men, we hoped to better understand the challenges they faced and the choices they made. Whether their experiences and attitudes reflect those of other poor noncustodial fathers who participated in PFS at the same or different locations, or to low-income fathers generally, is a subject for future research.

CHARACTERISTICS OF THE SAMPLE

Table 2.1 presents a demographic profile of the noncustodial parents interviewed for this book and of the full PFS demonstration sample. The majority of the participants (twenty-four) were African American, three were Latino, and five were non-Latino white. At the beginning of the study, participants ranged in age from nineteen to fifty-one (averaging thirty-two years). More than half (53 percent) had never been married, 9 percent were currently married and living with their spouse, 34 percent were divorced, and 3 percent fell into another status (widowed). Sixty-one percent had a high school diploma or a general equivalency diploma (GED). Although virtually all had prior work experience (93 percent), less than one in five was employed when first contacted, and only 28 percent had worked

Table 2.1   Demographic Characteristics of Participants in Parents' Fair Share at Entry into the Program

Characteristics	Qualitative Research Sample	Full PFS Demonstration
Average age of participant (years)	32.0	30.9
Average number of own children	2.4	2.5
Current marital status (percent)		
Never married	53.1	60.3
Married or living with partner	9.4	11.1
Divorced	34.4	15.2
Other	3.1	13.3
Living arrangements (percent)		
Living alone	34.4	9.9
Ethnicity or race (percent)		
African American	75.0	62.6
White	15.6	15.7
Latino	9.4	19.8
Other	0.0	1.9
Received high school diploma or GED (percent)	61.0	52.0
Receiving public assistance (percent)	25.0[a]	26[b]
Ever employed (percent)	93.3	97.8
Currently employed[c] (percent)	18.7	18.2
Ever arrested since age sixteen[d] (percent)	100.0	68.3
Sample size	32	5,584

Source: MDRC calculations from the Parents' Fair Share program.
[a] Refers to food stamps only for demonstration sample.
[b] Includes all types of public assistance (food stamps, housing assistance, general relief, general assistance).
[c] Refers to work status at the time of initial contact with the program.
[d] Refers to any arrests not related to child support.

full time at any point in the prior year (this information is not included in the table). Despite lack of earnings, only 25 percent were receiving any kind of public assistance when first contacted (primarily food stamps or general assistance). Every man in the sample had been arrested for something other than nonpayment of child support between his sixteenth birthday and our first contact. All had unmet financial obligations to the child support enforcement agency, had appeared in court for a hearing related to child support, and had been assigned to the PFS program. In many respects, participants in this study resembled those in the larger PFS research sample.

Each of the thirty-two noncustodial fathers in this qualitative sample brought his own personal history and dilemmas, and each followed his own trajectory (see table I.1 in appendix I for brief profiles of individual participants). Yet as the men themselves discovered in peer support groups (discussed in chapter 5), they had much in common. In this chapter, we look at the similarities and differences in their life experiences.

BEING POOR

> I can't get no money.
>
> > [Lover, May 1996]

Not having enough money to survive day-to-day, much less meet child support obligations, was a constant, inescapable problem. Nearly all of the participants lived on or near the edge of absolute poverty. Often they found themselves penniless, without enough money to pay bus fare to get to a job or a job interview, to make a phone call, or to use a Laundromat. The immediate problems of daily survival consumed what little money they had. Paying bills, putting food on the table, giving their children or their mother a little extra cash, and borrowing or repaying loans were a constant juggling act.

> Do I buy clothes to go on an interview? Do I take a bus to go to do the interview? Or do I hold onto the money to buy something to eat and have enough left over to chip in for my housing?
>
> > [Geraldo 1995]

Lack of money made it difficult to pursue job leads and, when they did find a job, to get to work in the week(s) before they received their first paycheck. Fila-G wrote this letter after receiving a small monetary gift from the program:[1]

> Thank you . . . [T]his was truly God sent. [U]pon checking mailbox, I was thinking where was I going to get $2.50 to get to work the next day . . . I just started working with Sears, through a temp service. [Y]ou know me, I talked my way in after finding out they needed some full-time help, spent my last money Friday on the bus, was told to return Sat[urday]. Open letter. [T]his will take me through the week till my first payday.
>
> > [Fila-G, July 1996, excerpt; some punctuation added]

At one point or another, almost all the men in the sample faced situations where their jobs (potential or actual) and personal well-being hinged on a few quarters or a couple of dollars. "Spare change" was not part of their financial vocabulary.

As a result, the men in this sample were vulnerable to the slightest fluctuation in their income or in the marketplace. A decision by the Los Angeles Transit Authority to raise bus fares a mere twenty-five cents caused a dilemma for Geraldo, who relied on buses as his sole means of transportation and often rode several buses each day to cover the various legs of his journeys to school and the PFS program. The fare increases forced him to weigh the value of spending the last of his $212 in general relief to get to a job interview against paying something for child support and for rent. He considered cashing out his food stamps for about two-thirds of their full market value. Otherwise, he did not see how he could afford to continue participating in PFS, buy food, and pay rent. Meanwhile, PFS program staff and instructors probably wondered why he had problems showing up for scheduled meetings and completing assignments.

Poverty complicated the men's relations with their children. Claudio's only steady income came from a part-time job as a recreation aide that paid between $140 and $150 a month, most of which went for child support. A forty-year-old Latino father of three, Claudio was estranged from the mother of his children and lived with another woman who had children of her own. When he could, he worked on the side to help her with household expenses and have a little something for himself. But often he did not earn enough to buy his children the things they wanted and needed, such as sports equipment. Lack of money (and pride) sometimes kept him away from them for weeks or months at a time.

> I'm doing some side jobs, doing something that I'm not supposed to be doing, working and making money . . . [But] I'm hurting sometimes because I can't see my kids because I can't give them what they want.
>
> [Claudio, December 5, 1995]

Repeated week after week, month after month, and sometimes endured for years, worrying about how to get from one day to the next took a toll. Jonesy, a forty-one-year-old African American father of three, came into the program to get his life back. A high school graduate and a veteran, Jonesy had made several unsuccessful attempts to run his own business in Los Angeles. Unemployed for almost two years and under pressure from the CSE agency, Jonesy was on the verge of losing everything—his apartment, his car, his independence, his dignity. With no money and no job, he faced homelessness. He feared for his family. Jonesy looked to the program to help him not only find work but also regain his self-confidence. Jonesy later left the program and disappeared somewhere in Los Angeles.

All of the NCPs in the study talked about how the stresses of poverty dominated their lives, interfering with their ability to plan ahead and follow through.

The precarious financial situation of participants was reflected in their living arrangements. At the time of our initial meeting, ten (31 percent) were living with a relative, often their mother. Like others, Nelson, who had been unemployed for more than three years when the research began, was fortunate to have a mother who had the space and means to help him. Nelson's mother allowed him to live in her home, but with certain restrictions, such as limited use of the telephone. This made it difficult for Nelson to "network" and "job search" but gave him a roof over his head and enabled him to stay connected to his immediate and extended family.

Fourteen (44 percent) of the NCPs were living with a spouse or girlfriend. During the more than three years when Trane was unable to find steady work, he lived with his longtime girlfriend, who supported him financially and encouraged him to keep in contact with two of his children from a previous marriage. Without her help, Trane might have lost contact with these children and ended up either homeless or back in his parents' home (a situation he wanted to avoid).

The other members of the sample lived on their own or moved between various household settings. In some ways, these men were more independent, but this did not necessarily mean that they were autonomous or better off. In fact, their living arrangements were more tentative and conditional. For these men, becoming homeless was an ever-present danger, and moving was part of everyday survival. Only a few men in this sample had been homeless for long periods. Few saw themselves as homeless or identified with others for whom homelessness had become a way of life (Snow and Anderson 1993). Yet a number spent days or weeks sleeping in their cars, on the street, or in the woods or juggling short-term options.

Jasper, a thirty-seven-year-old African American father of one, was without a regular living space when he entered PFS and remained so throughout the study. A recovering substance abuser, Jasper was intelligent, hardworking (when he could find work), and independent. He drove through a Grand Rapids blizzard to meet with the interviewer at a local restaurant, showing up with his car (which he no longer owns) filled with all his belongings. After dinner and a nearly two-hour-long conversation, the researcher asked Jasper where he was going to stay. He mentioned a friend "who works the late shift" and said his next move would be to his sister's home. He spent that subzero night in his car because he did not have a key to his friend's apartment (according to an informant who knows Jasper well). Because of personal differences with his sister, he did not move in with her at that time. Approximately one year later, he spent about a month living in his sister's home. Like other men in this study, Jasper depended on a pager. By giving his pager number to friends, family, and potential employers, he could respond to calls and stay connected to the outside world, without having to depend on others to relay messages. Another strategy of Jasper's was to use motels as "stop-off place[s]," when he had some money.[2] He would rather stay at a motel on the edge of town than in a shelter or other transitional housing. He liked the privacy of having his own room, even if it was only temporary.

Geraldo, a forty-three-year-old Latino father of three, had been a successful entrepreneur who once ran his own business in East Los Angeles. When he entered PFS, however, he had been on the road for nearly eight years and had lost almost all contact with his family (although relatives occasionally gave him news about his ex-wife and children). Unable to find steady work, Geraldo could not afford his own place and lived off and on with friends, strangers, and his adult son. When last contacted, he was living in a shed in the woods outside Los Angeles, doing odd jobs in the hope of saving enough money to try his luck in another city or state.

Jasper and Geraldo's situations were extreme but not unique for this sample or for low-income Americans generally, who periodically find themselves without shelter. This two-and-a-half-year research offers "snapshots" of participants' lives, not complete histories. Men who appeared at the time to be in a stable living situation were actually in a cycle of transition, on the verge of moving in or out of their current residence. During this research, most of the men moved frequently. They moved for various reasons: their current relationship was not working out, their stay with a friend or relative was straining that relationship, their living situation was dangerous, either because the housing was unsafe or because their personal freedom and safety were threatened by former associates or the law. Only one participant in this study, Willie, owned a residence, which was inherited from his relatives and later burned down. During three years of unemployment and underemployment, he was unable to keep up the insurance payments. When the house was destroyed, Willie was forced to sell the property for next to nothing to pay off debts. He and his family were forced to live in their car and later a motel until he could afford the security deposit for another apartment. None of the other participants owned a home or held a lease in his own name.

Transience and instability had a strong impact on how these men viewed and lived their lives. Employers are wary of hiring someone who puts the name of a third-party contact on a job application. If the NCP supplied an address and phone number, a potential employer might call and find that the man had moved on or that the number was out of service. The person who answered the phone might not deliver the message. Dependent on others for shelter, the participant's personal relationships with family, lovers, and friends were often tinged with necessity. The father's—and often the mother's—fluid living situation made keeping in touch with his children, arranging visits, and following through unpredictable. Frequently, a grandmother (usually the NCP's own mother, but in some cases the maternal grandmother) provided the main link between father and child. Lacking an address carries a social stigma. Employers, social service agencies, and family members, including the mother(s) of their children, might interpret a man's unstable living situation as a character trait, a symptom of unreliability and a "drifter" mentality. Temporary living arrangements and the threat or experience of homelessness contributed to the men's feeling of being "outsiders."

UN(DER)EMPLOYED, UNDERPAID

Without exception, the men interviewed saw the solution to their problems as a steady job at a decent wage. This was the main (although not the only) reason they participated in PFS. Typically, the men in this sample had moved from low-wage job to low-wage job, or from work to unemployment to work, for reasons ranging from temporary placement, to being fired, to quitting for another job that paid $0.25 or $0.50 more an hour, or to just quitting. None of the participants had a steady job when he entered the program, and many had been unemployed for a year or more. When they did work, it was usually at part-time, short-term, minimum-wage jobs. Although $5 an hour might seem like a lot to a teenager who is supported by his parents, it is not enough for an adult with responsibilities.

> I came into the program because I wanted a job, not no job that was going to pay me $5.05, minimum wage. I wanted a job that was going to pay me at least like $7 or $8, you know. I need decent pay, so every two weeks or a week I come home with something nice, you know, so I can pay child support, pay my bills, because, you know, I do have bills.
>
> [Chris Adam, March 7, 1996]

In fact, the minimum wage (as of September 1997, $5.15 an hour or $10,300 a year) has not kept pace with the cost of living. In the 1960s, someone who worked full-time, year-round at a minimum-wage job earned enough to keep a family of three above the official government poverty line. In 1996, the same worker earned barely enough to keep himself or herself above the poverty line and earned $2,064 below the poverty line for a family of two and $7,563 below for a family of four (Statistical Abstracts 1996).

The work histories of men in the sample varied widely (table I.1). A few had been successful in the past but had fallen on hard times. Some had never worked full time. Others had worked off and on, never holding a steady job for long. Several worked steadily, but at illegal activities, chiefly selling drugs.

Getting a Start

All of the participants were having trouble finding jobs. For the younger men with limited work experience, the struggle to find full-time work at $7 or more per hour was even greater. Young men with minimal or incomplete educations and few marketable skills found work mainly through temporary agencies.

Arron, who dropped out of school in the ninth grade, had never held a full-time job.

I was working, the times I was working, I never had a job over six months . . . I never got fired or nothing. It was always temporary like that, you know, two months on the job here and you know the first real job I ever had . . . it paid good, but it was just temporary.

[Arron, May 17, 1995]

A twenty-year-old father of five, Arron lived with the mother of his three youngest children in a two-bedroom apartment in a Los Angeles housing project. When his girlfriend got a job through a county welfare-to-work program, they devised a temporary arrangement. While she was at work or school, he stayed home and took care of the children. This allowed her to take advantage of new opportunities (without the cost of day care) and allowed Arron to devote time to his real love, writing rap songs and rehearsing with his band. When their money ran short, Arron got part-time work in warehousing or maintenance through a temporary service. But for the time being, Arron's primary role was homemaker and full-time dad, a role he enjoyed and valued yet would quickly give up should the right opportunity come his way. Sly, Hollywood, Viceroy, Kenny, and other young fathers were experiencing similar difficulties getting started.

Starting Over

Men in their thirties or forties who once made good money but had suffered a setback found it difficult to get back on their feet. Trane, a thirty-six-year-old African American father of three, had worked his way into a steady position as a store manager when, in 1992, the store was looted during the civil unrest in South Central Los Angeles, and he was laid off. He spent the next three years looking for work but never found anything stable. In 1996 he was hired as a temporary employee during the holiday season, working thirty hours a week in the shipping and sorting division of a major mail delivery company. When he was asked to stay on, Trane felt proud and confident, but at $8 an hour he still was not earning enough to make ends meet. A relative offered him a job watching over storage yards on the graveyard shift, and Trane worked both jobs for nearly a year.

[L]ike I say, they increased both my hours . . . both jobs increased hours, and I'm trying to hang, man, I'm trying my best to swing it. [My girlfriend] was just telling me she don't hardly get to see me anymore but I told her pretty soon it all would be okay, it'd be for a reason.

[Trane, April 1996]

Even with two jobs, Trane did not earn enough to pay all his child support obligations and support himself. But he was confident that he would soon get to that point if he could just keep both jobs going.

Near the end of the research, Trane called the interviewer in a panic because he had lost his job with the mail delivery company after failing to pass a promotion test. This could not have come at a worse time. He had just spent almost three weeks with the son he had not seen for nearly five years. He had been making enough money to start thinking about paying off his child support debt and getting his personal life in order. It had taken him nearly three years to get this job, and he was devastated; he had not told anyone but the interviewer that he had been fired. Eventually, the company hired him back at his original position, but he knew that in a year's time he would be facing the same test, and he would have to pass it or be out of a job.

At one time, Geraldo embodied the American success story of a self-made entrepreneur. The son of migrant farm workers, Geraldo spent his childhood traveling the southwestern United States, picking cotton or cherries beside his mother and earning as little as $4.50 for a day's work. He left the fields while in his teens.

I cannot see getting up at 4:00 in the morning, going out there where you can't even see where you're at, getting under a tree and getting soaking wet, and working like that till 7:00 in the evening, for the kind of money you'd make. Then you'd spend it all up, transporting yourself back to another state, and you got to start all over again. When you get there, maybe the crops went bad, maybe the hail came, destroyed the crops, maybe they're on strike at Campbell's, and there's no tomatoes to be picked. Now you got to borrow money to transport yourself to another state? No, I can't see it. There's no future in it. So at the age of thirteen, I quit.

[Geraldo, September 28, 1995]

Living with relatives in Texas, Geraldo completed high school. His first job, at a canning company, paid $1.25 per hour. Using his business savvy, he went on to run a successful medical referral firm with several employees. He owned his own home, was the sole breadwinner for his family, sent his children to private school, and supported a son from a previous relationship. When successive deals with his brother and then another partner went sour, however, he lost his company, and, with the hope of starting over somewhere new, left his family. He had been on the road ever since. In a sense, Geraldo had come full circle, back to the migrant existence of his childhood.

Outside the Mainstream

Then there were men who had worked hard since their teens, earning a lot or enough, but at illegal activities. Some were tired of the wild, hectic lifestyle, disenchanted with what it had to offer, and wanted out. Leaving a career on the streets often meant learning to live with less money and influence and sometimes under threat of danger. Contacts and acquaintances from their former life do not necessarily know or believe they are "out of the game."

Big Joe was a twenty-five-year-old African American father of seven from Grand Rapids, Michigan. Big Joe lived with his wife and three of his children. He kept in touch with his other children from previous relationships who lived all over Grand Rapids, saw them when he could, and enjoyed his role as daddy. Big Joe did not appear to have a job. Yet he could pay his cellular phone bills and buy expensive clothes from one of the chic boutiques in Grand Rapids. He ran his business very close to his chest—as he must, to stay out of jail. Every week after entering PFS, Big Joe went down to the child support agency and paid his child support—in cash. The last thing he wanted was for the Grand Rapids police to find some reason to arrest him.

Big Joe was a very smart young man, as he had to be, to be successful in maintaining his business interests. He was well aware that life on the streets is dangerous. He was trying to figure out a way to go legitimate but hesitated to give up what he had already established for the unknown. Big Joe came into PFS for one reason: to stay out of jail. A friend told him in so many words that the program was safe, so he dropped in now and then. During the period of this research, Big Joe did not find any alternative work he considered worth giving up his comfortable lifestyle or his street prestige. As of this writing, Big Joe was still working outside the mainstream but was seeking to launch a legitimate business in industrial interior design.

Bob, a native of Dayton, Ohio, and a graduate of the Dayton public school system, was a twenty-six-year-old African American father of five. At one time, Bob had been a major drug dealer on his "side of town." After a personal brush with violence and the death of a close relative, Bob decided to "go straight." His first venture into the mainstream landed him a $6.25-an-hour job in the stockroom of a local business, which he kept for more than eighteen months. Bob was proud of his decision and his job but quit as a result of personal and racist affronts by the manager's son. On entering PFS, Bob had been unemployed for two years and was living with his mother. Staying straight was a struggle.

BOB: I wasn't working. I felt that being in the streets was not the right thing to do, and I wasn't getting no income, which was keeping me mad, you know what I'm saying? Angry—and I was wanting to go back to the streets. But I was saying, no, that's all right.

INTERVIEWER: Where were you living?

BOB: When you're in the streets, man, you can have whatever you want. You can have whatever you want. It's easy. It's easy. It's easy out there. I could live with a friend, a girl, or anywhere.

[December 1994]

Asked about going back to the streets, Bob responded, "Yeah, I've been there. I've been there before. I don't want to go back—it's just like a dog going to the pound . . . don't wanna be there." Holding a job had given him confidence: "I know that I'm successful, and I'm not going back to the streets to get what I need. I can work." So far, with his family's help, Bob had resisted the lure of the street in the hope of a job offering him stability and a moderate wage.

At one time or another, many other participants, who were not major players, sold drugs and engaged in other illegal activities as necessity dictated and opportunity allowed.

Getting By

For most NCPs in the sample, chronic unemployment was a fact of life. Many were only able to find work through temporary employment agencies. These agencies offered immediate, stop-gap, low-skilled jobs—not what the men wanted, but often the best opportunity they could find. Sly was a nineteen-year-old African American father of one from Trenton, New Jersey. Bored with school, he frequently got into trouble and dropped out in the ninth grade. Sly's work experience consisted of a series of low-paying, temporary jobs.

INTERVIEWER: So what are you doing, man? How are you doing this on your own?

SLY: The best way I can, you know, just me and my little things I've got to pull off now and then, my little jobs or something. You know, just life. Got to save money, you know, things of that nature.

INTERVIEWER: So about how much have you worked this year?

SLY: Not that much. I mean, I maybe had—I had like nine temporary jobs. I had a lot, though, but nothing permanent, though, you know, not even—

INTERVIEWER: Not even close to being—

SLY: Part-time, a week at the most, or a couple days, something like that.

INTERVIEWER: That must be frustrating, man.

SLY: It is, but you take what you get, you know what I'm saying? Be happy. Yeah, it's like that.

[November 28, 1995]

Most of the older men in the sample (thirty or older) had been employed at regular, full-time jobs at some point in the past, but none had steady work when they entered the program. From their perspective, part-time and temporary jobs were the norm.

Willie, a thirty-seven-year-old African American father of two who had been married to the mother of his children for thirteen years, was a life-long resident of Memphis. In the early years of his marriage, he was able to find (though not always keep) full-time jobs. But according to Willie, times had changed.

The only jobs that I've had here recently has been from temporary services. And that means when you walk into a place, that's—it's really self-explanatory—you're just temporary. You don't mean any-thing to this company. You just here, just for now, and that's the way they treat you . . . I have been on jobs where they tell you, look, if you come here every day, and you work your butt off, we'll hire you. But it's a scam. I was at this one job where the man said if I stayed there thirty days he would hire me. The twenty-ninth day, because I was coming right with it, the twenty-ninth day he told me, "I have to lay you off, man."

[Willie, March 2, 1995]

To make ends meet, or simply to survive, virtually all participants depended on "hustling": seizing any opportunity, legal or illegal, in the formal or informal economy to make a little money (Wilson

1996, 142). The term hustling covers a broad range of ad hoc activities: doing odd jobs and working off-the-books for legitimate businesses or neighbors, working for a numbers parlor or after-hours social club, selling small lots of clothing, radios, or other goods on the street, shoplifting for acquaintances, playing cards for money, running scams—whatever might bring in a little cash.

PERSONAL OBSTACLES TO EMPLOYMENT

All of the participants in this study faced multiple obstacles in seeking employment. Although a few had attended college, some had not completed high school. Although some, such as Trane and Geraldo, had been successful in the past, others had erratic work histories that, in themselves, tended to alienate potential employers. Most had arrest records. For several, like Jasper, drug use or heavy drinking interfered with finding and holding a regular job.

Education

Nearly two out of three of the men in this study had either graduated from high school or obtained a GED certificate. For the majority, formal education stopped at this point, a common pattern in their communities (Fagan 1992; Kasarda 1992). Some dropouts, like nineteen-year-old Sly, felt they needed to finish school to get a decent job.

INTERVIEWER: What are you looking for? What kind of jobs, man?

SLY: Oh, primarily anything for right now, anything that can get me through, because jobs is like so scarce around here, now, you know. Just so I can really work the schools for right now, you know? While I'm trying to go and get my GED.

INTERVIEWER: Is that hard?

SLY: Oh yeah.

INTERVIEWER: Do you like it? What are classes like?

SLY: I mean, you just sit in the class and you know, just do a book, like answers and questions and all that. And you work through the different levels up to when you're up to take your GED test.

INTERVIEWER: Have you taken any of the tests yet?

SLY: No.

INTERVIEWER: No? When are you going to do that?

SLY: You have to work to, like, a certain—you've got to go through so many books, you know, and learn all the parts of the GED test and then you can take the test.

INTERVIEWER: Okay. Are you close?

SLY: Not really, because I just really started.

INTERVIEWER: Okay. What made you start this?

SLY: Because I know that's something that I need in the long run. You know, that's like, common sense.

[November 28, 1995]

But others were not convinced that a high school diploma or GED would open doors. Kenny, a twenty-five-year-old African American from Trenton, his girlfriend, and their daughter lived in his mother's house.

INTERVIEWER: Do you ever regret not finishing high school?

KENNY: Yeah. I mean, I think I regretted more or less having the fun, you know what I'm saying. 'Cause, I mean, the school—going to class and everything, and a lot of sisters . . . that I liked to deal with, I mean, and the brothers and everything, you know what I'm saying. Stepping out of high school—basically I lost the swing with everybody else . . . I would, like, kind of do my own thing—created my own little friends and things like that, so I would—I would have liked to have . . . you know, the high school diploma and everything, walked down the aisle, made my moms happy, but I mean, it didn't take no inspiration out of my life—and made me feel bad about myself or anything . . . I'm saying that I'm happy with how I turned out . . . and the type of person that I am, so I'm cool.

[November 6, 1995]

Observing that young men like themselves who graduated from high school were only marginally better off than those who dropped out, they saw little connection between completing school and getting a job. In fact, the value of a high school diploma compared to a college degree has declined since the 1970s. In the 1970s a college graduate earned about 20 percent more than a high school graduate; by the 1990s, the difference was more than 50 percent (Harrington and Fogg 1994).

A few men in the sample did have some higher education, but for them it had not paid off.[3] Willie, who earned a bachelor of science degree in the physical sciences from one of Tennessee's state universities, had been struggling to find work in Memphis since he graduated ten years earlier. Although the medical field in Memphis was booming, Willie was unable to get even an interview for an entry-level position at any of the number of hospitals or clinics in the city. Discouraged about finding work in the medical world, he sought jobs in warehousing, shipping, and delivery, dubbed and mixed music tapes, and finally sold drugs to make ends meet.

Lack of formal education did not necessarily mean that these men were unskilled. Several were accomplished cooks, who produced meals that satisfied large parties of discriminating diners; others were talented mechanics, who could fix almost anything with minimal equipment. But skills acquired in the informal economy—cooking for a relative's catering service, fixing the neighbors' cars, or working in mom or dad's corner store—did not translate into credentials and jobs in the mainstream economy. Several of the men were talented artists who lacked the connections with mainstream producers to be published or recorded.

Illegal activities, such as running or playing the numbers and dealing drugs, require intelligence and skill. A major drug dealer has to analyze markets, keep tabs on the competition, assess new products (crack versus heroin), deal with regulatory agencies (avoid the police), handle personnel problems (street runners), and often keep accounts in his head or in code.

> Organized drug selling also may be seen as a substitute form of business training that instills entrepreneurial skills. Adolescents who otherwise would be considered surplus labor are taught how to conduct business—how to buy wholesale and sell retail, keep books, pay bills, manage inventory and cash flow, calculate profit margins, and deal with competitors and unpredictable customers.
>
> [Harrell and Peterson 1992, 99]

These skills and work experience are, obviously, inadmissible on résumés for legitimate jobs. Arron spoke for many of the men in the community who had never established a foothold in the world of work.

I sit down and think about it, and I see some of my friends, they were a lot worse than me, but they have jobs and stuff. How's that? I have more education than they do and attempted to do more better things, but they get the best of everything and me, I'm just me . . . I'd of been going door to door trying out for jobs, I was getting desperate, I work anywhere, I work here, you know, doing whatever it is they want me to do, but the frustration stresses me out. I'm under a whole lot of stress, really, you know, because I had all these kids now from having fun back in the days, and the fun had to stop and it's time to be serious. But now that I want to be serious, there's nothing out here for me. I see there's nothing out here for a person with a Ph.D., can't even get a job these days! . . . So it's about competition, and *I can't compete in this world.* I really can't, and that's why at times I just really want to give up and forget it."

[Arron, May 17, 1995; emphasis added]

Locked Out

Past mistakes (often arrest records for these men) may become permanent obstacles to gainful employment. Participants sometimes found there were no second chances. G Man was a thirty-one-year-old black man who grew up in Texas and Los Angeles.[4] He had five children. For twelve years, he worked as one of the chief mechanics for a local utility company. He made good money, lived in the San Bernardino Valley suburbs with his longtime girlfriend and off and on with children from their respective relationships. He paid his child support and maintained contact with his other children. When he was laid off, he and his girlfriend moved back to South Central Los Angeles, just one house over from the one in which he grew up. According to G Man, the neighborhood was tough then, and it is tough now. Returning to his old neighborhood was a severe setback. He hated living there, but an old family friend had offered him a place to live, and he could not afford to move. Before the layoff, his children "[h]ad a ball, man. They loved to come to my house . . . Disneyland, you know, horseback ride in Griffin Park, take them to the park and let them go swimming, you know." After the layoff, he began falling behind in child support payments and, with little money in his pocket, found it difficult to maintain close relationships with his children. His girlfriend recalled, "It was boring [for the children]." He kept up with his children's activities but no longer had the space or funds to take them in for any length of time. Moreover, he did not want his children to be exposed to the poverty and violence in which he had grown up.

When G Man entered the program, he had a definite goal: to acquire a long-distance trucker's license. Working very hard to master the new technology of trucking, in addition to handling the trucks themselves, he became a certified truck driver. Shortly thereafter, on a cross-country trip, he received a message from the company asking him to return as soon as possible. When he got back, he learned that the company had discovered his past police record. He was dismissed immediately and had struggled to find work ever since. G Man's experience was not unusual. Many (though not all) trucking companies conduct background checks, mainly to keep insurance costs down. As a result, it becomes more difficult for men with prior driving and other violations to secure work in this industry.

INTERVIEWER: How are you surviving?

G MAN: Shit, any way I can.

INTERVIEWER: So nothing's changed for you, though?

G MAN: Nope.

INTERVIEWER: No. You working a little bit, man? Nothing?

G MAN: Nothing . . . Not even nothing, man, nothing. Most people want experience for the driving thing, you know. Then the ones I do get, they run a [record] check, then they don't want me.
[May 6, 1995]

Despite his skills and certification, G Man's past encounters with the law may always be a problem. All of the participants in this study had prior arrests for offenses not related to child support enforcement. Hence all lived with the possibility that their past history would disqualify them for a job or a promotion or would provide their employer with an excuse to fire and replace them.

Substance Use

Drug use and alcohol abuse presented another obstacle to employment for a number of participants. At one PFS site, job developers found that a number of participants, who knew each other before they entered the program, smoked marijuana regularly. This habit contributed to their inability to hold a job, mainly because they failed drug tests.

A few participants had serious problems with stronger drugs or with alcohol. Some individuals asked staff members for help; others, who chose not to discuss their issues with PFS staff, were open with the interviewer. Fila-G, a thirty-six-year-old African American father of seven who lived in Memphis, admitted that his drinking problem had haunted him for many years. He had lost a number of jobs, his marriage of thirteen years, and contact with his children because of his alcohol and drug use, which he successfully concealed from PFS staff. He did not want, or feel he needed, "outside" help.

> My, uh, drinking, you know—this is something that, you know, I'm gonna have to deal with, you know. I've been through supportive groups like that before, rehabilitation and, you know, AA [Alcoholics Anonymous] and all that . . . You know, just trying to let everybody else know how I feel is one thing, but doing what's real is another thing, you know, that all up to me . . . I could go to a AA meeting, sober as I don't know what; upon leaving, reach up under my seat, you know, by the time I get home, I'm half high, you know . . . So, this is just something that Fila-G is gonna have to tackle, you know, Fila-G and my, uh, good lord, you know.
>
> [Fila-G 1994]

As of our last meeting, he had not stopped drinking.

At one point, Jasper disappeared for three or four months. When he returned, he confessed to a facilitator that he had been using drugs regularly and drinking heavily, lost his job, and checked himself into a rehabilitation program in another state. Jasper was proud that he had stopped drinking but knew that he might relapse in the future and needed someone on whom to call for support.

Casual conversations and observation suggested that nearly all the participants had used illegal substances—most often, marijuana—at one time or another. Typically, these men did not see marijuana as more dangerous or addictive than beer or cigarettes, nor did they have a negative view of someone who smoked marijuana.

MEN AND WOMEN

At first contact, seventeen (53 percent) of the men had never been married, three were married (but not to the mother of their youngest child[ren]), and eleven were separated or divorced. One participant was married to and living with the mother/stepmother of his two children (Willie), and one was a widower (Lover). (See table I.1.)

A majority of participants in this study had one or more children, in some cases with more than one woman, before settling into a serious relationship. A smaller number had been married to the mother of their first child(ren) but later divorced. Whatever the pattern, relationships with the mother(s) of the child(ren) for whom they owed child support usually were strained. They and the mother had separated, often years before. However, most of these men, regardless of age, were committed to their current relationship. Within the sample, this primary relationship usually had lasted for more than three years. Peer support facilitators in Trenton and Dayton who asked the men how long they had been in their current relationships were told four to five years, on average. But marriage was not necessarily in their immediate plans.

Views of Marriage

> I really want to be, I want to be a family man. That's what I want to be.
> [Chris Adam, March 7, 1996]

Almost all of the younger men in this study wanted and expected to get married and to settle down—someday. But they tended to be cautious, primarily because of the financial responsibilities associated with marriage. Several studies have found that low-income women are equally wary of making commitments.[5] Given the high rates of unemployment in their communities, a husband is as likely to be a liability as an asset (William J. Wilson, *The New York Times,* July 27, 1998, A12). The older men seemed more settled in their ways, and marriage was not a driving force in starting or maintaining relationships.

Nineteen-year-old Sly felt, quite simply, that he was too young to settle down. Sly lived with his mother, who was very protective of him and helped him make ends meet. He loved his child; many times when the interviewer called, Sly was at home taking care of the child while his girlfriend was out. She and her family carried most of the responsibility for the child's care, however. He hoped eventually to get a job that would allow him to start making it on his own and to help out his child. He was also in school, trying to complete his GED. But giving up his youth to marry his child's mother was not part of his plans.

Other young, unwed fathers were involved in a steady relationship but were not ready for marriage. Chris Adam, a twenty-year-old African American who had broken up with the mother of his two children, was committed to his current girlfriend.

> She means, like, good things, like she want to do good things, you know, she want a job and this and that, you know. She got good values, let's put it that way.
>
> [Chris Adam, May 22, 1996]

Chris felt they were too young to get married, noting that his girlfriend was "only twenty." He was quick to add, however,

> I want to stick with her. I wouldn't mind marrying her, but until I get settled down, like I said, until I get settled . . . we just got to get settled, you know, job—J-O-B—with benefits. That's what I'm going to shoot for. All the kids—not just one, you know, all of them.
>
> [Chris Adam, May 22, 1996]

Like Chris Adam, a number of young fathers said that they wanted to be financially secure before they got married. Given their chronic insecurity, the wedding was not likely to be soon (although two young men did get married for the first time during the research period).

A few participants were living with the mother of some or all of their children but were not married. Contrary to widespread assumptions, getting married would not necessarily have disqualified these couples from receiving AFDC or other public assistance benefits. If neither partner is employed, or their earnings fall below a minimum level, married couples might be eligible for AFDC benefits under the unemployed persons provision. Nor were these NCPs breaking the law by living with the mother. It appears that reasons other than "beating the system" led to the decision not to marry.

Jah, a twenty-nine-year-old African American who was born and raised in Trenton, had lived with his girlfriend ever since the first of their two children was born. For Jah, getting married was not a prerequisite to being a "family man." To the contrary, he saw formal marriage as interfering with his personal freedom. (Whether his partner agreed was unclear.) By choosing *not* to hold a marriage license and to have children outside of marriage, Jah was not attempting to evade his role and responsibilities as a parent. Rather he wanted to be free to care for his family on his own terms. What counted, in his view, was that he was actively involved in the life of his child(ren) as a parent.

> They saying a noncustody—they call me a noncustody parent, but I'm not. I'm a custody parent 'cause I could be with mine and take him to anywhere I want to take him, any time I want to take him . . . Because me and my girl is not two people. See, they separate [us]— see, that's the United States and they problems, they always separating the family . . . You know? This is not a separate family right here, no matter if I'm married or not—we are one family, you know. We laid down, we had him. This is our family.
>
> [Jah, November 1, 1994]

Arron, who lived with the mother of his three youngest children, also saw being committed to his children and being an active daddy as more important than marriage. But he felt that if times got tough, the marriage bond could provide both partners with emotional security and thus become a stabilizing force.

> [I'm] married enough, shoot. I'm already married—this is all the marriage there's gonna be . . . One of these [days I'll change that]. I know I am one day, but not now . . . If we end up strugglin' too much, then I do. But other than that—nah, I don't think—we, we strugglin', but we makin' it enough to—we livin', you know . . . We can do little things, stuff, you know. But once times get harder than hard, then . . . I think about marriage, I'll consider it.
>
> [Arron, September 27, 1995]

Jah and Arron were exceptions, however. The majority of participants were estranged from the mother(s) of the child(ren) for whom they owed child support.

Supportive Mates

Current relationships, the interviewer found, were often a source of support and assistance in an unstable life. The only child of a widowed mother, Chris Adam began "running the streets" of Trenton in his early teens and dropped out of high school in the twelfth grade due, he said, to bad advice from his school counselor. Since then, he had bounced from one part-time, minimum-wage job to another and vacillated between being "a player" or hustler on the streets and trying to "go straight." Chris became a father at age seventeen and again a year later, both boys. He said he left their mother after a four-year relationship because "she played me with one of my friends, and it hurt." During this time, Chris was arrested for domestic violence and spent nearly a week in the county jail. His ex-girlfriend remains close to his mother, however, and he sees his sons often.

Chris was involved in a new relationship with a woman to whom he said he was genuinely committed. He credited her with changing his old mentality, which held that women were only after his money and could be neither trusted nor respected. He said he had learned to walk away and give himself time to cool down, instead of lashing out, when he was angry at her. Because of her, he had given up old ways and old friends. He wanted to be the kind of man she could respect, a provider. When, near the end of the research, his new girlfriend became pregnant, he became even more committed to his goals of getting a regular job, giving up marijuana, and "going straight."

Jason, a thirty-two-year-old white father of two, grew up in Dayton, Ohio. A high school dropout, Jason had a drinking problem that all but ruined his life. His wife and the mother of his children divorced him; he could not hold a job and had no relatives to whom he could turn. When he was hitting bottom, he met his current wife, who helped him to stop drinking and encouraged him to attend PFS after he was assigned to the program. Jason took to the program and its offer of education. He worked hard, got his GED, and then began a nursing program. While in the program, he worked with his current wife to get back into his children's lives. Integrating his children into his new life with his second wife and her children was not easy. Jason took great pride in helping his stepdaughter reacclimate herself into the family after she spent two months in jail followed by placement in a detention home.

> Well, she's not in jail anymore, she's in rehab and she's doing fantastic. Her out-date's in February. I'm really proud of the progress she's making. Things are going relatively smooth around here.
> [Jason, November 14, 1994]

Tyrone, a fifty-one-year-old black man and father of five, was born in Jacksonville, Florida. Most of Tyrone's children were grown and on their own, living up north. Tyrone also lived up north for a good portion of his life, and much of that time he lived with his children. He admitted that he was not a good father when they were growing up. He said that he did not spend much time with them because, frankly, he was not interested.

After he moved back to Jacksonville, Tyrone entered into a new relationship that "opened his eyes" and gave him a son he adored. He attributed his effort to be active in his youngest child's life to his new partner and to his experience in PFS, which not only made him think differently about fatherhood but also provided strategies and tactics that he tried to incorporate into his life. He began to spend as much time as he could with his child, taking him to the zoo and to church, things he rarely did before. Tyrone also reestablished ties with one of his grown sons who lived in Jacksonville.

Of the participants who used PFS for their personal betterment, pursued education or training, attempted to disassociate themselves from life on the street, or reestablished contact with one or more of their children during the study period, many credited a supportive relationship with their current partner.

Overlapping Relationships

For most men in this sample, a long-term relationship with a woman whom they *might* marry, or a live-in relationship with a woman to whom they *might as well* be married, was only part of the story. Typically, these NCPs were involved in a set of overlapping, sometimes conflicting relationships with current and ex-girlfriends or wives, their own and their ex's mothers, and their current partner's children from her former relationships as well as theirs. Often a man's own mother, or in some cases his ex-girlfriend's or ex-wife's mother, served as an intermediary, enabling a father to see his children on neutral territory.

Trane had lived with his girlfriend for eight years, but his children kept him involved in past relationships. Trane became a father at age twenty, and after he and his son's mother broke up, he married another woman and had two children, both girls. This marriage ended in divorce, and the children lived with his ex-wife and her mother. He had good rapport with the grandmother and was in regular contact with his daughters, by phone and in person. However, his ex-wife was a longtime drug user, and both he and the grandmother worried about her influence on the girls. When he entered PFS, he was working with his parents and the maternal grandmother to create a safe environment for the girls, possibly in his parents' home. He said that he would like to get custody of these children but did not believe that the Department of Children's Services would grant this, in part because he did not make enough to support them on his own.

At the same time, the mother of his first child wanted him to take custody of their son, who she felt was at an age when he needed his father. Given Trane's financial situation and concern for his daughters, he was reluctant to take on the additional responsibility, although he often contemplated the possibility. As a result, the mother limited his contact with his son. Over time, however, they came to an agreement whereby Trane and his son could spend several consecutive days, and occasionally a week or two, together. Although the process of father and son becoming reacquainted was gradual and often difficult, the mother continued to be supportive. Trane's relationship with his ex-wife, however, became even more strained. When last contacted, he was negotiating with her for joint custody of their girls and for a reprieve from his child support obligation. Trane is just one example of men who have to negotiate their way through networks of overlapping relationships to remain involved with or reengage in their children's lives.

FATHERHOOD

The number of children these NCPs reported ranged from a low of one to a high of seven. Half of the men in this sample were fathers of one or two children (see figure 2.1). More than half (nineteen) had children with one partner only, seven with two partners, and six with three or more partners.

The age of fathers with four or more offspring ranged between twenty and fifty-one years. One common pattern was that most participants became fathers between the ages of nineteen and twenty-four. The oldest father in the sample had most of his children in his twenties and his most recent child at the age of forty. As young men, they were struggling to become independent, to make enough money to be self-sufficient, and to remove or distance themselves from their recent past. These still-unresolved issues of youth affected their ability to assume the responsibilities and challenges of fathers—to be present, attentive, supportive, and active participants in their children's lives.[6]

Figure 2.1   Range of Children and Partners of Noncustodial Parents

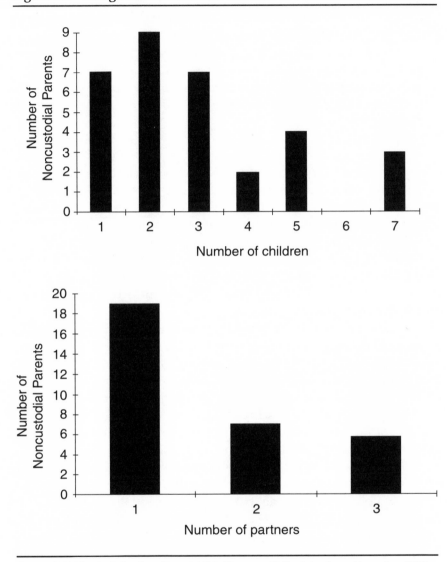

Source: MDRC calculation from Parents' Fair Share qualitative interviews, November 1996.

Yet contrary to stereotypes, few of these noncustodial fathers simply walked away from their children and never looked back. As one participant emphasized,

> Out of the whole class [PFS peer support], everybody—there was only two people that did not love their kids and did not want to be with their kids. Two people—and we're talking about [out of] easily fifty people.
>
> [Mack, March 6, 1995]

Observing other groups at other research sites confirmed this assertion. In informal conversations with the researcher outside the PFS program, noncustodial parents expressed their feelings and beliefs about fatherhood, responsibility, and obligations to their children, families, and selves. The researcher also had opportunities to observe NCPs' interactions with their children. With few exceptions, the men expressed love and concern for their children. Although most were unable to make formal child support payments, they often brought their child(ren) gifts—bags of groceries, money for clothes, games, toys, sports equipment, and the like—even when this meant doing without necessities for themselves. Likewise, other relatives (especially the NCPs' mothers) made informal contributions to the children's material well-being.

The participants in this study distinguished between the roles of daddy and father. "Daddy" implied the emotional and social aspects of fatherhood: spending time with their child(ren), playing an active role in parenting, acting as a role model, and providing guidance, as well as bringing them presents, showing them off to family and friends, and basking in their admiration and affection. "Father" connoted the practical and instrumental aspects of fatherhood: assuming financial responsibility through child support payments, when possible providing a stable living environment, and being an authority figure. Discussing their experiences as "daddy" brought smiles to their faces as they recalled shared interactions with their children. G Man told the interviewer with immense pride that the first thing he did on returning from his first truck-driving job was to pick up his children and take them for a ride in the cab of his truck—he felt like a "real" dad. "Father" always seemed to follow "noncustodial," implying debt and failed obligations, as well as denied access to the "daddy" role by the mother or the courts.

Given limited resources and varying personal circumstances, participants in this study perceived and handled fatherhood in different ways. Relationships with children ranged from full-time, live-in dads to no contact at all. In some cases (Claudio, Fila-G, and Geraldo), lack of contact with children was the NCP's own choice, in part because he felt financially unable to fulfill the role of father. In other cases (Jasper, Lover, and Ventura), the mother took the child and left, failing to inform the father of her whereabouts or denying him access to their child. Some NCPs had to meet certain conditions (formal or informal) in order to see their child(ren). When Trane would not agree to take custody of his first child and only son, the boy's mother banned visits, although she later relented. An ex-partner may disallow visits because the father is living with another woman or she has a new man in her life, because he fails to contribute to her household expenses, or for other reasons. In a few cases, the courts banned contact between a father and child(ren). Conditions for visits may become so daunting that noncustodial fathers give up.

Full-time Dads

I was with my family before I even entered that club [peer support]. I was with my family no matter what we go through or what we go without. I'm going to still be with mine. My baby's mother and my baby. Them things that I can't neglect and I know that from the day he was conceived. So, that's my lifetime goal—is to raise my son, you know what I'm saying? That's a must.

[Jah, November 14, 1994]

Jah was a live-in, full-time father. He worked as a laborer and was fairly well paid. He and his girlfriend were talking about buying a car so that they could be more independent. Just before their second child was born, however, he was stopped for a traffic warrant and then arrested and jailed for alleged possession of an illegal substance. Jah's girlfriend, who had been receiving public assistance (housing, food stamps, and medical benefits) for herself and the children, was angry with him for "messing up," because he had been doing so well. As soon as he got out of jail, he was back at home with his family; within a few months, he was back at his old job, and child support payments were once again being taken directly out of his paycheck. When the interviewer asked how he was doing, Jah responded:

> Who me? Well, it ain't for me no more to be doing all right, man—as long as my kid is all right, man, I'm all right. Yeah. As long as he don't have to ask nobody for nothing, do you know what I mean?
>   [this statement was made before his second child was born;
>   [Jah, May 8, 1995]

Jah was the only father in the study who lived with the mother from the time their first child was born and did not have children from any other relationship. But because Jah was not married to the mother, in the eyes of the law he was considered a noncustodial father, a designation he resented.

> You know, with my son, that's every day, you know? This ain't a weekend thing or where it begins on a weekend or on a Friday, no; this is every day for me, you know. I'm changing Pampers, I'm feeding him, I'm making bottles, I'm doing the regular things that a father suppose to do, that's me . . . So, I ain't trying to get custody, because I have custody . . . You know what I mean?
>   [Jah, November 1, 1994]

Arron, also unmarried, explained his live-in relationship with the mother of his three youngest as "staying together for the sake of the children."

> Nah . . . I only—I [am here] for the kids' sake, you know . . . I do anything to be around my kids, and nobody [can] say I was a deadbeat, or anything like that, you know . . . I don't ever want to be known as something like that. I take care of my kids, I'm gonna do like my father did with us. He struggled, he did a whole lot of strugglin' to make sure that we, you know, was a family. Although he and my mother didn't get along, he never hit her and stuff like that. You know, he—they stayed together just for us, and then once we got older, they divorced. Soon as we were grown . . . But I respect them for that, you know? . . . and I'm looking at it like, well, I could do it like that. I mean, although me and her may not get along too well at all times . . . I can see—she, she's still bearable, you know. She's not a unbearable person.
>   [Arron, September 27, 1995]

Arron also felt a sense of responsibility toward the two children with whom he did not live. When he heard that the mother of his other son was disciplining the child in a manner that he had learned through PFS might not be most effective, he called the child welfare agency in Los Angeles. An investigation found no evidence of child neglect or abuse. The boy's mother retaliated by denying Arron access to her apartment and cutting off his informal visitation rights, so that he only learned of the child's well-being through his mother.

Part-time Dads

More than two out of three men in the sample kept in touch with at least one child. But their relationships were more complicated than this figure suggests. Noncustodial fathers may have children with more than one mother and may have regular (unrestricted) contact with one child, but conditional (restricted) contact or no contact with another child or children. As a starting point, figure 2.2 shows the percentage of NCPs in this sample who were in touch with one or more of their children at least once a month—in person, by telephone, or through letter. Nearly two-thirds had at least monthly unrestricted contact, and about 15 percent had monthly contact under restrictions imposed by the other parent, other family members, or the courts. Slightly more than 20 percent had no regular monthly contact with any of their children.

Figure 2.2   Contact and Type of Contact NCPs Have with Children

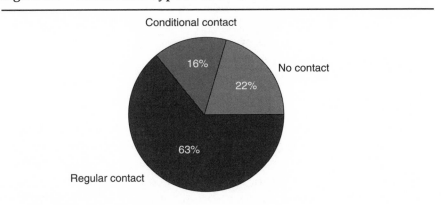

Source: MDRC calculations from Parents' Fair Share qualitative interviews, November 1996.
Notes: Distributions may not add to 100 percent because of rounding. Regular contact is defined as being able to see or talk with one or all children without restriction (informal or formal). Conditional contact refers to restrictions placed on NCPs by custodial parents, family members, or the courts.

Although one contact a month may not seem like much, given their often tense relationships with their children's mother(s), their lack of economic resources, and the children's location, for many of these NCPs seeing or contacting their children required significant effort. A number of NCPs in this sample wanted to remain connected to their children but, because of other problems, were unable to do so. When a father was jailed, for example, contact was limited and often cut off. Many of the men who had been arrested said that they rarely were visited by their friends, children, and their children's mothers. Like Jah's girlfriend, the mother may blame him for "messing up" and stay away as an expression of her anger and disappointment. The trip to a prison, jail, or detention center might be costly and time-consuming.

Fathers may lose touch when their children are moved out of the state or even out of the neighborhood. Even if the children live in the same metropolitan region, getting back and forth via public transportation may require hours of travel and numerous transfers, and the father may not have the cash for bus fare. In many cases, neither he nor his children's mother has a phone, so that visits cannot be planned in advance. If he makes the trip, his children may not be home when he arrives. Few participants had a permanent address where their children could write to them, or a private phone so their children could call them, much less a place of their own where their children could visit them. Nevertheless, these low-income NCPs contacted and visited their children about as often as middle-class, divorced, noncustodial parents do (Seltzer and Brandreth 1995; Furstenberg and Harris 1993).

Losing Daddy Status

Other NCPs in the sample were involuntarily separated from their child(ren), either by the mother and her family or by the courts. Lover, a twenty-eight-year-old African American father of three, was devoted to his children. But due to a complex series of events, the courts took them into custody and denied him visitation. A promising athlete in high school, Lover never graduated. Nevertheless he was recruited by one of the California state universities to play football and basketball. Although he attended some college classes, he dropped out before finishing his first semester. After leaving school, he looked for work and landed a number of jobs, none of which lasted. Frustrated by his inability to find steady employment, he joined the reserves and toured in operations Desert Shield and Desert Storm. Not long after he returned, his wife of four years died, leaving him to care for their two children. (His third child lived with another woman he had been seeing before he got married.)

Living with a relative, Lover worked hard to be a good single father. One day, when he was not at home and a friend was baby-sitting, his daughter was injured. Lover was arrested and incarcerated for a month; on being released from jail, he was placed under house arrest and ordered to wear a monitor or "tether." At the same time that the family courts declared him an unfit father, the child support enforcement system demanded that he live up to his responsibilities as a father. Admitted to Parents' Fair Share, Lover worked exceptionally hard to acquire credentials for a job in the travel/leisure field and found a stable, relatively high-paying job. In terms of employment, Lover was a PFS success story. But his problems with the judicial system were not resolved.

> Hey, I'm empty. I'm literally empty. Without my kids, it's like, every-thing I've done in my life, I've done with a goal and a purpose. My goal and sole purpose in my life right now, right now—and it has been since my kids is born—was to make life better for them than it was for me, you know. So, by their mother passing away, that laid a lot of responsibility on me. So I'm doing this, you know, I'm trying hard to do this, 'cause they gonna take my kids away from me, and they don't even know what the hell's going on! It hurts.
>
> [Lover, June 7, 1995]

The children were placed in foster care, waiting to find out if their father would be able to take care of them again.

Ventura, a white twenty-three-year-old with one child, had lived on the outskirts of Springfield, Massachusetts, all of his life. Ventura dropped out of school in the ninth grade to run the streets and become, as he put it, a "Mac Daddy" like the rest of his friends. To make money, he worked off and on as a craftsman. Ventura was twenty when his child was born. He and his girlfriend got along for a while, but she grew tired of the situation and left with their baby. She stayed in Springfield but had little contact with him. Because of his very poor relationship with the mother, he rarely saw his child. Ventura came into the program to get work but was more concerned about repairing his relationship with his girlfriend than about employment. He recognized that the first step would be giving up his street life.

In certain situations, lack of contact—at least until other issues are resolved—seems like a necessary choice. Marcus, a twenty-six-year-old father of one, entered PFS shortly after being released from jail. Like a few other fathers in the study, Marcus had a difficult time controlling his temper. While he was serving time for domestic violence, his wife divorced him. Acknowledging his feelings of anger toward his ex-wife and his inability to express himself in ways that were not hurtful to them both, he stayed away from her and, consequently, from his children as well.

MARCUS: And you know, my divorce is final . . . It became final as of February. See, I was in jail then. Yeah, so I got the papers and everything when I was in there.

INTERVIEWER: But you still don't have visitation rights to the kids, right?

MARCUS: Well, it's like this. Legally, no. But the kids haven't been wanting to see me . . . So I heard of this mediation thing. I really gotta think about it, because to see her again, I really have to keep from jumping in her ass . . . If I were to do that, that would make me a three-time loser, under the three strike law. And you know, I ain't ready, because I know my temper, man. And if I don't see . . . come, like, June, I haven't seen her for a whole year.

INTERVIEWER: You haven't seen your kids for a whole year?

MARCUS: Yeah . . . Two girls and a boy, and, you know, father's day came around, and I kind of broke . . . but I had a good woman by my side, you know, and it wasn't easy, man, but I made it through, and life goes on.

INTERVIEWER: Did they send you a card or anything?

MARCUS: No.

INTERVIEWER: All right. So are you still thinking about mediation, though?

MARCUS: Well . . . I don't want to think about it right now. I mean, this much I will say, it has crossed my mind.

[July 21, 1994]

Later Marcus did try to participate in voluntary mediation with his ex-wife, but she refused and he remains out of contact with the children.

Relinquishing Fatherhood

For a variety of reasons, other NCPs in the sample abdicated their roles as fathers. Fila-G had three children with two different women before marrying and settling down with a third woman who bore him four children. After thirteen years, this marriage ended in divorce. Fila-G struggled with a serious alcohol problem, sometimes combined with drug use. Given his problems with substance abuse, his moods, and the fact that he rarely had any money, the mother of his oldest children essentially wrote him off, and contacts with these children were minimal. After he and the mother of his four children divorced, he rarely saw them either. He loved his children deeply but hesitated to reach out, relying on the oldest to act as his intermediary. Although he rarely initiated contact, when they asked for help, he did his best to give it.

One spring Fila-G received a call from his oldest daughter, who had a problem she could not confide to her mother; she needed his financial and emotional help. Fila-G worked (by way of part-time jobs and drug sales) to get the money for his daughter, sought advice from a PFS staff member on how to handle and address the particular issues, and then helped his daughter with her decision. He stood by her the whole time and respected her resolution not to tell her mother. Sometimes hot-tempered and volatile, Fila-G was supportive and thoughtful in his handling of this situation. But he did not see any of his children on a regular basis.

Ralph, a forty-something white man from Trenton, was physically as well as emotionally detached from his family and relatives. When Ralph entered PFS, he had not seen his son and only child for nearly eighteen years. He and the boy's mother never got along, and he left her when the child was very young. He had lived all over the United States, for the most part by himself. Three or four years before joining the program, Ralph lost his job as a trucker and had been out of work ever since. At first he was withdrawn and distant from his peer support group, but over time he confessed that he had been homeless for two weeks. This was a particularly difficult admission for him, because he strongly believed in being self-sufficient and resisted asking anyone for help. Eventually Ralph got a job and was able to pay rent for an apartment. One day in February 1996, just before a scheduled interview, the interviewer phoned him at work and discovered he was gone. He had not given a forwarding address. He had just packed up and left.

Like Ralph, Edmond left his wife when his child was a baby and had not attempted to reestablish contact when he entered PFS. Geraldo left when his children were teenagers and was afraid that as time passed with no communication between them, the rift would grow greater and less likely to be repaired. Claudio moved in and out of his children's lives, depending on his financial circumstances and their mother's willingness to "forgive" him temporarily for leaving her and moving in with another woman. Jasper's girlfriend took their baby and went back home to her parents, who refused to allow him visitation—in part because he was of a different race and in part because he had an ongoing drug problem. Chapter 5 discusses how Parents' Fair Share attempted to help these men address and resolve some of the issues concerning their roles as fathers and their relationships with their child(ren)'s mother.

PLANS AND DREAMS, FRUSTRATIONS AND STRESS

Nearly all of the men in this book had spent years looking for steady work, with little success. Few, maybe three out of the whole sample, wanted help "straightening out their lives"; the others were particularly interested in getting a job. Some participants, however, had a vision of their life's direction from the first day the researcher met them. They had clear goals and saw the PFS program as a stepping stone toward their future accomplishments.

Ambitions

Lover set his sights on a career in travel and leisure. Given his meager resources (he was surviving on general relief and food stamps), completing the ten-week training program meant considerable personal sacrifice, but he stuck to his plan and succeeded not only in completing the course but also in getting a job in his chosen field. G Man worked hard to achieve his goal—a trucker's certificate to drive sixteen-wheelers—although the certificate did not translate into stable employment because of his arrest record.

Forty-year-old Ben, father of seven, came from an entrepreneurial Jamaican family who moved to Los Angeles when he was ten, started their own business, and invested in real estate. He entered

PFS for computer training so that he and a relative could start a computer-generated magazine geared toward the African American community. Ben struggled with school but kept at it and began to make progress in the field of computer technology.

Big Joe was already making a reasonably comfortable living selling drugs. He dreamed of starting a legitimate business and serving his community but lacked the resources needed to make the transition, such as educational credentials, the ability to raise capital, and access to bank credit. He had sought the help and advice of a local community leader but still hesitated to give up the prosperity he had achieved for the uncertainties of "going straight."

Kenny from Trenton also had ambitions of becoming a businessman in his community. Determined *not* to succumb to the lure of the street, he saw getting a job and "gettin' paid" as the first step toward starting his own legitimate enterprise. Kenny enthusiastically told the interviewer about creating his own opportunities in a location that did not offer many.

> We the ones that really goes through the suffering, you know what I'm saying, 'cause, well, I'm saying, well, economically- and financially-wise, because we're not really gettin' the money, you know what I'm saying? . . . These drug dealers that's constantly destroying us as a people—well, they gettin' all the money . . . And this is what the young brothers and sisters is saying . . . they killing the young before they can even make up their mind what they want to be, when they get older. Most of 'em is startin' . . . 'bout ten, eleven, twelve years old, selling drugs . . . Gettin' paid. You know what I'm saying? So my thing, I'm gettin' my—gettin' me a job, you know, sayin', I want to start me a little . . . a little sellin' clothes business . . . You know, by the time the weather breaks. So, through the winter I'm just gonna build my money up, so I could start my own little thing. Hopefully I could open me up a store by next winter . . . really I want to specialize in kids' clothes.
>
> [Kenny, September 25, 1995]

Dreams

Having faith enough in the future to be able to dream was a formidable task for many of these men. Over years of struggle, and regardless of age, increased pragmatism and focus on survival narrowed many participants' vision. For some, PFS opened windows to a view of what they might accomplish.

There were men who had dreams of pursuing careers in the arts and entertainment industry. Claudio was interested in fashion and photography. He had taken a photography class in high school and wanted to attend further classes on his own, because "that's where I got all my—my good grades." He felt he took "good pictures" and "with a side job I'm saving money to get my camera," a Nikon with a micro lens, "because I like close-up shots." He thought a job in the garment industry might move him toward this goal. Arron, a talented rap lyricist (see box 3.1 in chapter 3), spent much of his time writing songs and rehearsing with his band. Chris Adam also dreamed of making it in the world of rap music. He said his band was "tight" and that their first step was getting known around New Jersey. But Chris was not counting on fame and fortune; first he needed a regular job. One day he mused, "Five years from now I want to be working, I want me and my girl and my kid to be staying, you know, in our own house, paying mortgage—not no rent—mortgage." Given that Chris had been unable to find more than temporary, minimum-wage jobs (when that), this modest version of the American Dream appears as challenging as his goal of becoming a rap star.

Then there is the simple, emotional dream of many of these men—to be with their children, to show how they care for them. Geraldo, who relinquished his role as father, remembered being dad and held onto this dream with difficulty.

> It's very difficult to deal with my, my children, which are now adults . . . Somehow, someday, I will have a chance to talk to 'em . . . And I will be there to say, look, I'm here, I love you. Maybe I've proven otherwise, maybe I did wrong. And if you won't give me another chance, all I want to know—all I want you to know is I'm here to help you, whatever I can do for you . . . And they'll decide if they'll let me, or they won't. But that's the way it's gotta be. I, I've accepted that.
>
> [Geraldo, September 28, 1995]

Daily Stress

> Sometimes I just need a vacation.
>
> [Sly, March 1995]

Every NCP in this book has expressed how the stresses of poverty interfered with their plans and dreams. Efforts to attain independence, stability, and a decent standard of living were often over-whelmed by immediate problems of daily survival. Many of the men in the sample told the interviewer that they had to take time out from the PFS program, or from things in general, to get their heads together. Hollywood, who felt continually pulled to help his grand-mother and other relatives, as well as his child and the child's mother, went to live with his father in Kansas for five months.

> I just had a break. Like I say, I got my break. A lot of people don't get that break . . . When I left, went up to, uh, stay with my father. I got—just needed to get away.
>
> [Hollywood, October 18, 1995]

Sly, who was participating in the Trenton PFS program during the day and working in the fast food industry at night, was pushing himself hard. When the pressure got to be too much, he went down south for a while. After a short respite with relatives, he returned to Trenton. Eventually he was brought back into the program. After his break, he felt energized, was able to refocus his efforts, and started school again.

Jah also dreamed of getting away.

JAH: We have a little money now. I'm trying to get this truck, and then I'm going to take me a nice trip down south.

INTERVIEWER: You're going down south to visit the folks down there?

JAH: Yeah! I just want to go on a nice vacation and take the family. Get out of this ghetto for a little while, anyway, man!

[May 8, 1995]

The notion that men who are unemployed and who cannot support their children may need a break is difficult for many people to grasp.[7] Our culture tends to link stress with high-powered jobs and life in the fast lane. But poverty is not idleness; surviving with min-imal economic resources is hard work. For Sly, Trane, and others in this book, stress was constant and time off, rare.

A ROCK AND A HARD PLACE: THE COURT AND CHILD SUPPORT ENFORCEMENT SYSTEM

The men in this sample stated that their two main problems were staying out of jail and paying child support. Every man in the sam-ple had been to jail for circumstances ranging from a CSE infraction to driving without a license and from disorderly conduct to more serious offenses. All were in debt to the child support system. Men who had experienced the harshness of the criminal justice system anticipated the same from the child support system, which they viewed as biased, self-serving, and hypocritical. Virtually all believed that the officials they encountered did not care about them or their families.

Mack, a twenty-seven-year-old African American, lived in Grand Rapids with his longtime girlfriend (whom he often called his wife) and three of his four daughters. His other daughter lived with relatives of his past partner. Although a high school graduate and a veteran, Mack had never found a steady job that paid enough to allow him to support his family and himself. Rather, he alternated between low-paying jobs in the mainstream economy and hustling with his friends. He had spent time in jail, but every time he came out of jail he went back home to the projects and tried to make it again. Mack felt strongly that the interaction between the court and CSE systems ultimately thwarts noncustodial parents in their attempts to deal with their obligations:

> Court—I hate that . . . In his courtroom once you stand before them and say your name, they're God. They can take your life away from you . . . To me, if these people are having a bad day, then you're having a bad day, and when it comes to the category I'm in, they call it deadbeat dad . . . A lot of us, out of the whole [PFS peer support] class, everybody—there was only two people that did not love their kids and did not want to be with their kids. Two people—and we're talking about [out of] easily fifty people. And they make it seem like we run away from our kids, we have babies and run—it's not like that, man. But I hate guys in court. They're unfair, they really unfair. They don't care about us, you know.
>
> [Mack, March 6, 1995]

> You pay to stay out of jail, simple as that. "If you don't pay us [CSE agency] our money, you go to jail." It, it destroys [the family]. They, they say, "Well, this is gonna help." How in the world can you help if daddy's in jail? 'Cause daddy is not just all about money.
>
> [Mack, October 18, 1995]

Like other participants, Mack felt trapped between a rock and a hard place. If he evaded the CSE system he could be jailed; likewise, if he answered a CSE summons and could not pay current and past child support, he might be jailed or severely reprimanded, and an admonition that goes on his record may be counted against him in future CSE hearings. Either way, he would be removed from his family and be unable to contribute to their support. (The issues of child support enforcement and jail are addressed in more detail in chapter 4.)

The choices and decisions these men made, the risks they took, and their conception of their opportunities and responsibilities reflect the social and economic environment in which they lived day-to-day.

Chapter 3

THE WORLD OUTSIDE PFS:
AN INSIDER'S VIEW

Every ghetto has a different name, but they are all the same.

[Coolio 1996]

There's nothing out there. What they're doing, they're selling drugs, they're working here and there, they're living off of different women, you know, off each other. They're trying to keep up with their payments. I don't even know if that's as much . . . you got men out there that are trying to survive and get educated, but the ones in my community, the ones that I see, education's the farthest thing from . . . they hear all this stuff on TV, and they just don't seem to have any hope for the future.

[Harry 1995]

At one time or another, every man in the qualitative sample echoed Harry's feelings of desolation, entrapment, hopelessness, and hardship. Such is the world in which these men must live, work, play, and survive. Others—notably William J. Wilson, in his recent book *When Work Disappears,* which is set in Chicago—have analyzed how the lack of opportunities within the nation's ghettos and isolation from the world outside the ghetto have pushed many African Americans out of the workforce and trapped them in socially and economically marginal environments. Poor Latino neighborhoods, although distinctive in some ways, exercise a similar undertow; likewise, poor whites may drift beyond the social and economic mainstream. Rather than focus on the structure of innercity poverty, this chapter looks at poor neighborhoods from the insider perspective of participants in the research.

We begin with an overview of the broader metropolitan communities and then focus on the neighborhoods in which participants live, the challenges these communities present, and the strengths on which the men can draw as they confront daily life.

COMMUNITY CHARACTERISTICS

Participants in this book are from seven metropolitan areas around the United States: Grand Rapids, Michigan; Jacksonville, Florida; Memphis, Tennessee; Springfield, Massachusetts; Dayton, Ohio; Trenton, New Jersey; and Los Angeles, California. These locations can be viewed through different lenses.

Greater Metropolitan Areas

Looked at through a macro-lens, the broad picture is one of cities that are rebuilding, growing, and changing. Chamber of Commerce brochures and mayoral or city managers' plans and projections highlight expanding economies, new business opportunities, and social and cultural attractions such as museums, theaters, libraries, symphonies, restaurants, historic districts, and public parks and gardens. Sports teams (professional or semiprofessional) located in the city or county are also showcased. By displaying these resources, a city or county advertises itself as a healthy, budding community— one that encourages individuals and families to move in, do business, and participate in the community's vibrancy. But not all districts, neighborhoods, or populations within these metropolitan areas are being revitalized.

The Inner City

In contrast to the glowing pictures projected by their cities' chambers of commerce, the men introduced in chapter 2 describe a world of scarce resources, deteriorating housing, neglected public facilities, and diminished opportunities. As the maps in appendix B show, most of the NCPs in this sample and in the full PFS demonstration live in areas that are densely populated by people of color (in most sites, African Americans, but in Los Angeles, African Americans and Latinos) and in which 20 to 40 percent or more of the population live below the official poverty level. In these high-poverty census tracts, rates of unemployment, high school dropouts, crime, arrests, chronic illness, and premature death are double or triple national levels.

Residents of these high-poverty areas tend to be socially and economically isolated. In their everyday cultural, economic, and social routines, participants in this study have little contact with the booming metropolis in which their community is located. For example, driving around Memphis in the fall of 1995 with Willie, a life-long resident of the city, the researcher and participant came on Memphis's major private university, located no more than a mile from Willie's home. By reputation both expensive and selective, it was, for Willie (a college graduate) also exclusive—not only as a result of cost, but also of accessibility. Over the many years that Willie had lived in Memphis, and despite his family's prominence in the local community, he had never once stepped inside this gated campus. Even now, he entered with apprehension. But once on university grounds, he thought he would have liked to have gone there. After touring the campus, he gathered materials for his daughter, who was about to graduate from high school and had decided to go into the army before starting college. Yet Willie had difficulty imagining her at a university that had always seemed out of bounds.

Participants had never entered numerous other "public" spaces. In Ohio, a job club instructor took the men in his class to the local library after discovering that many participants had never been to a public library and did not know how to use its resources in their job search efforts. This was common at all of the sites. With some exceptions, the only reason these men knew about their city's museums, civic centers, theaters, gourmet restaurants, and other resources was that they or someone they knew had worked there. Most were strangers to their city's main business and shopping districts. Few had attended a game at their city stadium or sports auditorium.

Participants were skeptical about urban renewal. They saw little to be gained in *their* neighborhoods by local officials' and politicians' plans to build a better city or stronger business community. In a conversation about his views on life in Trenton, Jah challenged the interviewer to explain how his neighborhood would benefit from the urban development taking place in his city. In his analysis, a new baseball stadium located in a poor area would reap profits for outsiders, but few benefits for local residents.

I'm going to [take pictures and send] them back to you because you need to see what's going on.[1] You won't see what's going on, but

you'll see what the people are living in, the credibility of abandoned
houses. Listen here. This is Mercer County. Here they is building
baseball stadiums over there, right, for the Caucasian people, right?
Baseball stadium. Half the black people don't even like baseball here,
you know? Matter of fact, it's more white people with baseball than
it is black. And they done built that big, giant stadium that I've never
went to and nobody else has ever went to in Trenton, but the money
from Mercer County and from Trenton pays for it. And here it is, all
these abandoned houses here that they should fix up and set up for
subsidized rent or something, you know? It's a business. They ain't
going to get no money from that, so what the fuck? Fuck them. Let
them live in abandoned buildings. I know millions and millions of
people here—I mean thousands of people—that live in abandoned
houses. That's just barely living, man.

[Jah, February 6, 1996]

Dismissing the claim of city officials that the stadium would improve
surrounding neighborhoods, Jah believed that most local residents
would never set foot in the stadium, either as fans or as employees.
He saw high unemployment and drugs on the streets as the primary
images of community he had to offer to his two young children.

Disparities between the macro-community and the micro-
community in which many participants live show where the NCPs
in this book actually *came from* as opposed to where, within a larger
social context, they resided.

ECONOMIC AND SOCIAL BOUNDARIES

William J. Wilson, in his recent book *When Work Disappears* and in his
earlier work *The Truly Disadvantaged,* has analyzed the origins and
consequences of the "new urban poverty" (Wilson 1987, 1996). The
deindustrialization of America—the transformation from a manu-
facturing to a service economy—began in cities (Wilson 1996). Fac-
tory jobs that, in the past, offered low-skilled workers entrance to the
mainstream economy have moved to other countries and to semi-
rural areas in the southern and central United States; warehouse,
sales, and many office jobs have moved to the suburbs. Government
cutbacks have reduced the number of entry-level civil service jobs
(clerk, postal worker) open to women and racial minorities. New
jobs in the service economy tend to be skewed, with high-level, high-
paying, fast-track positions for highly educated workers (lawyer,
stockbroker, and the like) and low-level, low-paying, dead-end jobs

for unskilled workers (waiter, janitor, service industry clerk), but little in-between. In central cities, even the "lousy jobs" that used to be available through informal networks are drying up (Waldinger 1996; Fagan 1992; Mason 1996), leaving many inner-city residents stranded. Wilson's stories of hopelessness, dismay, and anger in economically depressed, socially isolated neighborhoods in Chicago are echoed by the men in this sample.

Limited Opportunities

I know at least 200 guys that been tryin' to find jobs for years and still can't find nothin'.

[Bob, September 20, 1995]

As any of the men in this book will explain, they do not have enough money because there are not enough jobs of any kind and almost no steady jobs that pay living wages in their communities. Furthermore, although newspapers may carry pages of want ads, prospective employers outside their communities may not want to hire these men—either because the men lack the required education and work experience or because employers distrust inner-city, minority males.

The redistribution of jobs in metropolitan areas has had a direct impact on the attempt of inner-city NCPs to find work. In Trenton, for example, men frequently complained that potential jobs are located far from their neighborhoods and that public transportation services are so inadequate that they have to walk miles to return to their homes. Many times, a car and valid driver's license are requirements for employment, excluding many NCPs from better-paying jobs. Such barriers to newly forming labor markets are not specific to Trenton; they exist in all PFS sites, where access to the labor market is severely limited, and jobs with wages that would enable them to become economically and socially independent are nearly impossible to find (see table 3.1 for occupational wages by site).

Directly or indirectly, these NCPs described their isolation and recognized the importance of personal connections, which they lacked, in getting a better job. Arron explained how he would like to be able to maneuver through this job-market middle ground:

I need a chance. I need—I want to be like one of the people who just— you know, I want to—I'm the back door man, in other words. I want to come in through the back door. Not the front. The front door hard

Table 3.1 Mean Occupational Wages by Site (U.S. Dollars)

| | Median Wage | | | | | | All Sites | |
Site / Occupation	Los Angeles, California	Jacksonville, Florida	Springfield, Massachusetts	Trenton, New Jersey	Dayton, Ohio	Memphis, Tennessee	Mean Median Wage	Mean Median Salary[a]
Occupation								
General maintenance worker	10.77	10.00	12.52	11.98	10.50	9.50	10.88	22,360.00
Motor vehicles worker	18.60	13.85	—	—	15.00	14.05	15.38	31,668.00
Forklift driver	12.00	10.45	—	—	12.92	9.25	11.16	23,202.40
Guard I	6.50	5.00	—	10.56	6.50	5.25	6.76	14,064.96
Janitor	6.80	4.50	10.23	—	18.26	4.75	8.91	18,528.64
Material handling laborer	—	6.25	9.38	—	—	7.38	7.67	15,953.47
Shipping and receiving clerk	9.40	8.52	11.15	10.25	—	9.25	9.71	21,717.44
Truck drivers Medium trucks	14.96	11.73	—	—	10.40	9.82	11.73	24,390.55
Tractor trailers	14.00	15.55	—	—	13.95	10.15	13.41	26,832.00
Warehouse specialist	11.95	10.00	—	—	12.75	7.71	10.60	22,053.20
File clerk (general)	5.07	3.42	3.76	4.10	4.60	4.23	4.20	8,770.00

[a] Calculated using median wages, a forty-hour work week, and fifty-two work weeks excluding sites for which information is not available.

to get in, you know, everybody knock at the front door. I want to just go around to the back . . . real easy and smooth, you know . . . Like rather than have to go to college for something—hell, just tell me what to do . . . Oh, all right, I know you have to know a + b = c, but it—what it's gonna have to do with the job that I'm doing any damn way . . . ? [F]rom my working experience I see, right, aw—they make you go through all of this . . . just to get this kind of job . . . [when] all you got to do is just put the basics, the surface of it, to use . . . That's why I say college is a waste of time. Waste of money.

[Arron, September 27, 1995]

Unconnected and unemployed, Geraldo looked back on his days as a successful entrepreneur with nostalgia:

I was still in the ball game where I knew people, you know, business people that could have got me going . . . But then, that [would have] required moving out of California. Because nothing's happening in California and hasn't happened in the longest time.

[Geraldo, June 19, 1995]

Even men with training and work experience, including men who were veterans of the armed services (such as Lover, G-Man, Trane, Geraldo, and Mack), found that employers shied away from hiring them, without explaining why. As frustration set in, many gave up the search for meaningful work, instead returning to a job-by-job existence. Negative experiences compounded frustration. Trane described an experience where a seemingly legitimate job offer turned out to be a "hustle" (an employer's attempt to take advantage of a prospective employee):

[T]his job really pissed me off, this one job [a PFS staff member] sent me on . . . the guy goes, "Uh, yeah, Trane, we like your background and everything, you, you know, uh, you're just the man for this job." Ten bucks an hour . . . they guarantee me bringin' home four hundred bucks a week . . . So, he goes, "So, okay, Trane. You got the job." The job was supposed to have been, uh, warehousing, um, sales, and, um . . . inventory . . . So I goes way to Buena Park . . . we goes way, deep into East L.A . . . And this whole time we ridin', I'm thinkin'—I goes, "Man, where is this warehouse?" . . . [W]e get all the way on First Street, downtown L.A. . . . And he goes to his trunk, and he pulls out three big old bags, right? And, uh, he goes, "Here's yours, here's yours, here's yours," and I'm goin', "What is this?" And he goes,

"These are many radios. Start sellin'." . . . [H]ere I am in a shirt and
tie, right? . . . Smelling good . . . And he goes, "We'll want ten bucks
apiece for each one of these radios"—they had like thirty radios in
each bag—. . . I said, "Man, you know what?" I said, "This is illegal."
And he goes, "Who cares?" . . . I goes, "You know, I don't need a job
that bad where I have to panhandle." . . . And he goes, "You guys
always talkin' about you want a job and all this, and soon as someone
lend out a helpin' hand to help you, then you don't want to work for
it."

[Trane, September 19, 1995]

Trane walked away, feeling insulted and misled. Experiences like
this one contributed to the suspicion and skepticism many of these
men felt toward employers and their jobs.

The Impact of Race and Racism

Just as lack of educational credentials and erratic work histories hin-
dered the efforts of NCPs, so did social perceptions of inner-city residents, especially African American men. Wilson (1996), Massey
and Denton (1993), and others have shown that for African Americans, and to a lesser extent Latinos, living in or near severely economically depressed and racially isolated communities increases
the individual's vulnerability to unemployment and poverty. Moreover, the longer people live in these environments, the more problems they accumulate. Waldinger (1996) and Wilson (1996) suggest
that opportunities are extremely limited and that inner-city people
of color are scrutinized more thoroughly than their white counterparts. Indeed, PFS job developers reported that some employers
asked that "certain people" (men of color) not be sent for interviews.

Willie articulated the problem implied by many men in the sample:
racism. Willie had a criminal record, but he had avoided any long-
term incarceration. He had skills, patience, and humor and was
keenly aware of what he saw as the bias inherent in the "southern way
of life." In one conversation, Willie described how he lost a job despite
his efforts to fit in as the only African American on the work crew.

So at 11:45 every day they would give—everyone was chipping in—
give money for a pizza. So this particular day, I walked over to the
girl and hand her my money that I was chipping in with and walked
back to where I was supposed to be at. So this . . . lady came up to me
and said something in [a language other than English], which—I'm

no idiot—it was very harsh. You can tell by the expressions on her face. And so I told her, well, I don't understand. Then she turned around and in English is saying, "I can't tell you something you don't understand." So I said, now this woman's talking [in another language] and English to me. She walks off. She said that I left my post. She walked off, and she came back and told me that I was dismissed.

[Willie, March 2, 1995]

Later in the conversation Willie explained with great animation why he, like other men, quit jobs in the past even though he needed the pay and had no other employment prospects.

Afro-American men want—well, I can only speak for the Afro-American man who wants his family to look up to him. I can only speak of that man only. And I can speak for other men, too, the one that's naive and uncontrollable at times. I can also speak for him, but for right now, let's just deal with the family man. The black man who wants to just pay his bills, see his wife with some nice things, his kids with nice things, and just live. Okay. That man now is kicked so until it is unreal and yes, you are made at times to quit your job. They put so much amount of pressure on you still that sometimes it's not worth it, not even your own advantages, not even sometimes even [for] your family. It depends on how much pressure has been applied. No family man, no black Afro-American family man wants to depend on his wife to manage things. But as men, not as black men, but just as men, I mean, treat me [with respect].

[Willie, March 2, 1995]

The men in the sample reported that their experiences on regular and even temporary jobs were tainted by the distrust of employers and coworkers. Believing that they were on trial and considered "guilty until proven innocent" (because of their personal histories as well as stereotypes about minority men), these men sought to avoid confrontation at all costs. Their efforts to "stay cool" or "straight" sometimes were interpreted as sullen or even hostile, as "attitude." The men of color in the sample reported that consciously or unconsciously, employers and coworkers deliver small insults and subtle slights. The men become angry, and suddenly, or so it seems, tensions boil over: the minority worker is laid off or quits, confirming the worker's suspicion that *they* are against him and the employer or coworker's suspicions that *the worker* does not fit in. In some cases, of course, dismissal is the result of simple financial calculation: employers hire and fire temporary workers as a matter of policy, to avoid paying benefits and making long-term commitments. Some men also believed that such short-term hiring practices are designed to evade regulations covering minority workers.

Viceroy worked for a packaging company; after five months, he was planning to move out of his relatives' home and into his own place when he was suddenly dismissed. In an attempt to understand why he was laid off, Viceroy considered the ailing economic climate as well as racism.

> From my understanding, the reason why they laid people off is that they lost a contract with the military. They make milk, or they pasteurize milk, and they lost a big contract with the military. So, you know, they couldn't make as much money. The military's one of their big moneymakers. But the exact reason, I don't know. There was people that was working there through a temp service and they didn't lay them off, but they laid me off. So, I don't know . . . I think there was a lot of favoritism. A lot of favoritism. You do a lot of brown-nosing, from my understanding, you get what you want to get. But you know, that ain't me. I would say that they were being racist, but the guy that was the temp, he was black, and I know he did a lot of brown-nosing. But I don't know, man.
>
> [Viceroy, March 26, 1996]

When hard times hit, these men rarely used legal remedies or the few social services available to them, except for food stamps and some unemployment insurance, when they qualified for them. Experience had convinced them either that the safety net did not exist for them or that the benefits were not worth the efforts and hassle.

> I missed a couple of days and when I came back to pick up my check . . . he said, you're laid-off. He really didn't ask no questions, he just said, you're laid-off, just like that. And unemployment—went down there, and I told them what happened, so they turned my benefits on, and they gave me $209 for three weeks . . . Then they sent me a letter telling me I had an interview. I went in for the interview, they said, your benefits have been denied. I said, how are you going to deny something that's never yours? That's my money . . . simple as that. I said, you-all didn't tell me how I had to be fired or how I had to be laid-off when you took this money out my check. They didn't tell me that. They just told me, we takin' this money out your check, this is for whenever you don't have a job, you can come back here and you can get this money to put you back on your feet till you get a job. But that's a lie. United States still lying . . . So I left it alone, see, 'cause

we used to people taking stuff and not being able to do nothing about it, and now I still can't do nothing about it. You go to appellate court, you appeal, your appeal don't necessarily say you're going to win . . . And when you appeal, more than likely you're going to lose. Especially if the job have no union, so you have nobody backing you up, saying this is how you got fired—you have no witnesses at all. So I have no tools to win.

[Jah, November 1, 1994]

Jah voiced the widespread belief among the men of color in this sample that the deck is stacked against them, in the public as well as the private sector. These unsatisfactory encounters on the job and with social service agencies were not unique to African American participants; they also affected Latinos and whites who had fallen out of mainstream employment. Their experiences differed on certain levels, however.

A Racial Comparison

A major difference between white and African American NCPs in the sample is that, when they entered PFS, the majority of African Americans had participated less in the mainstream economy. Moreover, isolated in or near the inner city, they had relatively little contact with individuals who had succeeded in the mainstream. In their efforts to find regular employment, many of the black men were not starting over; they were starting from scratch. African American families can (and do) offer young men food, shelter, odd jobs, cash, and noncash support, but rarely jobs that might lead to self-sufficiency or economic stability. Latino communities foster small businesses that serve local residents and create jobs (albeit low-paying) and opportunities for entrepreneurs such as Geraldo, who enjoyed success as an independent businessmen (albeit short-lived). The legitimate businesses in low-income, inner-city, African American communities tend to be owned by outsiders or, in the case of African American–owned businesses (barber and beauty shops, pawnshops, liquor stores, Afro-centrist clothing stores), are too small to hire many employees or are not quite legitimate (unlicensed repair shops).

In contrast, non-Latino white NCPs, no matter what their situation at the time of initial contact (unemployed and homeless, under-educated, with a substance abuse problem, emotionally unstable), were able to start new chapters in their lives or at least continue with the confidence that they were going to succeed. With the exception of one NCP, all the white, non-Latino fathers in this sample found jobs relatively quickly, either through a friend or relative or through the program.

White NCPs in the sample were also more mobile geographically. Once they gained employment, they usually worked for a time, then moved out of the county and state (this was confirmed by the observations of many PFS program staff). By the time they began a second job, most stopped contacting the researcher, and attempts to find them through key informants were generally fruitless. This was not a common pattern for NCPs of color in the sample; as a rule, whether they gained steady employment or not, they generally stayed where they were, lacking the resources and often the desire to move far. This suggests that when the white men in the sample fell out of the mainstream economy, unless they hit bottom (long-term homelessness), they were able to climb back up. And once back on their feet, they were able to pack up their work experience and move on in search of better or different jobs and living situations.

Latino men in the sample did not share the white NCPs' confidence that they could sustain their accomplishments or obtain improved or meaningful work. But they did manage to maintain a level of stability that the African American NCPs could not, especially a stable residence and accessibility via telephone. During this research, all but one of the Latino fathers could be reached at the same number or offered a contact person who knew how to reach them. Latino participants in this study were also more likely than whites or blacks to find jobs through friends, and these jobs often were located within their communities.

Given severely limited opportunities, the puzzle is that the African American men in this study were more likely than white or Latino participants to remain within the neighborhoods in which they were born and grew up. This does not mean that they never left their communities, only that they were more likely to return home eventually. To be sure, their living situations were unstable, but usually within a limited radius. Why do the inner cities function as a magnet?

COMMUNITY STRENGTHS AND WEAKNESSES

Midway through the study, in 1995, talk of the Million Man March began to circulate in neighborhoods, PFS groups, and the mass media. Viewed in the press as a separatist (antiwhite) movement, participants and sympathizers saw the march as a step toward reclaiming their self-esteem and pride. It was a challenge issued to the African American community by African Americans themselves to stop the hemorrhaging and decimation of their vast community. The underlying message was that men who have been stigmatized, isolated, and marginalized by the larger society have something of value to offer their communities. The call to stop hurting and start helping one another, to stop blaming "society" or personal circumstances, and to assume responsibility was heard by the million or more African American men who joined the march in Washington, D.C., in spirit, if not in person.

In one of his rap poems, Arron captured the delicate balance between the bravado of a street-wise survivor and the plea of a young man crying "stop" (box 3.1). This poem, like the Million Man March, recognizes both the hopes and the challenges facing the African American community and speaks to the need of African American men to do more than just survive. Caught in a trap partly of his own making, Arron saw little way out, yet dreamed of escaping. In different ways, all of the men in the sample expressed the ten-

---

Box 3.1 "Blue in the Sky"

I want to come up, like the blue in the sky,
so I maintain my focus
when I get high. I can't be trippin',
a nigger gots to do somethin'. It ain't easy livin'
in the East Side of Compton.
Niggers bumpin' down the avenues, while we havin' brews,
what the fuck I'm gonna do, when I have nothing to use?
So I had to learn hard, from the ruckus—I'm out there
slingin' the weed, makin' the deed,
gatherin' up suckers. Checkin' all busters, actin' like they the big boss,
tryin' to [rip] from me—that monkey ass got tossed. You're lost.
Now that I'm takin' what you came with,
while I'm aimin' at your head with a high power Tech,
chains from your neck
is now in my possession.
What a fucked-up way for you to learn a valuable lesson.
Niggers should have told you 'bout me, bro,
because I'm givin' 'em second chances, only want to let you know.

[Arron, August 1995]

sions between risk and responsibility, survival and spirituality, the pull of family and the call of the street. The challenge for many of these men was to prevent their children from being consumed by the sense of hopelessness and futility that often engulfed them.

The Neighborhood

The neighborhoods in which most of these NCPs lived had little to offer in the way of formal institutions (banks, safe recreational facilities), voluntary associations (block associations, parent-teacher associations), or other social supports. A walk through one of these areas reveals a history of neglect and abandonment: boarded-up stores and theaters, vacant lots, decaying and burned-out housing, convenience stores instead of supermarkets, check-cashing and lottery shops instead of banks, street vendors instead of department stores. The men described their worlds in terms of despair:

> Trenton is mostly drug-infested in every area you go to—it's drug-infested, man. Your kids, no matter you walk to the store, take your kid to the store, he sees it. You take him to the pizza place, he sees it. Or you take him to the mall, and he sees it. Take him downtown to buy him a pair of sneakers, he sees it. Wherever you take him! There ain't nowhere you can take your kid that he ain't going to see drugs anyway. You take him to Chuck E. Cheese, he'll see it.
>
> [Jah, May 8, 1995]

> What about the homeless? That's, that's the biggest issue in this country. What about the drugs? That's the biggest issue in this country. What about the hun—the hungry people? I mean, what about the families who—the reason the family's corrupt, the reason the kids are in the orphanage homes, is because they know that the mother and father had no opportunity.
>
> [Willie, August 14, 1995]

At the street level, in individual dwellings, the notion of "the greater community" held little real meaning for most men in this study. Communities are created by individuals with their own strengths, weaknesses, expectations, and issues. Although the men in this study may be considered, and considered themselves, part of a macro-community—the larger racial community, for example—they were isolated from the larger society (especially the economic community). For many men, their sense of community—of similarity or identity, participation, and sharing—began and ended inside the apartments or houses where they and their families lived. What was happening in the world, the nation, or their city seemed irrelevant, overshadowed by the challenge of their own basic survival. They could not ignore what was happening on the streets, but their primary social circle consisted of their mothers, fathers, friends, girlfriends, and children. For other NCPs, however, the street life *was* their community. Bourgois (1995) and Anderson (1992) have discussed the lifestyles and networks that develop through "working the streets."

The men in this sample had hidden vitality, strong family bonds, deep spirituality, generosity, and heroism—qualities too often overlooked in descriptions of the ghetto. Much has been written about the breakdown of formal and informal institutions in poor, inner-city neighborhoods. One enduring institution, dating back at least to the carry-out shop described in Eliot Liebow's book *Tally's Corner*, is the neighborhood restaurant. Because the men in this sample often were "guests" in other people's homes, they did not feel comfortable using the kitchen and often found buying a meal to be more affordable and convenient than buying groceries. The local take-out also functions as an informal community center, where residents make and maintain connections, keep up with local news, and perhaps find a temporary job or a helping hand.

One day, the researcher met with Claudio in East Los Angeles. After a tour of the school where he worked as a part-time aide, they went to a local hangout for some lunch. This eatery was frequented by students from the local high school and friends of Claudio's, as well as by local construction workers and a few people who were once from the area and knew where the food was good and inexpensive. We both had large lunches for less than $6, a luxury in Los Angeles. We picked a spot near the service window and talked; the researcher was the only monolingual (English) speaker in the spot. During our conversation, people came up to Claudio, speaking in Spanish, laughing, and leaving with their take-out orders. After a young women left our table, a somewhat boisterous man staggered up, locked his gaze on Claudio, and started speaking to him in Spanish. Claudio spoke patiently with the man for about five minutes. Finally, the conversation ended, and Claudio reached into his wallet, which contained literally two dollars. He took out one of the dollars, handed it to the man, and told him in Spanish to get something to eat. As the man exited, Claudio explained what had transpired:

CLAUDIO: He was just asking that he—he's homeless, he said he needs money for something to eat. I told him, like you say, hey, you know how it feels.

INTERVIEWER: Exactly.

CLAUDIO: I ain't got much, but I tell you, that's the only buck I have (but I'm not going to give him my other checks that I have [Claudio had just been paid])—hey, when you been through it, what could I say?

[December 5, 1995]

Most of the men in this study had been through not just poverty and homelessness, but also violence, crime, and incarceration. Yet the interviewer witnessed many such examples of compassion and camaraderie.

The Street Life: Gangs, Violence, Drugs, and Fear

Many of the participants in this study had experienced drugs, gangs, and violence. G Man described the pressures on himself and his immediate family when they moved to Los Angeles.

My stepfather got killed in Texas, my mother moved down here to try to get away from it . . . The number one thing when we came out here, you have to be in a gang . . . If you're not in a gang . . . with them, you know, they're going to be around you, so you might as well be in one. My brother's been in trouble ever since we moved here. In and out of penitentiary, he's thirty-three years old . . . I've been in trouble with the law myself, but not consistently. I'm through with that.

[G Man, May 19, 1995]

Los Angeles is the only home Arron had ever known. As a young man, he made his living in the streets, establishing a powerful presence and making enemies. Yet Arron, like others in and outside of this study, remained close to his family. Arron's mother cared deeply for her son and prayed that he not meet the same fate as her other two sons, one of whom was killed and the other paralyzed as a result of gang violence. Arron himself developed a bleeding ulcer at the age of fifteen and did not expect to live past thirty.

See, I've been trying to stay on the right foot for the last two years now, you know, but nothing's been working out for me; that's what frustrates me and makes me want to go back into the devious things that I used to do . . . in order to get by, because you don't have no choice. I mean, generally, on GR [general relief], generally you get $212. Nobody don't want that. I mean it's good to have, but it's no money. It's spent before you even get it, and it's spent on something that you won't have anything to show for it, a meal or something, maybe, if that. It's hard out here, it's so hard, it's frustrating . . . And now I'm trying to do it the right way and been trying for the past couple of years, but it's frustrating because nothing, nothing comes in from it. The only thing that came through for me is the one little job for two months, not even that much.

[A]t times I just really want to give up and forget it. I'll just start slinging dope and something, but I don't want to do that because it's even getting—that's when you go to jail. And that's how the world is set up, so people like me, bam! go to jail. Nobody want to hire you.

[Arron, May 17, 1995]

These men described a world in which it is easier to get arrested and jailed than it is to find steady work. This became more and more clear as the research progressed (see Wilson 1996; Kasarda 1992; Jencks 1994; and Waldinger 1996). All the men in this sample had been arrested at some point after turning sixteen years old. Almost half spent at least a day in jail during the course of this research, while only thirteen had a full-time job at some point during the same period. The recent work of Freeman (1987, 1996a, 1996b) supports the finding that men, especially men of color, experience frequent and close contacts with the criminal justice system, either by being incarcerated or under its watchful eye (being on probation, under house arrest, awaiting trial).

Nearly one-third of the men in this sample acknowledged that they had earned money from illegal activities (this did not include working "under the table," which almost all reported as a source of some income). As the data from Wilson, Fagan, Freeman, and others suggest, participating in illegal activities, especially related to drugs, may be one of the only reliable ways to make money within inner-city neighborhoods. However, the return for such work is not as profitable as many people believe.

Not one person in this sample claimed to enjoy dealing drugs or being involved with criminal activity. To each, it was a way to make money. The men themselves felt it was wrong to be selling. Yet the alternatives, as they perceived them, were so limited that dealing appeared to be the only game in town. During a car ride, Lover lamented his financial situation. Almost in tears with anger, he declared in resignation, "Maybe I'll be a drug dealer like they want me to be." As on many occasions over the previous few months, Lover had spent yet another two hours in two different courts, trying to regain custody of his children, with no success. He did not have enough money to buy over-the-counter medicine for his flu, and he did not have access to any medical system or doctor. Money was not the main cause of his frustration, but rather the fact that he did not see any opportunity to improve his circumstances. He did not feel that any individual or organization was willing to give him a chance to prove himself as a productive citizen. Lover did not turn to selling drugs, but other men who reached similar levels of need and desperation did.

Drug dealing often provides low-income men with a substantially higher income than most could earn in the legitimate labor market. In another conversation, a participant who requested anonymity explained how he provided for his family:

INTERVIEWEE: I don't have no rent, no car note . . . That's the only thing I got going for me. That's what keeps my head above water. I mean, I have drowned several times, but shit, I always float back up. And that's the reason why I'm able to float back up . . . Because I don't have house note and a car note.

INTERVIEWER: Say you're doing your hustle and stuff—about how much a month do you make?

INTERVIEWEE: Hustling? . . . Depend on what kind of hustle . . . If it's drugs, then—$2,000, $3,000 a week . . . If it's legal hustling—'bout $170 a week.
[Anonymous, September 20, 1995]

For this man, as for others, dealing drugs was a last resort, a kind of safety net.

Dealing is a dangerous game, as all readily acknowledged. Over half the men who had been serious players in the drug world were, at the time of the initial interview, trying to go straight. They wanted to distance themselves from "the game" because it was getting "too wild." Bob, a big-time dealer for nearly ten years, explained.

I don't want to be over there in the rowdy part of town—I have to be the wildest out of all the bunch, and I don't wanna be like that. I wanna just live, I don't have to be all like that. I didn't come in like that, so I don't have to be like that. I finally learned that I don't have to worry about what another person thinks. It's what I know. Forget what they think, it's what I know. I don't care what they think about me. I know that I'm successful and I'm going to stay successful and I'm not going back to the streets to get what I need. I can work . . . I can work. I could've did it from the jump, it's just that I was lazy and I wanted to sit back and make that money. But that's not what's happening.

[Bob, December 1994]

For men like Bob, who was working at a job that paid $6 an hour at the time of this interview, going straight meant a substantial reduction in income. Leaving "the game" is not equivalent to quitting a job or getting divorced. The stark realities of this lifestyle—being unwelcome in the territory of former rivals, being arrested and incarcerated, or getting shot and killed for past or suspicious behavior—shadow the men who once were players. Men who, during the course of many conversations, admitted to being in life-threatening situations or having a cousin, brother, partner, or acquaintance who had been killed or seriously injured usually spoke emphatically about going straight and looking for less dangerous work. This change in awareness was not related to age; it happened to the youngest and oldest as well as to some who were in their late twenties and early thirties.

Drugs are a major concern in the neighborhoods in which these men lived and dealt. Yet if a community mobilizes to rid its streets of drugs and crime, it inevitably places its sons and daughters in jail for trying to bring money into their homes. For almost every person determined to get rid of gangs, dealers, and drugs, a mother is praying, "Not my son," or a woman, "Not my man," or a friend has to "pour out some liquor" and wonder if his own time is coming.[2]

Families know when a son, brother, boyfriend, or neighbor is engaged in illegal activities. In most cases, they do not condone dealing or hustling, but neither do they condemn the men in their lives. Living side by side with them, in the same harsh environment, some see such activities as the key to survival. They may lecture, cry, and pray, but they rarely turn him out. Over time, many are willing to offer emotional support and share their own limited financial resources to help the men survive and maintain contact with their children. Immediate family, kin, and girlfriends often stick by their men in bad times and provide the inspiration and courage for them to go straight.

SOCIAL NETWORKS AND KIN

The networks of kin, friends, and associates of participants usually had as limited resources and as few contacts with the mainstream as they did. In general, inner-city blacks (male and female) are less likely to know someone who is steadily employed, has some college education, or is married than are Latinos living in similar environments (Wilson 1996). According to our observations, they are also less likely to receive help from a relative or friend in finding a job. But although family and friends might not be able to help these men achieve certain mainstream dreams, they are vital in helping them to stay afloat. In many cases, NCPs were only able to live in an apartment or house because someone else, integral to their inner circle or community, was covering the cost of the residence. During the course of this research, every apartment or home visited was modestly furnished and decorated. There was nothing fancy or extravagant. A typical household inventory might include a kitchen table and chairs (usually occupied), much-used and often tattered furniture opposite a television set, and assorted children's toys. Whether the place belonged to family or friends, was well-kept or not, or was a single room occupancy (SRO), the men had to respect the owner(s) and behave like guests. This connection both to a person who cared and to a secure domicile allowed some participants to feel grounded enough to pursue economic opportunities. Men whose personal lives were less stable, whose living situations were more precarious, and who were disconnected faced a more difficult struggle.

Family Connections

Mothers and kin often played a key role in helping NCPs stay afloat and connected to their children while they got established or attempted to straighten out their lives. Bob and his girlfriend had lived together off-and-on since their first child was born. During most of the study, however, Bob was unemployed and lived with his mother, younger brother, and various "drop-in" relatives. His children and their mother were regular visitors, too, because he wanted the children to have a sense of who he was, to get to know their father. But he felt that he and his girlfriend needed to work out personal and employment issues before he moved back in with her, which he planned to do eventually.

Bob had been a well-known drug dealer—as he put it, "the wildest out of all the bunch." He came into the program because he had not paid child support and because he wanted to find a job and turn his life around. He credited his family, especially his mother, with never giving up on him, helping him to put his street life behind him, and making him conscious of his responsibilities as a father and a black man. "Yeah, my mom always be behind me—no matter what I do, she always be behind me."

Kenny lived with his mother in a house in Trenton that was given to her by an aunt. Their door was always open to relatives, and visitors frequently came and went. Kenny and his stepbrother spent much of their time improving the townhouse their aunt had given them—fixing walls, repairing plumbing, and expanding their mother's bedroom. Kenny dropped out of school in the ninth grade. At the time, he was running the streets and drinking heavily. After his first child was born, when he was nineteen, Kenny began to settle down. His family was a major source of emotional support and financial backing, helping him to find jobs and to care for his child.

Kenny had held many low-to-moderate-wage jobs in hospitals and nursing homes, but never for very long. He did not work steadily at any job during the nearly two years he was in this study. Yet Kenny's family, both immediate and extended, did whatever they could to help him and his baby get by. His real passion was cooking, and he sometimes worked for a relative in the catering business, earning good, but irregular, money. The owner of the business believed that Kenny was talented but needed formal training before he could cook for a living; this same relative also housed Kenny when he needed a break from his mother's home. After a disagreement, however, her new husband forbade him to come around. Unable to contribute to his mother's household expenses, Kenny, his girlfriend, and their daughter lost their telephone privileges.

When Kenny entered PFS, he was caring for his first child, who had lived with him and his family for nearly a year. Two days later, he was awarded legal custody of this child. A second child, whose mother had a drug problem, had been "dropped at his doorstep" by the mother's sister, for the protection of the baby. Unsure that the second child was his, he was awaiting the results of a paternity test. But he cared deeply about the baby's well-being and was prepared to take on the responsibility of fatherhood, regardless of whether or not he was proven to be the biological father. His family urged him to check his potential child support obligations with the CSE agency, to protect himself in case the new baby was not his, and supported him when he decided to take legal responsibility for the child.

Family Demands

Living with family exacts a cost, however. Many of the men in the sample, both young and older, expressed their feelings of obligation and responsibility to provide for their mothers, brothers, sisters, and grandparents. Sometimes, the burden was overwhelming. A twenty-three-year-old African American father of a one-year-old child, Hollywood (a name he acquired on the street for his flamboyant style) was a high school graduate who had been helping his family since he was a young boy.

HOLLYWOOD: I'm just tryin' to help people, not—you know, just tryin' to help all—everybody I know.

INTERVIEWER: And yourself?

HOLLYWOOD: Yeah. See, y'all don't understand . . . court be on me . . . I have a grandmother I'm trying to help, I got a mother I'm trying to help . . . None of 'em work. I've got two little brothers who're talented as heck, you know . . . And they messin' up in school, they—I'm tryin' to help them . . . Then I got my fiancée, you know . . . She want to get married. Plus, I got to raise my son, then I got my nieces and nephews, my brother in prison, so, he got two babies, and . . . one of the baby's mothers ain't doin' . . . so I got to try to take care of that. You know, I got my hands full.
[October 18, 1995]

Like several other participants, Hollywood began selling drugs in his early teens and became a known dealer in his part of town. He looked at drugs as an opportunity to make good money and be a man, a provider, to his family. Near the end of the research period, Hollywood and his child's mother got married and moved into a place of their own. Whether this move will lessen Hollywood's burden—and help him to "go straight"—remains to be seen.

Disconnected

In contrast, some participants had little or no contact with their relatives and few friends. While other men reached points of desperation from time to time, these loners tended to be habitually dispirited and hopeless. Fila-G, a thirty-six-year-old African American father of seven, lived in his grandmother's house. Although he felt much love and pride for his children, he had little contact with them. At times, he aspired to turn the situation around, but finding the trust to approach his family and open the door to ongoing communication was no easy matter, for either side. His manner was often one of resignation.

> I'm just sittin' on the porch. Well, right now, I could truly say I don't foresee much of nothing, you know. Gotta get over, see kids, or something like that, and, uh, you know, it ain't much a broke man can do.
> [Fila-G 1995]

A life-long resident of Memphis, Tennessee, Fila-G had a high school diploma but had never held a regular, salaried job. Instead he survived on part-time, short-term jobs for hourly wages and at times sold drugs. Fila-G had three children with two different women before marrying and settling down with a third woman who bore him four children. After thirteen years, this marriage ended in divorce. Fila-G struggled with a serious alcohol problem, sometimes combined with drug use. He admitted to the researcher (but not to PFS staff) that his drinking contributed to his problems with employment and relationships.

During the study, Fila-G was living in his grandmother's house, where he had moved a few years earlier after he and his wife divorced. A stepbrother and other relatives occasionally stayed there, too. But his relationships with his relatives were tenuous. During the spring of 1995, Fila-G was mostly unemployed, scraping by on the part-time work he was able to get from an uncle who owned a general maintenance business. When his uncle unexpectedly became very sick and was hospitalized, instead of letting Fila-G take over the existing jobs, he let both the jobs *and* Fila-G go. He did this knowing that his nephew was in desperate financial shape. Later in the year, the uncle agreed to loan him some money to pay the taxes on his grandmother's house. Fila-G's relatives did not expect much from him, and he felt the same toward them.

As a rule, the disconnected men in this study had more problems than did participants who were connected to family and kin and were less likely to make concrete steps toward financial independence. Fila-G and others like him tended to end the program much where they began (see chapter 7).

Family Values and Spirituality: Sources of Strength

Family and religion played key roles in these men's lives. In one long, contemplative discussion, Kenny described his philosophy on family sacrifice.

> That's why we as blacks here, and the women in America, we need to go back to our cultural [heritage], living like family, loving one another, caring for one another, so the way we going through things now, get with a sister . . . time go on, you . . . you don't want to deal with it no more . . . Suppose she pops up pregnant, you know what I'm saying? Then you have most brothers who don't want to deal with her nor the baby. You have some brothers who don't want to deal with her and deal with the baby. You have some brothers that may sit there and deal with her and the baby and still have to pay child support because she's getting welfare.
>
> I've got a good mother, man, that loves my daughter, man, that would lay down and die for my daughter. My sisters, they do anything they can for my daughter, anything, and what's so good about it is that . . . me and [my daughter's mother] have a good friendship, and we communicate a lot. That's why it's not really—we won't have to argue about things that my daughter needs—she's going to get it . . . I owe these people this money now, and she knew from day one when she got pregnant that my daughter would never have to want for anything because of the position that my mother and them is [in].
>
> The way they live, the money they got. The money my father got. They knew that my daughter would never even have to want for milk, Pampers, anything like that, clothes. My daughter got $100, her shit cost more than mine, you know what I'm saying? My daughter would never have to want for nothing'. [M]y daughter did need that health care, and you know they need to get checked out, when they get pregnant they have to go every month for a checkup. She needed that, so I can't really fault her for going and doing that, because I wanted my daughter to be born healthy, you know what I'm saying?
>
> [Kenny, February 22, 1995]

Neither Kenny's philosophy nor the support he had received was unique among the men in this study. Sometimes the support came from sources other than the family; sometimes it came in conjunction with the family's assistance. Trane, who spent three years unemployed, stood up to his family's ridicule for "living off of a woman" and fathering children who were distant. As he made efforts to find work, maintain his relationship with his two daughters, and reengage with his son, his family gradually became more supportive and caring toward him and his daughters, who were living under very difficult circumstances with their mother and grandmother. The grandparents started talking to one another in the hopes of finding a better situation for the two girls. Trane began working two jobs to try to help his daughters and regain access to his son. Throughout all his efforts, he had the steadfast financial and emotional support of his girlfriend of eight years. He eventually was able to reunite with his son.

Nelson's mother, who lived in Memphis, highlighted how their family's tight network continued to serve her son, as it did herself and her siblings before him:

> Because a lot of times, you know, when parents try to correct things that they see wrong, they think we're still chastising them. When they get a certain age, they don't feel like they need it . . . So I have to bag up . . . You have to bag, you know, we have to bag up and let you-all see it you-all's way first. Yeah, and when you realize it, well, you says, "Mmm, mama's way wasn't so bad after all."
>
> Oh, that little boy [Nelson's son], he come to see me all the time. He stay with his grandmother. And if I'm home with him when he pass by—I don't stay too far from school—he'll stop by and eat a piece of cake . . . Yeah, and come and look at TV for awhile and keep on going . . . This one here, I got from diapers, the oldest one. Now, the other one, she calls . . . I been in touch with her since she's a baby. So [Nelson] keep in touch with his children.
>
> We have a close-knitted family. Like my sisters and brothers, we was very close, and we all have our children raised in that way. They're pretty well—we're a pretty, well, close family.
>
> [Nelson's mother, April 29, 1994]

For many of the men in this sample, spirituality was a major source of support and strength. Not all of the men in the sample went to church regularly, if at all; nor did all consider themselves religious. But more often than not, when these men discussed their struggles and life experiences, and what gave them hope, courage, and purpose, spirituality ranked with family and community. A few of the men explained how their spiritual beliefs enriched their lives.

'Cause our thing now, like I said, is just to come together for a better world . . . It's just everyone is in the world, we accept them all, as the human family of the planet Earth . . . You know, 'cause one thing that definitely links us all together is the red blood that runs through our veins, you know. So we just, you know, create on that type of aspect. We don't get into the, um, racism part or blamin' the white man for this or blamin' the white man for that, you know what I'm saying. More or less we have learned to become the guards of responsibility, to take responsibility for our own ways and actions, you know, 'cause as we are taught, the world doesn't need to change, it is each and every one as an individual who needs to change . . . and take respon- sibility for the world and what's going on in the world, and do their best to make it a better world.

[Kenny, November 6, 1995]

Well, I go to church, and it's not to hear the choir, it's not to see who's dressing. What I wear now is what I wear to church. It's to hear the Word, and if you hear the Word and listen and take it your own way, not the person sitting next to you, don't take it their way . . . nobody's way but your way, and you and God will deal with that on a one-on- one basis . . . I thank God every morning. It's the first thing I do, is get on my knees and thank God for letting me see another day. If I can't do nothing else, I can at least do that!

[Viceroy, March, 7, 1995]

[The church is] everything to me . . . It's always been. But now that [my baby's] here, it means even more to me because I know that I'm giving him something that my grandmother and them gave me. Nobody holds it on me, and nobody threatens me. Come Sunday morning, I may wake up sick and say I don't feel like I'm going today, but I go anyway. I go anyway, because I know there's a blessing for me, there's always a blessing.

[Tyrone, February 10, 1995]

Spirituality helped these men, and others from their communities, to overcome anger (Kenny), maintain hope (Viceroy), carry on family traditions (Tyrone), and generally find the strength to carry on and, in incremental steps, move forward when an opportunity presents itself.

CONCLUSIONS

When poor NCPs talk about themselves, the communities in which they live, the personal and social obstacles they face, and how they cope day-to-day, stereotypes of "deadbeat dads" fade. Men such as Lover, Mack, and Jonesy served their country honorably in the military. Jah, Viceroy, and Derrick took whatever jobs were available in order to continue living and staying connected with their children, mostly on an unofficial basis because of the rules governing TANF, AFDC, and public housing. Others like Bob, Kenny, G Man, and Claudio made efforts to be successful within their communities by seeking ways to do right. Each of these men faced, head-on, the lack of opportunity within their immediate and extended communities and was, on more than one occasion, knocked down.

The challenge is to discover ways to help these men and their families do more than simply subsist.

Chapter 4

THE NONCUSTODIAL PARENTS' PERSPECTIVES ON CHILD SUPPORT AND THE CHILD SUPPORT SYSTEM

"I always see my kids" is a common assertion of the men in this sample. As shown in figure 2.2 in chapter 2, these economically poor NCPs reported having more contact with their children than the public and policymakers might expect of "deadbeat dads" who have not met their support obligations. How much contact is enough is another question.

Taking the perspective of the poor noncustodial parent, this chapter examines two pivotal questions. First, does paying child support through the child support enforcement system make sense to low-income noncustodial parents? Second, does paying child support make NCPs feel more connected to their child?

Mack, who lived with three of his four children and their mother, described his feelings toward the child support system:

> So they, they take this bill, and they say, "Well, we want you—the money you owe us." You know what I'm saying? This is what they do. That's, that's all they care about. They want the money they owe it—they—that you owe them. That's it, that's, that's plain—plain and simple as that. You owe them some money, you payin' them money, or you go to jail. [Sarcastically] I love this, man, this is—this is the greatest thing in the world, all right? [The child support agency] is the biggest pimps in the world, all right?
>
> [Mack, October 18, 1995]

Although some men were not as vehement in their disdain, most had had negative encounters with the CSE system. While participating in the PFS program, a month or so after he went through the court process, Mack described his experience in court.

INTERVIEWER: What happened when you were in court and they told you that you were going to be in Parents' Fair Share? Tell me about that.

MACK: Even at that time, I didn't want to go there. I was telling them, I was like, you all want me to go to this program, what am I supposed to do to make it? They was like, listen. We don't got nothing to do really with what you're going to do to make it. All we're concerned about is the kids, you know. That's what they told me. They were like, whether you go, that's your choice; if not, they send it back to court, and they're to get the police on you. That's exactly what they said.

INTERVIEWER: How did you feel then?

MACK: Like a piece of trash. I'm not saying they gotta care about me but it's like, forget you, we don't care what happens to you, you just better get down there if you don't want to be in jail.

[March 1995]

Despite the anger, resentment, and alienation that many of the men in this sample felt toward child support enforcement, unlike other NCPs, who chose to avoid the system, they decided to appear for a hearing. The following sections describe what they received in return and how this process affected their lives.

TURNING YOURSELF IN: WHEN THE CSE OFFICE CALLS

All of the men in this sample received at least one official letter, phone call, or, in some cases, direct visit from a public or municipal representative (police person or social worker) requiring that they appear at a hearing to address the issue of their failure to meet their child support obligations.

> I was supposed to have been in this program since 1994, but I wasn't—I signed up for it, but I just wasn't coming, you know, so years has gone by, you know, I wasn't paying child support, but then I got employed, and then I started paying child support. I mean, not the full amount. I just was paying what I could pay, you know what I'm saying? So then I got unemployed again. They took my income tax. I mean, that brought the money down a little bit. And then I still wasn't

in the program then. I got in the program recently, like last month, because I went to court, and the officer, he was like—the officer told me, he was like, if they don't accept me back into the program, I was going to be incarcerated. So . . . [PFS] gave me another opportunity, and now here I am, back in the program.

[Chris Adam, March 7, 1996]

As Chris Adam indicated and others would concur, getting the letter, notice, or telephone call was not always enough to persuade them to deal with the child support system. Rather, they came forward because they thought they would personally benefit by reporting to the court or to the CSE agency. They gave three main reasons for coming forward: to stay out of jail, to find a job, and to straighten out their lives. These motives were not mutually exclusive.

The men in this study, and others who participated in the PFS program, believed it was possible and *not unlikely* that they would go to jail for not paying their child support.[1] Bob went to court specifically to avoid incarceration:

Okay. I was court-ordered into it. That's because I went to court for the child support hearing. So, they gave me a chance whether to go to jail or come to the program, and I came to the program. When I first got into the program, it was . . . it's always been all right for me. It's not been like they've been wasting time and stuff, because they haven't. Everybody's been real helpful to me. They got me a job and stuff. The first time I got into the program, I had, uh, lost friends and stuff and things just wasn't going my way.

[Bob, December 1994]

Spending time in jail, however briefly, was an all-too-real threat to these men, all of whom had been incarcerated in the past. They joked about it—"I can do [thirty days] on top of my head" [Fila-G, 1995]; "It's fun, and I get to see my friends" [Mack, 1995]—but it is not an experience that they truly wanted to repeat. For many, avoiding jail was a prime motivation for facing their child support debt. A peer support facilitator reported a discussion in a group session held near the end of 1996:

It was great . . . [the group members] took over the group. They were trying to tell these three brothers who weren't going to the Urban League job club that they should go. I just sat there. It was unbelievable . . . They told these brothers that they had better get their asses over there and do right before they were sent back [to the CSE agency] and put in jail. This was the best part—one of the brothers told them, "What are you going to tell them when you're in jail and you're all sitting around going, What are you in for? Murder, burglary, drugs . . . *child support?"*

[November 1996]

According to the facilitator, although the group laughed heartily over this example, each recognized himself in the story and was warning others of the possible consequences of failing to pay their support. Ralph, who spent ninety-six days in jail for not paying child support, offered his perspective, based on experience:

The fixation is this: knowing that I dwelt among people that committed homicide, and try to put that on a set of scales and try to make sense of it all, saying, I guess this is the answer to child support debt, is to let you dwell amongst a bunch of people who committed murder and arson and child molestation and rape and the sale of heroin to children. I guess this is their way of saying, this is the answer for being a noncustodial parent, is to let you dwell among murderers for three months. Food for thought, don't you think?

[Ralph, December 21, 1995]

The second reason for appearing at a CSE hearing and choosing to participate in the Parents' Fair Share program was the possibility of job opportunities. Many of the men who came into PFS had been out of the regular labor market for some time. They had not worked at a job that provided benefits and some security for a year, two years, or longer.

I'm a good cat, man, and I used to pay my child support when I was working, you understand what I'm saying? . . . It's just the economy went bad, and I lost my job.

[Geraldo 1995]

The opportunity to get a "good" job meant that they might have the means to pay support and spend more time with their children, two deficits usually held against the NCP by the court system and the custodial parent. In some cases, obtaining respectable work that paid decent money appeared to be the first chance these men had seen in a long while to "get back on the right track," enabling them to receive recognition for making the effort to be responsible. This effort was often rewarded by family members, friends, and current and ex-partners who subsequently would include them in social activities. Although the men's financial goals were modest and often fell short of their real needs, their efforts did get them some "social capital" to expend. Chris Adam explained what he thought he needed to earn to be able to survive and meet his financial obligations.

INTERVIEWER: How much money do you need to make per week, or per hour?

CHRIS ADAM: An hour? I probably—I'm not greedy. It'd probably be like $7.50 an hour. In two weeks, you'll probably bring home like probably $350 or close to $400. If I could get a job that would pay me something like that, I'd be in the game because again, I would start looking forward to other things, I mean, like, probably get a car, you know? So me and my girl will be happy. I mean, I want the best for her. She needs the car, and I go to work in the morning. She might work in the afternoon, and, I mean, I take her to work, you know? I'm just trying to do everything like that.

[May 22, 1996]

Making $7.50 to $9 per hour was perceived as enough to meet their support obligations and to stabilize their lives. For some, the possibility of getting work through PFS was worth coming forward and risking jail.

INTERVIEWER: You're not getting anything else—general relief or anything like that? General assistance?

FILA-G: No. I sure wish I could. If you know about anything, let me know. But, uh, I not, uh, not receiving anything else, uh—like every now and then I do a couple of odd jobs for my uncle, you know . . . that may put $40 or $50 in my pocket or something . . . This is maybe every week or biweekly . . . Or something like that, you know—when something come up, you know. But other than that, uh—it's just my [food] stamps. That's about it.

INTERVIEWER: Hopefully you will be able to get a kind of regular job through this program.

FILA-G: Yeah, man, I hope so. That's why I'm here, you know . . . It's what I'm in for, you know, because I—you know, although I don't wanna go to jail, but then I can deal with juvenile court, you know . . . If I was going through for anything else, but . . . you know I wouldn't be in it, you know. I mean . . . you can lock me up, that's almost thirty days for contempt—I can do that on top of my head, you know . . . I don't want to sound like I'm looking forward to it, but understand: if I was in the program for anything else but, you know, trying to gain, uh, some good employment . . . you know I wouldn't be there.

[November 9, 1995]

A third reason that some of these men entered the courts and eventually the PFS program was that they wanted to untangle and make sense of their lives. These men had been struggling with multiple personal, economic, and social problems for some time. A number stated that there was not "anything else like [PFS]" in their communities. Many saw going to court and acknowledging their obligation as a first step toward becoming involved with their children, resolving painful issues from the past, and taking a chance on a first-time opportunity to create a better life for themselves.

SLY: [My girlfriend and I] get along, but it's just not—you know what I'm saying? It's time for us really to, I say, get our lives situated, and just the perfect time to do it while we're still young, so another time we can be together; but right now is not right, you know what I'm saying? All that lovely-dovely and that . . . It's time for us to get our lives situated, get our little careers together or whatever, and start now while we still young, because our parents aren't going to be able to help us out forever. It's getting hard as it is. So it's like that.

INTERVIEWER: Yeah, I hear you. You're nineteen, right? . . . Did they ever talk to you about going back to get your GED?

SLY: That's what I was planning to, before my counselors told me about this program. This lady that comes down to our school . . . a lady from [a local college] . . . she runs this . . . program. So she was telling me that she would give me a computer course so I could brush up on, like, my math courses and my English and all that social studies before they send me directly into the classroom, so I can brush up a little bit, and then she was supposed to send me in there, but it seems like every time I go talk to her, she's out in the field.

INTERVIEWER: Would you still do that while you were doing the apprenticeship?

SLY: Oh, yeah, if I had the time. If it's like a day job, which I think it will be, I'll probably go to school at night and try to knock that out. Because I need that, at least the equivalency.

[March 22, 1995]

Sly, like many other young fathers, had not graduated from high school, had no work history aside from temporary jobs, and had few if any marketable skills. As he explained, his community does not hold many opportunities for him or his peers. The glimmer of hope offered by Parents' Fair Share was worth a try, given the scarcity of alternatives.

INTERVIEWER: As a young man in Trenton, what's it like? A young black man in Trenton? . . . What were your options before you started PFS? What were you doing?

SLY: Really nothing, man, because the only option I really had was going to the GED program, and maybe they have a full tech school on Mercer County . . . I could have went there maybe, or maybe the job corps in Edison, New Jersey, or something like that, but other than that, it—here's really no options, you know what I'm saying. I had to resort to crime or something to get money. Really, that's how hard it is, because there are so many dropouts, rates going up so much, it's like half of the teenagers that are going to school is dropping out. And nobody really want to go to school no more, and they don't really want to know how important it is until they miss it, you know what I'm saying? It's a big mistake they made. Just like every day I sit around, I regret that I'd dropped out of school, you know what I'm saying? Because I know how hard it is to get there, and I know that's what you really need, the whole story. To really survive, you can't even, even—people that just graduated out of college not really finding jobs these days, so it's really hard for people that don't really have no education to get anything—not even a minimum-wage Burger King job, and who wants to work there? You know? It's hard, man, it's hard up here.
[March 22, 1995]

A drug dealer with a substantial reputation in the not-too-distant past, Bob was determined to change so that he could feel respectable and comfortable sharing more of himself with his children and family.

I'm at an entry level now, at the job, that's doing . . . I'm stocking wine at a wine store. That's not what—I'm not trying to make that no position. I want to be a laborer, I want to be in a union. I want to be in something that I can look forward to ten, twenty, thirty years from now, having my son go out and use me as a reference and work in the same job that I have. I don't want to have to tell my son I busted my ass for ten years in the wine store. I was the only full-time black guy in there, and to this day, I bet you couldn't go in there and get a job because they're not going to give you props like that out there . . . I was getting all this attention [from the PFS program] and . . . they started to try to keep me in the basement. They like, why is this nigger getting all this attention? . . . And then when I told my boss . . . Shit, he says, "Well! I can't treat you like you're special or nothing." I said, "I'm not asking you to treat me special! Just be lenient with me, be a little lenient with me, because you'll never find nobody—not like me, not like me. You never find nobody who come in here, used to making thousands in a day, and going to give that up for $6—I don't think so."

[Bob, December 1994]

Others reacted to the offer of job training and opportunities by the courts and CSE with suspicion and bewilderment. On countless occasions, men in Los Angeles and other locations said that they thought the letter from court was part of a "sting" operation.[2] When they learned that PFS was not simply a lure, they began to trust PFS staff and to accept the offer of help.

PERCEPTIONS OF THE CSE SYSTEM

The child support enforcement system was created to ensure that fathers meet their financial obligations to their children. The law is explicit on this point. According to a 1994 report of the U.S. Government Accounting Office (GAO) to U.S. Senate, Committee on Governmental Affairs (U.S. Senate 1994, 2, 3), exacting compliance was intended "to help obtain the financial support noncustodial parents owe their children and to help single-parent families achieve or maintain economic self-sufficiency." The law requires noncustodial fathers with children who are receiving or have received AFDC benefits to repay the state for these benefits. The 1994 report further states that, "Federal and state governments first became involved in child support enforcement activities with the aim of recovering government welfare costs. Child support owed by noncustodial parents of families receiving welfare was to be collected by state and local child support programs and then returned to the government, with a small portion going to the families."[3]

Underlying the child support enforcement system is an assumption (reflected in federal and state law) that if a custodial parent and children are in poverty and relying on the taxpayers for public assistance, the noncustodial parent has an obligation to provide some support, depending on his financial resources. Looking at research based on large nationally representative samples of noncustodial parents, McLanahan and Sandefur (1994), and the U.S. House of Representatives, Committee on Ways and Means (1994) (known as the Green-book) have concluded that noncustodial parents are financially better off than custodial parents. This has led to the assumption that NCPs are able but *unwilling* to pay child support. Neither the research nor the CSE system fully considers noncustodial parents in poverty or near poverty who may be willing but *unable* to pay child support. One reason for this is the fact that these men are vastly underrepresented in major national surveys because they are difficult to locate. Another reason is that public policymakers have concluded that these men are not financially worth chasing. Most of the men in this sample, for example, did not make enough money to cover their rent consistently for a year, let alone meet other financial obligations.

A majority of men in the sample saw the CSE system as designed primarily to retrieve money for the state. Jah understood child support enforcement in its most pragmatic form:

> It's always a money thing, man. It's a business. Everything is about money. Everything is a business here. Child support, rearing people. That's a business, you know? I don't know who getting the money for it, but it's business.
>
> [Jah, February 6, 1996]

Mack, Jah, and others like them resented the CSE system because of what they saw as its hypocritical message and implementation. In their experience, CSE agency does not care about them or their families (that is, children), only about the money owed. When these men were brought into court and asked why they had not been paying child support, they perceived that their responses were heard with suspicion, contempt, and little empathy. They believed that prevailing notions about them are based in prejudice, founded on scant direct experience, and upheld by a variety of personal, moral judgments about how fathers ought to behave with regard to children. The love that these men felt for their children was obvious. Time and again, they told of the contributions they made to their families, yet under federal and state statutes, only child support payments made through government agencies are credited against the NCP's obligation when the custodial parent is receiving public assistance. By ignoring the efforts of poor NCPs to support their children outside this formal system, the CSE system conveys the message that failure to make official payments is equivalent to not caring for one's children, causing hurt and resentment.

Jah described the struggle of being a noncustodial parent who nevertheless lived with his children and kept up with his current support payments. When he entered the program, he owed approximately $3,000 in arrears.

> I want to live. I want have everything, man. You know, everybody's dream is to have everything that they need to get by, that's all. I'm not talking about five, ten million dollars where I can say, "Ha, ha, ha, how you like me now?" You know? I want to have just enough so my kids won't have to ever need anything, so when they run out of Pampers, I can go get another bag, you know, shit like that, man. It's hard when you're trying to be a father, right, and then you turn around saying you're the best father in the world to your kids, which you're trying to be, and then all of a sudden you can't even buy a pack of Pampers, you know?
>
> [Jah, February 6, 1996]

For men like Jah, child support is more than money. In many ways, it is about showing their children a way of life unlike what they themselves experienced growing up. When these men said, "I'm supporting mine," they were often talking about their contacts with their children and how this contact binds them closely together. Authentic, spontaneous interaction between the noncustodial parents in this sample and their children was observed throughout the research period: fathers took enthusiastic and numerous photos of their children, put the interviewer on hold on many occasions to tend to a fretting baby or chase after a playful one, recognized that their daughters had "become . . . young lad[ies]" and their sons, independent young men, attended to crises regarding their children's own pregnancies, and responded when they requested their father's help. These are major challenges for parents who do not live in the home and are generally on the periphery of their children's lives. But many men made these contacts—spent limited funds and made personal sacrifices to help their children, even when they received no acknowledgment of their efforts from the court or, sometimes, the custodial parent. The court's failure to recognize their efforts to be child-supporting fathers in any form other than by making payments to the state is one reason the NCPs gave for avoiding or evading the CSE system.

A frequent criticism voiced by men in the sample was that the people who run the CSE system do not care about NCPs who, if they used their meager resources to pay their child support obligations, would have little left over on which to survive themselves. According to the participants and the researcher's observations of court proceedings, some procedures that might help noncustodial parents meet their obligations to pay child support either are not conveyed to participants or are poorly used. For example, a noncustodial parent who is unemployed or has had a reduction in earnings might be eligible for a "modification of obligation" (see Doolittle and Lynn 1998 for an explanation of downward modification).

In the following passage, Edmond described his experiences with the CSE system. He did not deny that he had an obligation; he just struggled with the inflexibility of the system to hear out his particular situation.

INTERVIEWER: You were brought in because you weren't paying child support. Now you're—

EDMOND: I still believe that a man should be responsible for his offspring . . . to an extent. But the law doesn't recognize special cases. They just say you owe because he's genetically your—you fathered him, you owe him. But I—you know, it's just how come society decided they were gonna throw down as a rule, and I just disagree with it. I think we should let it help the mothers in court, but don't make this massive law that applies to everyone. But—yeah, so a lot of people are caught up in this thing, but honestly, can't do anything about it. I find it difficult to understand why I owe child support when I haven't been earning any money . . . So I'm going to—I'm going through a paralegal right now to try and get my child support reduced . . . I've already paid him, actually. We just gotta do the paperwork . . . And I think I should be successful. I just don't understand—if I had been married to her, and out of work, I wouldn't owe child support. I wouldn't, you know, there wouldn't be a bill running up in that regard. And so that's why I feel like it's wrong, you know, that, you know, just a big net. And it gets some of the innocent people, and—as well as some of the dastardly—oh well, the whole idea is, they take you there because you're supposedly avoiding paying your child support.

INTERVIEWER: How long have you not worked? You've worked part-time?

EDMOND: Well, steady. Yeah—I haven't had a steady job since '92.

INTERVIEWER: And were you paying child support before that?

EDMOND: Yes. It was coming straight out of my paycheck.

[May 16, 1996]

One of the things that most angered the men was their belief that the system and the people who work in it do not care about their families or communities. Participants often pointed out how many men have taken to selling drugs within their communities, to children and the parents of children, in order to meet their child support obligations and other responsibilities. The court knows that these men do not have "official" jobs but does not check to see where the money is coming from. It simply accepts payments made toward child support, and the noncustodial parent is free to walk. As Bob told it, the money he made selling drugs was spent in the same spirit of disregard for the "system," the community, and himself with which it had been earned.

The struggle for the men who earn money through drug-related activities is not so much paying their support, but rather making sure that, no matter how much they are out of sight, their children stay out of trouble. Not falling prey to the negative aspects of their environments can become a major challenge. As Sly pointed out, the temptations and danger are especially hard for a young African American male.

INTERVIEWER: I want all of you guys to do well. I'm tired of seeing young fellows whose primary option is going to jail.

SLY: Yeah, man! 'Cause that's where a lot of them at, man! And that's really the hardest thing to stay away from—for young brothers in Trenton—is jail. That's the hardest thing, because everything is temptation. Really, now, even if you fucking spend $50 and make $100, but you risking your freedom—that's too stupid!

[March 22, 1995]

According to Sly (and others), if he paid his child support obligations by dealing drugs, he would have a "clean" record with the CSE. If he got arrested and jailed, he would be removed from his children and family for years. And if he got shot on the streets—one of the costs of the drug business—he would be gone forever. Sly wanted to "go straight," but his opportunities to do so were limited.

The men in this sample, and economically poor NCPs in general, dealt with the CSE system in different ways. Early in the project, the researcher sat in on an introductory peer support session. The facilitator conducting the session asked the men to discuss why they were in the program. They all knew why—because they had not been paying their child support. Then a twenty-seven-year-old father of seven, in a soft and shy voice, told the group that he had stopped working and as a result stopped paying child support because too much money was being taken out of his paycheck and his family could not live on what little was left over. The conversation that followed, and the interviews with other men, indicated that this young man was not the only person to opt out of the system.

Claudio, a perpetual part-time worker and day laborer, quit working full-time because he had nothing left after his child support obligation was deducted from his check.

CLAUDIO: You know, that's what I was gonna take that to [PFS staff person] so she could see it 'cause in 1989 they said that I owed $11,000 and something, and then in 1990 I received a letter that I had a $4,000 credit, and then I received another statement that I was [owing] $7,000 the following month after. In February I received another letter that I was [owing] $12,000. You see, I was gonna take that to [the staff person], fax it to the DA [district attorney], and say, "What the hell went on?" 'cause I told her about it, and she goes, "Okay, Claudio, bring it in, I'm gonna fax it. Let's see what they tell me." I go, okay, 'cause I told her I took the DA . . . but the judge didn't want to hear me, 'cause I didn't have an attorney with me. So far, what I'm getting right now, I owe, like, $15,000.

INTERVIEWER: $15,000 right now. Wow. What is your monthly payment?

CLAUDIO: $212 . . . See, but what the DA doesn't understand is that I didn't stop working for not to give child support. I just stop working because they were taking my whole money. See, I had some check stubs, when I was working at [a local high school], I was working only three hours after. I was making $500 and something a month, and they were giving me back $105.

INTERVIEWER: That's amazing.

[July 14, 1994]

Although there are many rules on the CSE books about what proportion of income can be taken out of a paycheck during a given pay period, as well as provisions for adjusting payments, the court does not always apply the rules with consistency, giving rise to situations such as Claudio's.[4]

The CSE system is often incomprehensible to the general public, let alone to the noncustodial parent, who faces a large legal obligation:

INTERVIEWER: Let me ask you this: once you graduate and get certified, say you get the job that you want—will you make child support payments then?

TYLER: Oh, yeah. Well, what I'll do then is I'll just—they can take it out of my check before I even see my check. That way it's out of my hair, the courts get their money, and everybody's happy, you know. I mean, to me, I realize it's a big problem, and I want to get this problem off my back. See, that's what the Parents' Fair Share made me at least realize—it's a problem, it's going to be there for the rest of my life, you know, it's not going to go away when my kid's eighteen, like I thought it would, you know, it's going to be there, and it's always going to be there until I pay it. So with Parents' Fair Share, at least they opened my eyes to, like, "Hey, it's going to be there whether you want to pay it or not," but this is where my reality comes in at now, is I know I have to pay it. It's not only for my kid, but it's, you know, when I have my child, like I say, and her mother will vouch for it—you know, I do tend to her, I do support her and stuff like that, and I do give her cash on the side. But I'm going to stop all that. I'm going to have her—what my intentions are, because we've been talking about it—stop the money for the child support, stop asking the courts for the child support. I'll start paying the child support [directly to her], and it's like she'll be getting that money still. I'm going to be paying [arrears] for at least the next five, six years, no matter what, anyways, so once I get a job I'll just have them take [what I owe in back support] out of my paycheck.

[March 22, 1996]

Tyler knew that he had debt but was unsure why he owed so much, given that his children lived with him and he and his mother provided for them while his ex-partners tried to get their lives together. Tyler told a group of facilitators that he was going to avoid paying the debt for as long as he could, because he thought the system was unfair. Although he was taking responsibility for his children, he received no economic relief from CSE. But by convincing the mother of his children to stop collecting AFDC in exchange for some monthly amount of money he would provide to her, Tyler felt he could at least begin paying down his child support debt and stop its growth.

Other NCPs left their families in the course of attempting to sidestep CSE. Ralph had never had any relationship with his family and spent a good portion of his life avoiding both his financial obligation to pay child support and his social and emotional responsibility to his offspring—decisions he later regretted.

> As far as being the "good daddy"—and I don't want you to interpret that with sarcasm (it probably has a taste of sarcasm)—"Is Ralphie being a good daddy?"—no. Totally inappropriate behavior on my part as a father in regards to presents, cards, et cetera, being there as a loving, caring, nurturing, strengthening—the whole ball of wax. It was null and void, it was missing. And these are the things that have been just like I told you previous, have just been ripping me apart.
> [Ralph, December 21, 1995]

Geraldo left his family when his business venture failed. He kept moving and had little or no contact with his children for years. When Geraldo stopped running, he owed more than $60,000 in arrears.

In some cases, the father was not responsible for the separation. Derrick had lived with the mother of his two youngest children for nine years and was trying to meet his obligations as a father and provider. But he had little contact with his oldest child, a daughter born when he was thirteen and the mother was seventeen years old. He and the mother simply drifted apart.

DERRICK: I used to see her when I was in junior high school, you know, seeing the baby then, and once she got married and stuff, and basically, she'd move and be in an area for six months, and—boom—she'd move again. So it was like, the last five years, I'd see her in a store and say, "Oh, where'd you move to?" She'd tell me, blah blah blah, and—boom—the next day they've moved again. So it's more or less I can't keep up with her, you know. I said, when I did see my daughter, "It's nice to see her," and I handed her a little bit of money and everything, but it's more like I can't get a relationship with her, you know. I know I could—I would love to, but it's more like she just moves so much I gotta still go on with my life . . . trying to catch up with her and find out what's going on. She treats her very well.

INTERVIEWER: She does?

DERRICK: Yeah. You know, she's dressed, washed, clean, and everything. You know, me and her never had no problems. It was more or less when I'm doing my own thing, and she's doing her own thing, you know, our schedules—between me and her, where she's at, you know, it's hard to find.
[August 1, 1994]

JUSTICE OR INJUSTICE?

Decisions to avoid or evade the CSE system reflect participants' perceptions that the court's treatment of poor NCPs like themselves is oriented toward money (not family), is arbitrary, and often is racially biased.

WILLIE: These people [from CSE and the PFS program] aren't doing [a] thing for these black men. It's still the same way! [The system doesn't] give a damn about you, it's just the kids.

INTERVIEWER: Some of whom will be growing up as black men.

WILLIE: Exactly! Still, it ain't helping now. What is money? What is money when you don't even see your father, what's money? What's money when a mother take the money and do anything other than what she's supposed to be doing? But hey, you can't open your mouth to the mother. You can't say, don't do it like that! You can't say that, because once you take it down there to juvenile court, it's out of your hands; once you pay that money to them, it's out of your hands! Your child's life is out of your hands, and that's—I thought that was the main issue. But it's not about the child, not to welfare—it's about the dollar, it's about your salary, it's about you paying the state back their money that they have given your child. It's not about the welfare of the child or the mental status of that child. It's not about that! It's not about you bettering yourself! It's about paying back the white folks, that's what it's about.

[March 2, 1995]

Feelings that the system can reduce one's status as a father to this level is a major issue for many of these men. Willie captured the widespread feeling among NCPs that because they are poor, black, and male, they do not count.

All of the men in this study had had frequent contact with the judicial and CSE systems and harbored a great distrust of both. Their lack of faith stemmed from past and present experiences in these legal arenas. For example, at a peer support session in Los Angeles, a facilitator brought in a legal aid representative to discuss the issue of child abuse and to offer some guidelines on the levels or degrees by which a child could be disciplined. As the representative stood before the group of about fifteen men of color, and after a few awkward moments following her introduction, she stated, "You know, when you go before the judge, you will be treated differently than the father from Beverly Hills."[5] Most noticeable after her comment was the protracted silence. One person asked a question that she could not answer, and although she promised to get back to him at a later date, she never did. From the men's point of view, the legal aid representative was telling them the story of their lives: as poor men of color, they could not expect the same consideration—the same justice—as wealthy, white men from affluent neighborhoods; nor, given their limited resources, could they expect the same level of legal advice or consideration.

Willie described, with painful irony, what it was like to try to be a good father in a dangerous environment *and* know that the justice system might descend at any moment and take you away:

> I'm scared every day . . . You've never waken up in the morning just afraid? . . . Well, I wake up like that every day . . . Afraid that maybe one day your wife might say—wake up one morning and you get a letter in the mail from juvenile court saying, come to court with me, come. Bring some money or go to jail. You wake up in the morning, your lights might be turned off—afraid of that. Might wake in the morning, and you're afraid you might just walk out the door and somebody blow your brains out. Accident. There are gun shots around the neighborhood all night long, 9 millimeter automatic shot guns, I mean, you name it. I'm trying to raise a family, wife and kids, around dope dealers, addicts, thieves, rapists, murderers, and I could go to jail for not having money.
>
> [Willie, March 2, 1995]

Willie was not alone. Lover was battling the fear that he would have to go back to jail and lose his children forever because of his constant struggle with the judicial system, child welfare system, and child support system. There were many reasons for the noncustodial parent to feel this way.

Personal experience had led these men to believe that they could, at the discretion of powers beyond their control, be detained or incarcerated at almost any time. An administrator who had been working with a PFS participant recently released from jail and new to the program related the following. Upon his release, this man was told to report to the child support office, where a case manager informed him that he could either enter the Parents' Fair Share program or a bench warrant would be issued for his arrest. If he attended the program as advised, the warrant would not be issued. He reported to PFS but remained concerned about the warrant. A PFS administrator who investigated his situation discovered that in fact the warrant *had* been issued—despite the man's regular, diligent participation in the program.

In the reverse case, during a child support case conference in which PFS staff were involved, the name of an "inactive" participant came up—an individual whom PFS had been trying to get to return to the program for some time. PFS staff suggested that a bench warrant be issued for the participant's nonparticipation, strategizing that once he appeared in court, he could then be routed back into the program. But as it turned out, no warrant was issued because the CSE case manager disregarded the situation, making an exception because he felt this particular individual had been under a great deal of stress.[6] This seemingly arbitrary discretion wielded by people in positions of power angered and frustrated the men in this sample. They saw that the rules are not always consistent, and when severe penalties are applied it is usually against men like themselves.

There is an inherent conflict between personal needs and administrative discretion. Because of their prior contacts with the judicial system and the relatively small size of their communities, coupled with their lack of real mobility, these men felt paralyzed beneath the watchful eye of the system. At least they believed they were, and the fear and wariness of constant surveillance weighed heavily on their day-to-day activities. Another incident illustrates the degree to which these men felt they had to live with certain rules and social codes. After spending an afternoon and part of the evening together, Mack and the interviewer went to pick up one of Mack's running buddies, Big Joe. The two friends were inseparable and had shared many experiences. Big Joe squared things away with one of his girlfriends, after which he needed to visit his other girlfriend's house to pick up his car and check in on one of his children. The interviewer was behind the wheel during the twenty-minute drive, with Mack in the front passenger seat and Big Joe in the back. Mack and his friend were laughing and catching up with one another when suddenly Big Joe cautioned the interviewer to slow his speed, because the police would not hesitate to stop a car filled with black men driving through a white neighborhood. Mack emphasized that this was no joke, and the interviewer slowed his car to five miles an hour below the speed limit. When they arrived at their destination,

Big Joe went into the apartment, and Mack spoke informally with the interviewer, explaining simply, "That's the way it is in this town"—a man could count on being pulled over by the police if he was black and in the "wrong" neighborhood. Although there was more laughter that evening, the warning to keep a watchful eye at all times was a poignant reminder of the precarious state of these men's freedom.

These illustrations make two key points. First, they highlight the power of discretion that people in positions of authority hold over these men. The threat of jail is both credible and potent. Second, racial bias plays a not so subtle, yet sometimes intangible, role in explaining why men of color do not have particularly high regard for the legal or child support systems. The majority of black and Latino men perceive the police and "the system" as offering them very little respect or justice. As a result of past experiences and interactions with various agencies in the system, these men are reluctant to seize opportunities offered by such agencies.

In conclusion, most men in the sample were not "eagerly awaiting" or overly optimistic about the PFS program. But the threat of jail, the possibility of finding a decent job, and the desire to straighten out their lives led a group of noncustodial parents to participate in the program. As Willie put this,

> When you're down there, they make a scene, like, well, we're interested in you! You know, all of that talk that they did, that went on in orientation—it sounds good, it had me enthused, and I said, this is great, this is—something is finally looking up in this city.
> [Willie, March 2, 1995]

The next chapter discusses what happens when a group of NCPs are assigned to PFS and decide to try out the services that the program has to offer.

Chapter 5

THE ONLY GAME IN TOWN: WALKING THROUGH THE DOORWAY OF PARENTS' FAIR SHARE

What opportunities did Parents' Fair Share offer to those non-custodial parents who chose to participate? Is this type of intervention able to serve individuals who bring with them a complex array of issues and problems that hinder their ability to gain or maintain meaningful employment? This chapter and the next examine the men's experiences while in the PFS program. These chapters try to answer the two questions through the voices and perceptions of those who participated in the PFS intervention. This chapter focuses on participants' experiences with the program portion of PFS, specifically the peer support component; chapter 6 examines employment and training opportunities as well as mediation (see box 5.1 for a review of the program's components).

These chapters are not intended to evaluate the program and its various components, but rather to provide an inside view of how thirty-two men, out of the several thousand who participated in the program, engaged and used the PFS intervention. Highlighted are the apprehensions, problems, anger, love, and courage that the noncustodial parents shared with the PFS staff. Also emphasized are the challenges facing individual PFS sites and staff in reaching, convincing, and encouraging NCPs that their goals were realistic and attainable.

ENTERING PFS

At all seven demonstration sites, few participants were ecstatic about cooperating with the program. To the contrary, they were

Box 5.1 Parents' Fair Share Program Components

Employment and training   The centerpiece of the Parents' Fair Share program was a group of activities designed to help participants secure long-term, stable employment at a wage level that would allow them to support themselves and their children. Because noncustodial parents vary in their level of employability, sites were strongly encouraged to offer a variety of services, including job search assistance and opportunities for education and skills training. In addition, because it is important to engage participants in income-producing activities quickly to establish the practice of paying child support, sites were encouraged to offer opportunities for on-the-job training, paid work experience, and other activities that mix skill training or education with part-time employment.

Enhanced child support enforcement   A primary objective of Parents' Fair Share was to increase support payments made on behalf of children living in single-parent households that are receiving welfare. Success meant that participants' earnings were translated into regular child support payments. Although a legal and administrative structure already existed to establish and enforce child support obligations, demonstration programs had to develop new procedures, services, and incentives in this area. These included steps to expedite the establishment of child support awards and flexible rules that allowed child support orders to be reduced while noncustodial parents participated in Parents' Fair Share and then to be raised quickly when they got a job or stopped participating.

Peer support   Background research and the pilot phase suggest that employment and training services, by themselves, will not lead to changed attitudes and a pattern of regular child support payments for all participants. Education, support, and recognition may be needed as well. Thus demonstration programs were expected to provide regular support groups. The purpose of this component was to inform participants about their rights and obligations as noncustodial parents, to encourage positive parental behavior and sexual responsibility, to strengthen their commitment to work, and to enhance their life skills. The component was built around a curriculum, known as Responsible Fatherhood, that was supplied by MDRC. The groups sometimes included recreational activities, mentoring arrangements using successful Parents' Fair Share graduates, or planned parent-child activities.

Mediation   Often disagreements between custodial and noncustodial parents about visitation, household expenditures, lifestyles, child care, and school arrangements—and the roles and actions of other adults in their children's lives—influence the pattern of child support payment. Thus demonstration programs provided opportunities for parents to mediate their differences using services modeled on those now provided through many family courts in divorce cases.

often reserved, withdrawn, angry, or resistant to the fact that they had been required to come to the program and actively participate.[1] PFS recruits wondered why they had been singled out to be "projects," as Jah referred to himself, and made to pay their child support, when they knew friends, relatives, and acquaintances who had children *and* jobs and were not paying anything. It seemed unfair to them that they had to attend the program while those in similar situations did not have to participate.

On a typical orientation day, the interviewer would see a group of noncustodial parents scattered about a room, slumped at the waist, with their faces in their hands and shaking their heads, waiting for the program to begin. A small group of men might strike up a conversation while they waited, discussing anything from neighborhood news or a mutual friend or relative to a sporting event or personality. These sometimes animated conversations helped to pass the time as well as alleviate their anxiety about what lay ahead. But generally on the first day, as NCPs waited for the program to begin, the overall atmosphere was solemn, and the mood apprehensive.

All of these NCPs had been assigned to Parents' Fair Share by the courts and the CSE system, institutions they perceived as biased and threatening.

INTERVIEWER: And then you take [your payment] to juvenile court or wherever?

NELSON: I'm finished. I don't want to go down there. I don't want to go close to the place.

INTERVIEWER: I don't blame you.

NELSON: I don't even want to go close at all.

INTERVIEWER: Is it really that bad, Nelson? . . . court and all that stuff?

NELSON: I just don't like going to it their way.

INTERVIEWER: It's really bad, huh?

NELSON: Yup.

[February 27, 1995]

Their own and their friends' experiences had made them cynical about the possibility of finding steady work and paying child support.

INTERVIEWER: So do you think most of these guys—you included—would have been making regular child support payments if you had a regular job?

NELSON: A regular job—right. I sure would.

INTERVIEWER: So tell me, how can you get regular work in Memphis?

NELSON: There's no way you can get regular work in Memphis. If you're not out of your house and trying to make some [contacts], you know they're going to take your money.

[December 14, 1994]

Nelson felt trapped: regardless of whether he was without a job and had no income, was looking for work, or was in the process of obtaining employment, he knew that CSE would keep trying to collect the money he owed them.

In addition, the interviewer found widespread initial confusion—among the NCPs in this sample and in PFS as a whole—over the intent of the program. The men did not know what to expect when they began the program. Some had visions of quickly obtainable and well-paying employment, while others expected little benefit.

In conversations held at orientation and other times during the program, the interviewer asked NCPs if they knew of any other program like PFS in their communities. The majority of participants, particularly the men in their twenties, said PFS was "the only game in town" or at least the only one they were aware of. Having tried the options that they knew and still coming up empty, they thought that they had little to lose by taking a chance on PFS. No NCP was literally forced to participate in the program.[2] Those who did participate hoped that PFS would lead to contacts, good jobs, and, more generally, positive changes and outcomes in their lives. Those who did not opt for the program took their chances with the court and the outside world.

On orientation day, the program staff and the noncustodial parents knew little about one another. Participants were unsure of what the program would expect of them; program staff was unclear about the specific needs, obstacles, and personal histories of the participants.

Program orientation was designed to be the first in-depth contact that the noncustodial parent made with program services.[3] Usually a program administrator, who led orientation sessions, began with a simple message: PFS was created to assist the noncustodial parent in finding employment and paying child support on a regular basis. This message followed the men throughout their participation in the program: pay your child support and be a responsible father. Administrators attempted to clarify that the program existed to *help* low-income NCPs find work but that they should not *depend* on the program to solve their problems for them. He or she described the range of services and service providers available to participants. Sometimes staff were asked to say something about what they did and how they would be available. The leader explained program requirements and other administrative details.

Participants usually described orientations as long (at least an hour and usually longer) and one-sided, with the administrator doing most of the talking. The NCPs listened, fidgeted, and occasionally inquired about child support payments, the child support system, and work. At times, they tested program providers by asking, "Do I have to come if I find work?" or "How often do I have to be here?" Some complained that they had better things to do with their time or that attending the program interfered with their regular schedules. Administrators and other staff heard grumbles about the CSE system and started to learn, albeit superficially, about the complexity of the NCPs' lives. Often the presenter had to repeat several times that many of these issues would be addressed in their peer support sessions. Although these comments did not necessarily allay the NCPs' concerns or apprehensions, they did keep the orientation moving forward and into the next phase: actual participation in the program.

From the point of view of CSE, active participation meant that an NCP showed up at the program site regularly and sat down in the activity to which he was assigned.[4] (The researcher did not attempt to measure whether participants were actively engaged in the activity, only that they were physically present.) Requirements varied from site to site. Participation in one core activity at least three times a week was standard, but some programs required a start-up period of five days a week and gradually reduced the days over time. Meeting with one's assigned case manager only was not considered active participation. To be eligible for the qualitative sample, an NCP had to have at least one contact with a program component; the interviewer attempted to maintain regular contact with members of the qualitative sample whether or not they were actively participating in PFS at the time.

Table 5.1 shows the program participation rates for men in the qualitative sample, juxtaposed with the sample of PFS participants who attended the PFS program during a similar period of time. In general, the qualitative sample had a slightly higher participation rate than the larger sample, making greater use of job-related activities such as skills training and on-the job training. The second part of the table (average number of sessions attended) clarifies some of the differences in participation. Participants in the qualitative sample used peer support about a week longer—or four sessions more—than the other sample. The qualitative sample also spent more time in basic education and less time in on-the-job training. These differences may be attributable to interactions between PFS staff and persons in the qualitative sample; staff may have felt that placement in on-the-job training would not be beneficial for these participants or that it offered jobs with relatively short-term tenures.

Some of the minor variations in participation may stem from differences in how peer support sessions were structured in the seven demonstration locations. The variation may also arise from differences in individual behavior, including a level of comfort or ease with the program gained by attending peer support sessions on a regular basis, over a long period of time (discussed later in this chapter). Nearly every person in the qualitative sample officially participated in at least one program activity, and the majority had numerous interactions with various components of the program. However, because a much larger number of NCPs given the option of PFS did not come to the program or use services to this degree, it is important to understand why those who chose to be active participants did so.[5] It is men like these who will participate in future programs and need similar resources and services.

PEER SUPPORT: AN OVERVIEW

Peer support was designed to run for eighteen sessions (see appendix C for a list and description of sessions), with each session progressing at its own pace, with no set time limit. Organized in modules with numerous interactive exercises designed to prevent sessions from turning into classes or one-way dialogues, there was room for flexibility if a particular session worked poorly or the group decided that another issue was more important than the planned topic. Sometimes the process of "checking-in" dominated a day's dis-

Table 5.1 Participation in Parents' Fair Share Activities within Twelve Months of Referral among Qualitative Research Sample and Participants in PFS Program Group

Sample and Measure	Qualitative Research Sample[a]	Participants in PFS Program Group[a]
Ever participated (percent)		
Any PFS activity	96.0	100.0
Peer support	88.0	90.9
On-the-job training	28.0	15.8
Skills training	20.0	10.9
Job club	80.0	71.9
Job readiness	72.0	54.0
Basic education	16.0	15.7
Mediation	0.0	3.7
Average number of sessions attended for those active in identified activities		
Any PFS activity	73.3	43.7
Peer support	18.2	14.2
On-the-job training	30.1	43.3
Skills training	60.0	50.4
Job club	15.3	11.2
Job readiness	15.4	11.5
Basic education	61.5	26.2
Mediation	0.0	1.1
Sample size	25	1,334

Source: MDRC calculations from data in the Parents' Fair Share management information system.

[a] A subgroup of the full qualitative research sample, as of July 1995. This sample was chosen to allow sufficient follow-up of participation in PFS activities.

[b] Includes all noncustodial parents referred to Parents' Fair Share, including parents who entered PFS as of July 1995.

cussion. As built into the program, this flexibility was encouraged. Facilitators were given the option of taking groups quickly through the curriculum; a minimum of ten completed sessions comprised eligibility to move on to the next component—employment. Working within such an arrangement, a participant might spend two to three weeks in a peer support group, attending as many as three to five days a week, with each session running approximately two to three hours in length. In some sites, such as Dayton and Grand Rapids, peer support sessions were run on a more open-ended basis, with participants encouraged to attend sessions for as long as they found them helpful. Although required to meet a minimum level of participation before moving on to the next activity, peer support "graduates" were not barred from reentering another group and sharing in the group process again.[6]

Peer support was designed to help noncustodial parents resolve conflicts and issues that interfered with their getting and keeping a job and eventually paying child support. In Kenny's words,

> [F]irst, you come in, your first thing is this peer support . . . You know what I'm saying? "Man, what type of father are you? How would you deal with situations with your children if this went on, if that went on?" . . . Then we do, like, different little plays: how would you get aggravated—you know what I'm saying, if somebody trying to aggravate you—could you maintain your cool? How to present yourself, you know, to society . . . And then, what's your most important things. What's your, you know, values, or health—you know, well, what's your most important things in your life, you know. Then you moves on to that, into, um, I think it was job search . . . And then the last one was, you know, just goin' out lookin' for it. So once you got the job search, you already had, you know, confidence and everything, what you—what type of father you needed to be. Now, the second step: gonna help you get a job . . . Now we gonna give you all the tools that you need . . . how to fill out an application, how to present yourself when you go for this interview . . . [Y]our third part, all you gots to do is go out and get it, apply what they done gave you.
>
> [Kenny, September 25, 1995]

From the moment the NCP first walked through the door, both he and the program faced numerous obstacles. Not only did many participants lack the technical and interpersonal skills they needed to be placed in existing or developing labor markets, preconceptions about who they were and how they got themselves into their present state of affairs dominated their interactions with court officials, case workers, prospective employers, and others. Beyond the immediate predicaments of owing child support and being underemployed, farther-reaching questions surfaced for these men regarding what they wanted to do with their lives and what adjustments they should make to feel part of their communities, families, and the working world. Other personal and social obstacles included issues involving family; racism, education, and substance use for the

African American participants; and ethnic bias and language barriers, specifically for Latinos. Respect for cultural sensitivities was essential to reaching these men.

African American participants lived in racially and economically segregated areas, as evidenced in chapter 3. Poorly educated, isolated from the mainstream economy and to some degree the mainstream culture, and disproportionately likely to have been arrested and imprisoned, they were accustomed to being treated with suspicion and judged as potentially dangerous. How did this environment and these experiences affect their belief in their ability to change?

Big Joe illustrates some of the complex issues and problems that NCPs bring to programs like PFS. A moderately successful drug dealer who had been in and out of jail, Big Joe was a high school graduate who made enough money to allow himself the luxuries of a cellular telephone (with telephone bills in the range of hundreds of dollars per month) and the ability to shop at local boutiques. With the talent and skills to "make it" on the streets, he had never held a job in the mainstream market for more than six months at a time. Big Joe did not like, trust, or want to associate with white people on a professional level.

One summer day, Big Joe discussed with a PFS program staff person his decision to get out of "the game." He needed to "do right" for a while: his main man had been arrested and "locked down," and he was feeling the pressure. He returned to the program after a month's absence and started making the minimum child support payments, putting himself in good standing with the CSE agency. He worked with an African American staff member to set up a job interview. For the first time, Big Joe seemed enthusiastic about the idea of legal employment. According to his job counselor, the company needed workers and liked the program. Before his interview, Big Joe, his counselor, the interviewer, and another participant went to lunch. The mood was positive and upbeat. Big Joe got some coaching from his counselor and seemed receptive. Everything was going well.

On the drive to his interview, Big Joe's mood suddenly changed. Minutes before he was laughing and confident; now he was guarded, reticent, cautiously alert to his environment, and increasingly uncomfortable. His voice fell to a soft murmur, and he seemed almost shy on being introduced to the owner of the company. He was shown around the corporate office and introduced to many of the people in management, all of whom were white and pleasant, although none seemed particularly interested in him, nor he in them. Big Joe's counselor accompanied him into the job interviewer's office and discussed Big Joe's many skills, the progress he had made in the program, and how he envisioned his client fitting into the open position. When the interviewer asked Big Joe some straightforward and relatively simple questions, he answered in a strained and forced manner.

After nearly thirty minutes, the interviewer discussed benefit packages and salary and told him she looked forward to his starting day. Big Joe made a quick exit. While waiting for his counselor to finish with the interviewer, the researcher asked Big Joe what he thought of the interview process. Grabbing a candy from the front desk and putting it in his mouth, Big Joe whispered, "I hate white people—I can't work for them. She was so patronizing, man." On the drive back to the PFS office, the counselor jokingly told Big Joe that certain things would have to change now that he was going to be a working man—for instance, he would have to keep up with his bills, and maybe it was time to give up that cellular phone. Big Joe chuckled and punched in the number of one of his buddies.

Big Joe never took the job. He continued to struggle with being on the street, partly because he did not believe that he could afford to make the financial sacrifice and partly because he distrusted the majority of employers both inside and outside his community. Working for nearly $8 an hour, with benefits, was not enough incentive for Big Joe to put aside his anger toward white people. A week passed with no word from Big Joe, but over time he rejoined the program and once again began working with the counselor.

Much of what stands in the way of these NCPs lies outside the realm of the job market and the enforcement agency. Instead, it is deeply imbedded in the social structural aspects of their lives and the lives of those who make decisions about whether to hire them, to adjust their child support payments, and the like.

Preparing people to make substantial changes in their way of life is not an overnight, or even a three-week, process. Nor is it easy to convince employers to change their perceptions of low-income, minority males (in particular) and to help these men make the transition into the working world.

At the outset, peer support might have been designated the activity least likely to succeed. Participants themselves were surprised by the scope and depth of the program—the degree to which PFS led many of these men to examine their attitudes, beliefs, fears, and anger in order to reach their objectives. How would facilitators approach such sensitive and personal topics with a group of NCPs who, for the most part, viewed their situations as solely their own business and responsibility? What would attract these participants, men primarily, to sit in close quarters and discuss intimate issues concerning their lives and the lives of their children? The answer lies partly in the design of peer support and partly in the skills and openness of its facilitators.

Peer Support as a Safe Place

PFS program locations are places of safety. In interviews with members of this sample and in larger group settings, the researcher frequently overheard comments such as, "This program is like my second home, my second family." Sitting in a peer support group for a week, the interviewer listened as people told intimate, sad, thought-provoking, and sometimes frightening stories about their lives, noting how they trusted the group to keep their confidence. Earning participants' trust was necessary, because trust came at a premium in many of these men's home communities. For men of color, this issue permeated every aspect of their lives: because of the color of their skin, they believed that they were not trusted to walk into stores, not trusted to raise their children, not trusted to pay their child support, not trusted enough to be offered decent employment. As a result, these men were suspicious of everything; even their relations with friends and lovers tended to be guarded. It was powerful to watch faith and confidence build in and among these men. These beliefs and experiences held true as well for the white men who ventured into the program and peer support component.

In the summer of 1995, the interviewer, who had visited the Dayton site on a number of occasions, returned for a week to observe some group activities and meet individually with several participants. It was Thursday, and all activities were in full swing. The job club/job search instructor had taken his group to the library. Peer support groups had also proceeded smoothly that day. Just before lunch, all noncustodial parents present were asked to remain on-site for an extra half-hour, if they could, to speak with the interviewer about the program. About twenty-five (not including staff) remained for this open forum.[7] The interviewer was familiar with most of the participants and, after assuring them that there would be no reprisal for expressing their thoughts and feelings, asked the group to describe what they liked and did not like about PFS. As frequently occurred during individual interviews, participants were adamant that their real names be used, an act of bold confidence directed toward the CSE agency, not PFS.[8]

After about twenty minutes of conversation, the interviewer asked a question using the phrase "deadbeat parent," prompting members of the group to respond that they did not, under any circumstances, consider themselves to be deadbeats. Quite the contrary, they felt that the system failed to understand and respond to *their* needs. One man, dressed in a sweatshirt and sweatpants, suddenly jumped out of his seat and in a raised voice began to lecture the interviewer. He was suspicious of the purpose of the discussion, he was angry, and he did not hesitate to voice his feelings. "We are not deadbeats here, so why are you trying to destroy this program? This place is like our second family, our second home. Why don't you just take your ass across the street to *them* and leave *us* the fuck alone!" [Anonymous, 1995, paraphrased]. This man had to be physically restrained. He was very protective of the staff who had been helping him and wanted the interviewer to know that PFS was a good program that cared for "brothers and sisters." He vehemently urged that an investigating eye be turned on the people who worked across the street in the welfare and child support offices.

What most impressed the interviewer about this incident was the passionate loyalty and commitment expressed toward the program and its staff. No one in the room disagreed with the man's defense of the program as a place that was safe and respectful and cared for its participants. These individuals had rarely experienced this feeling outside the walls of PFS, and it prevailed in many of the program sites.

The need for safety and solace was exhibited in every site visited during this research. The PFS program site was often the only place where a participant could put to rest the stresses of the outside world, at least for a couple of hours. One day in early March 1996, a facilitator was sitting in the relatively new peer support room in Grand Rapids, not expecting anyone to show up for the day's session because of an unexpected snowstorm. To his surprise, noncustodial fathers began to trickle in. Many were late because of the weather; the public transportation system had broken down, forcing them to walk to the site. About twelve men, almost all African Americans, finally assembled in a circle and responded to the facilitator's check-in question, "Why did you come today?" with standard answers: "I had to," and "I need a job." But one participant, a lanky man formerly from Chicago, took the opportunity to say that he came out that day because peer support helped him alleviate the feelings of stress that greeted him every morning and followed him until he laid down at night. This statement was answered with much nodding of heads and supporting comments; many NCPs felt that coming to the group sessions helped to reduce their daily tensions.

What made this man's confession so powerful was the fact that during the entire session, he had been sitting across the room from a member of a rival "fraternity." According to the group's facilitator, the two opponents had tacitly agreed to put aside their animosity during the sessions and to maintain interactions that were honest and respectful. The facilitator regarded this truce as a major accomplishment of the group process.

The importance of establishing and maintaining an atmosphere of safety and acceptance at program sites cannot be overestimated. Participants came into PFS with a variety of tough personal issues that had to be addressed before they could benefit from some of the more matter-of-fact elements of the program. Trust played a critical role in their honest expression, to PFS staff and to themselves, of what was blocking them from achieving their expectations of the intervention. For the program to be truly effective, staff members also had to learn to trust their participants.

The Group Process of Peer Support

Peer support rests on the basic principle of group therapy, which holds that the process of airing problems, speaking one's mind, and establishing trust are valuable in and of themselves. For the participation to appear worthwhile, individual members must feel that the group offers some ray of hope (see Yalom 1995, ch. 1, for an explanation of the key therapeutic factors associated with group work). The hope of finding a job, of establishing a better way of life, and of resolving personal problems motivated these men to participate in PFS and the peer support groups. Group members had to feel that they shared something in common—in this case, each member's unpaid child support. Yalom refers to this common factor as the group's "universality." Ideally, participants learn that they are not alone in their problems and derive a sense of belonging, support, and encouragement from participation. The group serves as a natural experiment in interpersonal relations, helping participants to discover how what they say or do affects other people, what attitudes or situations make them angry or resentful, and how to practice better coping strategies. In order for the group to move forward, this environment must carry no threat of retribution but must remain open to ongoing, candid discourse regarding the participants' lives and options.[9]

Yalom (1995, 5) writes, "Many patients enter therapy with disquieting thoughts that they are unique in their wretchedness." A major aim of the peer support component was to help participants see that they were not alone and to encourage them to trust one another enough to share personal details.

KENNY: [W]ithin, like, peer support, a lot of brothers got, you know, together, that was going through the same type of, you know, problems with the system, you know. [Peer support] was saying—it was teaching us how to overcome it . . . So that was the support right there, you know. It was givin' us that extra booster, that extra lift that we needed to overcome, you know, the trials and tribulations that we were going through at the time . . . And how to, you know, how to get over it and get through it.

INTERVIEWER: And you think that's important?

KENNY: Oh, definitely, definitely. 'Cause I mean, it's already bad enough that it's a struggle out here, you know . . . And with that support, it—it helps you greatly. I mean, 'cause some brothers wasn't working, didn't know how to present themselves, you know. Had a job, but maybe didn't have a good family or didn't have brothers that was real with 'em, you know what I'm saying? . . . So it was, definitely, you know, support. You know, I took the energy that I already had and just made it even better. Made it greater, that's all.

[September 25, 1995]

Sharing feelings of isolation enabled these men to explore other, perhaps similar, experiences that had been keeping them from moving forward in their lives.

For some participants, peer support created a space where they could express frustrations that they might not have expressed otherwise or might have expressed through violence.

INTERVIEWER: Did peer support sessions help you?

BOB: Yeah.

INTERVIEWER: What did you learn from them?

BOB: Um, I learned a lot from them peer supports because there was a lot of things that was going on that I was holding in, and peer support would help me bring all them problems that I had in me, out.

INTERVIEWER: How did they do it?

BOB: Well, we would sit around in a big group, all men. Well, we had one woman, you know. We didn't never disrespect her or nothing, but we still got a chance to talk . . . how we felt. See, they let you talk how you feel and what's on your mind, and you know, you could talk. Then when it get too tense, we take a break or something. Then we'll come back to the session and stuff, and talk. We had a lot of people. I had a lot on my mind that I needed to get off, and [the facilitator] and them had me talk through it, and the way that I knew I wouldn't go back and try to retaliate. I could get it right without doing nothing and keep trying to find a job. And after I found my job, it was really straight. Pretty straight for me, yeah. We would come in and have so many hours, you know—you feel better. 'Cause I would come here depressed as hell and when I left, I would feel good, 'cause I got it all out. You know, somebody would listen—that's all I needed.

[1994]

Peer support sessions were effective because they were interactive. It was not uncommon for a participant to seize the opportunity to be heard, as when Ralph lectured a group of NCPs on motivating themselves to pay their child support:

I said [to the other participants], "Come on, guys, let's cut it out." . . . I said, "How many in here are working?" Not one. I said, "Now," I said, "how the hell do you make it every day? How do you do it? . . . Who puts the money in your pocket? . . . How do you get by? You have no spending cash? Nothing? No job?" I said, "What, are you bumming money off the old lady, bumming money off the family, bumming money off of somebody?" I said, "But how the hell do you exist?" . . . You know, and the one guy . . . "Ahh," you know, "Fuck this," like, "Ahh, " you know, "I don't need a lecture. Who the hell are you?" . . . A da-da da-da da. I said, "Well, welcome to the real world, and, and, uh, that's how you make it, brother, you get up off that ass, and you take that healthy ass out there, and you give it a good eight and ten hours every day . . . That's what makes the world go round, kiddo." I said, "'Cause that debt ain't gonna get paid, unless you get a j-o-b."

[Ralph, October 4, 1995]

For some NCPs, it was important to realize that they had something to offer the group and could learn from one another.

One of the major strengths of peer support was that it offered an opportunity for honest communication. To some degree, peer support groups may have helped, at least temporarily, to fill the void left by weakened social institutions, such as the family and religion. As Nelson described this, "Peer support is like a regular thing. It's like a community group trying to get together, trying to improve things" [Nelson, December 14, 1994].

Issues and Activities

Peer support was guided by the Responsible Fatherhood curriculum, designed to help noncustodial fathers address personal issues that precluded them from being active participants in the lives of their children and paying regular child support. Family networks and connectedness were one of the many topics of the peer support curriculum. One of the first activities in which noncustodial parents were invited to participate was the creation of a family tree (see appendix D). Participants were given a drawing of a tree, its branches filled with circles labeled for different personal characteristics, and were asked to write in the names of the people in their lives who possessed those qualities. They were encouraged to work independently and to consider thoughtfully which people in their families could be represented by the characteristics highlighted in the tree. The goal of this exercise was to help participants better understand their origins—to take a look at the people who influenced their beliefs, values, and actions and how these legacies shaped their current relationships. After some reluctant grumbling, people filled out their charts, and a discussion promptly ensued.[10] At the Trenton site, during the discussion phase, Jah was asked why he had left his tree completely blank. He explained that his partner and their son were all the family he had (they later had another son) and that the tree represented him by himself within the forest. When the group challenged this explanation, he explained that his birth family was unable to give him anything and that he had to do it all on his own. Although many in the group that day had filled their branches with names of family members, they nodded with understanding. They, too, felt alone.

In a related peer support activity, the same men were asked to look at a group of pictures and to pick those that represented some aspect of their lives. A noncustodial father of two, seated across from Jah in the group circle, chose a single photograph: a picture of an African American family sitting together and watching television. When asked why he picked only one photo, and this one in particular, he said that the scene depicted something he would really like to do someday. There were nods all around. Two weeks later his telephone was disconnected, and he was arrested and incarcerated for burglary.

In contrast, Jah expanded his family's branches, despite some setbacks. In a conversation with Jah during the summer of 1995, he discussed some of the changes he had experienced over the past year and a half. One was that he was spending more time with his own and his girlfriend's family.

INTERVIEWER: Do you guys see your family at all, anymore?

JAH: My mom, and all? Yeah, I see them all the time. Seen her yesterday. Yesterday was Sunday . . . ['C]ause me and my girl was over at her grandmother's, playing spades. Not spades—we was playing poker for quarter[s]. We be having fun . . . We go and play cards . . . Moms was over there. [Jah's mother lives across the street from his girlfriend's grandmother.]

[June 19, 1995]

A year later, Jah was working hard at his public health and sanitation job but still struggling to put enough food on the table for his two children. Because of his efforts to get closer to his family, Jah's brother tried to get him some part-time photography work, which, despite Jah's enthusiasm, did not materialize. His brother, however, continued looking for ways to help Jah make more money.

Peer support was oriented toward people, not jobs. The basic goal was to help participants recognize and begin to change behavior and attitudes that were counterproductive to their progress. Once the NCP accepted that he was in the program, he often found himself challenged on a personal level. Personal issues surfaced in both group sessions and private conversations with facilitators. When it came out that Chris Adam smoked marijuana, a job developer who sat in on the sessions and had good rapport with Chris saw this as a red flag.[11]

INTERVIEWER: Let me find out where you are. What's happening?

CHRIS ADAM: Well, now, the program has helped me a lot. You know, well, I stopped—I got off, I got off the marijuana now—

INTERVIEWER: You did?

CHRIS ADAM: Yeah, I got off the marijuana. It took me, you know, it took me awhile to get off of it. But, you know, I stopped—I stopped smokin'—stopped smokin' like I used to. I used to smoke like a quarter [ounce] . . . that's about four plugs or five plugs—I mean, you see what I mean—I cut that down, it's like smoking one a day.

[May 22, 1996]

At a different PFS site, three men approached a peer support facilitator after a session and asked for assistance with their drug and alcohol involvement. In yet another, a peer group facilitator discovered that Junior, who had a history of domestic violence and substance abuse, was illiterate and frustrated, often to anger, by his inability to read. Parents' Fair Share helped Junior to enter an adult literacy program as a first step toward resolving other problems. Lover believed that participating in PFS would help him to regain visitation with, and ultimately custody of, his children.

During sessions, participants were encouraged to discuss racism, domestic violence, and custody and visitation problems. Peer support facilitators and other group members functioned as a sounding board, pushing NCPs to develop new strategies and tactics for coping with these issues.

Perhaps the most difficult and ultimately positive goal of peer support was its attempt to acknowledge and address racism as a relevant and constant presence in the lives of the participants of color. The topic of racism emerged from within the sessions and was rapidly incorporated into the curriculum. For many, dealing with white people on a professional and personal level evoked reservation and suspicion. Most lived in areas that are economically, ethnically, and socially segregated and where contacts with white people are rare (see appendix B). The few whites they did encounter—police, social workers, landlords, and store owners—were generally seen to hold poor people of color in suspicion and low regard and to use positions of power against them. The peer support curriculum attempted to help NCPs deal with the anger, hurt, and disappointment that resulted from their encounters with the child support system as well as with their family, partners, and friends by introducing and developing coping skills and strategies.

Discussions of racism accentuated the fact that whites were in the minority in PFS, a reversal of their usual experience in the outside world. Facilitators almost always tried to help white participants feel sufficiently comfortable to take part in discussions. This was accomplished by maintaining ground rules and by holding the group's safety as paramount. Without exception, no physical fights ever erupted over the subject.

When the group consisted of a mixture of cultures and ethnicities, one strategy was to have participants change roles. The facilitator would ask the group to write down on a piece of paper what would be the first thing they would do if one morning they woke up in a different skin: as an Asian, Latino, white, or African American. The activity often began with laughter and some joviality, but quieted down as soon as someone read what he had written, sharing his perceptions of the racism he had encountered or of racist acts he had heard people articulate but had never experienced first-hand.

The most common assertion voiced by African American and Latino participants was, "I would go back to the jobs that I applied for in the past and did not get, to see if they would hire me now that I was white." A number of white participants said that if they woke up black, they would "go into stores and see if people really followed me around, thinking I was going to steal something." These simple statements usually got the group moving into questions of stereotypes and how racism might or might not pervade their lives. By structuring the session in such a manner, the group maintained its atmosphere of safety, while sustaining respect for individual participants' points of view. Also, some of the participants learned from the process, borrowing strategies developed within the group to handle difficult issues relating to race and racism. Exercises like this one represent the best part of peer support and the group process—men offering help and behaving in a forthright manner with one another, in the hope of facilitating safety and change.

The Facilitator as Agent

The success of peer support depends on the skills and dedication of peer facilitators and their ability to establish rapport with participants.

> I have a lot to thank for this [facilitator] in here . . . because he's instilled in me one thing: I have no fear of sharing anything that has hurt me. There was years and years of me walking around not trusting anybody to talk to about it. Now I don't have any reservations speaking [about] what has troubled me for years . . . I don't walk around feeling as though I'm going to have an angina attack or I feel as if the top of my head's going to explode from blood pressure because I keep holding all this crap in me. It's got to come out.
>
> [Ralph, December 21, 1994]

For many NCPs, what was special about peer support was that for the first time in a long time they were listened to and heard.

Peer support facilitators strove to be empathetic, believing strongly in the purpose of their gatherings and the individuals with whom they worked.[12] This dedication did not go unnoticed by participants, who often admiringly referred to facilitators as "real" and "straight" and implied that in such an atmosphere of authenticity, they, too, could be "real."

> [W]ell, I say, like, [our facilitator], who was the head of peer support—he showed his love towards us, showed that he cared for us, you know what I'm saying? And that allowed us to sit back and express ourselves more clearly. And also we were—most of us were growing up here in Trenton together. Most of us know [one] another. Most of us come from basically the same type of lifestyle, where everybody sees different things from different angles, and they go through the situation differently; so we was coming from all different angles, and helping and seeing things that other brothers were going through made me realize how much really, basically, the system is against the black man here in America.
>
> [Kenny, February 22, 1995]

Sometimes the most important person in the group turned out to be the peer support facilitator, with whom the strongest bonds were formed. For instance, Jasper, who had a history of being independent, who was careful about what he chose to share with staff members, and who had not appeared at the program for a month, sought out his peer support counselor during one of Grand Rapids' big winter storms.

JASPER: Okay. Well, you know, when I was in this program earlier . . . I'll tell you how they worked with me to try to get me on [my] feet and everything. And what happened was, I kept getting job—you know, job hook-ups that was only paying me $6.50, $7.50 an hour. That just wasn't kicking the butt, you know?

INTERVIEWER: Yeah, I hear you.

JASPER: And I started getting depressed, you know, and actually I ain't gonna say I just went overboard, but I started sitting around, you know, drinking a little too much, and stiff at times . . . And just finally decided I'd call the hospital up in California.

INTERVIEWER: Are you serious?

JASPER: No. I'm in one of the greatest programs I would suggest to anyone . . . So they kept me in the hospital probably eight or nine days. And then they sent me to a recovery home . . . I stayed there probably another seven, eight days before they finally released me and let me come back.

[August 6, 1996]

Listening to Jasper's story, the facilitator realized not only that Jasper had lost another job and been hospitalized for alcohol abuse but also that he had been homeless since his release from the recovery home. Jasper did not come out and say that he was homeless; nor did he ask, directly, for help. But the facilitator could hear that Jasper was in need of some assistance. Working together, they found Jasper a place to stay; called Jasper's former employer, who had liked his work and wondered why Jasper had disappeared; and got Jasper reinstated in his job for a short period. But as Jasper pointed out, one of the reasons he needed help in the first place was, "I can't keep on working for seven bucks an hour." He soon became unemployed again and rejoined the program, because, in his view,

Tomorrow's gonna be an exciting day at school [PFS], because I'm gonna be looking at some real critical stages—decision[s] to make, as far as jobs. Because I am not—this is only the first week, I've been out of work since I've been back, but I don't want to get back into that world where I'm not working because I start to get lazy. I start to get, you know, depressed, and all those things start to fit in, and that not good.

[Jasper, August 6, 1996]

Jasper trusted his peer facilitator enough to call on him in an emergency; moreover, he saw participation in PFS, in itself, as helpful in preventing him from slipping into depression and heavy drinking.

For peer support to be useful, participants had to feel comfortable discussing the issues that were interfering with their ability to pay child support and see their children, including the difficult realities of struggling with alcohol and drug dependency, living with HIV, and living with racism, anger, and chaos. The challenge for peer facilitators was to transform this group of individuals into a cooperative whole, interested in having respectful and productive interactions.[13] This was a difficult process for participants. To meet a group's particular needs, the facilitator had to walk a fine line between adhering to the curriculum and allowing flexibility.[14]

The Glue of PFS, and Sometimes a Quagmire

Individual participants' opinions of peer support ranged from high praise to indifference and disillusionment. Some participants attributed much of their personal growth and progress to peer support.

BOB: I've been in the program for about seven or eight [months]. It's coming up time for us to graduate. But I think after I graduate I'll still keep in touch.

INTERVIEWER: Yeah. You like these guys?

BOB: Yeah. We done got real close, all of us.

INTERVIEWER: Is that important to you?

BOB: Yeah. That I can get along with the instructors and stuff, and they cared. That's what it was all the point of. 'Cause you know, we all grown and I was like, they cared like, you know, it was one of them in the situation. That's what kept me coming every day and kept looking for work, kept looking for work, then I finally find it. I stayed with it, and I had somebody on my shoulders to make me stay with it.

INTERVIEWER: That's important.

BOB: That was the most important thing.

[1994]

Others participated regularly and actively in peer support groups but still doubted their usefulness and were more interested in the other program services. One such participant was Jah, who described his perceptions of the types of men who attended peer support and what they really needed:

JAH: [In t]he poor world that I was in, Operation Fatherhood . . . is teachin' the young men how to go along with society . . . 'Cause you ever heard that sayin', sayin', "If you can't beat 'em, join 'em"?

INTERVIEWER: Right.

JAH: So that's how I took it . . . If I can't beat 'em—

INTERVIEWER: So you joined 'em.

JAH: So I had to.

INTERVIEWER: How do you feel about that?

JAH: I feel okay, right now.

INTERVIEWER: [I]s that a good message? From Operation Fatherhood?

JAH: Yeah, that's a good message.

INTERVIEWER: Why?

JAH: Because most of the guys that was there be a minority . . . If they ain't minority, they had to do something very, very drastic in order to lose what they had. Like Ralph . . . Listen: Ralph had it. Know what I mean? . . . Hear me: Ralph had it. He had a house, he livin' with his wife, he had his wife, they had a house, they had a son—you know, Ralph had it. Ralph had everything. Ralph had a car, his wife had a car, you know? . . . Ralph started drinkin' and lost everything . . . It's a choice, and Ralph—Ralph made the choice—well, he—it probably wasn't a choice when he found out how bad it was, makin' it.

INTERVIEWER: Right.

JAH: But Ralph put hisself in that situation . . . I'm sayin', Ralph is a— Ralph is a Caucasian person, and he had it, he had it . . . Him and his wife had it . . . When the divorce came through, he—she got the house . . . Her and the kid. So, most of the guys down there are black folks . . . And most of 'em is tryin' to be taught how to pay child support, or how to take care of they child. How to spend more time with they child, you know? . . . How to give they child that support. You know? . . . Most of 'em know that, already. . . . The only thing they lackin' is a job . . . Everybody can't wait to get the job club, job search . . . Everybody can't wait. Some of 'em is impatient and don't even go through the rest of the part and just go to job—just go, go look for 'em a job theirselves . . . And get out the program.

[August 9, 1995]

Even though Jah was willing to participate in the group, peer support did not meet his needs as he saw them, and he labored through the sessions.

Still others appeared at meetings but kept their distance. Fila-G completed his peer support program requirement but spent most of his PFS experience on the fringe, if not outside the group. In interviews, Fila-G admitted that his drinking had haunted him for many years. He had lost a number of jobs, his marriage of thirteen years, and contact with his children because of his alcohol and drug use, which went undetected in peer support. But he did not want, or feel he needed, "outside" help.

My, uh, drinking, you know—this is something that, you know, I'm gonna have to deal with, you know. I've been through supportive groups like that before, rehabilitation and you know, AA [Alcoholics Anonymous] and all that . . . You know, just trying to let everybody else know how I feel is one thing, but doing what's real is another thing, you know, that all up to me . . . I could go to a AA meeting, sober as I don't know what; upon leaving, reach up under my seat, you know, by the time I get home, I'm half high, you know . . . So, this is just something that Fila-G is gonna have to tackle, you know, Fila-G and my, uh, good lord, you know.

[Fila-G, 1994]

Although officially in the program, Fila-G continued to drink, to run the streets to make pocket change, and to wonder when the next crisis would hit. He tried to take action on his own, but this strategy was costly: eventually he spent twenty-eight days in jail for not participating in program activities and not meeting his reduced child support obligation. Fila-G's situation was not unusual or uncommon: PFS staff could not help unless the men were willing to communicate their difficulties and to participate in their own development.

As the experiences of Bob, Jah, and Fila-G demonstrate, for men who participated in a spirit of hope and cooperation, peer support and its facilitators could be agents of positive change; for those who were less ready or able to face their personal obstacles, even the support of the group forum failed to help. Although it is difficult to prove a direct causal relationship between the paths chosen by these NCPs and their having completed peer support, there was evidence of tangible changes in attitude for some.

As a rule, when the men completed peer support, they took great pride in their achievement. Because a large number of NCPs in this sample and in the larger study of PFS had not finished high school, graduating from peer support was one of their first experiences of completing something and being acknowledged publicly for their accomplishment. Some program sites held formal graduation ceremonies and awarded certificates of completion. The ceremony sometimes took place during the final peer support session, with the whole PSF staff present, or was held as a special event where NCPs were encouraged to invite family members to witness their success.

BOB: You know we just had our graduation and stuff.

INTERVIEWER: Oh, did you go?

BOB: Yeah, I went. I wouldn't miss that stuff for the world.

INTERVIEWER: How was it? Tell me about it.

BOB: It was all right. It was all right . . . and then [my facilitator] put me on the spot, but it was all right.

INTERVIEWER: He put you on the spot?

BOB: Yeah, he made me make a speech.

INTERVIEWER: You made a speech?

BOB: Yeah.

INTERVIEWER: I wish I had known that you were doing that. I would have been there.

BOB: I didn't know that I was doin' that! [Laughs] Till the last minute.

INTERVIEWER: So what did you say?

BOB: Man, I—I was so nervous, I really can't remember what I said. I know I just was—I said, "What you want me to talk about?" He said, "Just talk about how the class helped you." So I just told, you know, I was just tellin' 'em how the class helped me, in the situation I was in . . . how I first got in the class, and how the class helped me deal with that problem . . . And shit. By the time I was finished, everybody was clappin' and applaudin' and the cameraman was on me and I was sweatin' all nervous, and my mother was smilin' at me—I was like, oh . . .

INTERVIEWER: So your mom was there?

BOB: Yeah.

INTERVIEWER: Yeah? Was she proud?

BOB: Yeah . . . Yeah, my mom always be behind me, no matter what I do, she always be behind me.

[September 20, 1995]

Photographs of peer support graduates were placed on the walls as encouragement for NCPs who were just entering the program. These displays were designed to foster optimism and self-esteem. In many cases, completing peer support bolstered the person's self-confidence, allowing him to begin to trust in his own ability to attempt something new. With the knowledge that the PFS program was behind them, some participants reached out to children infrequently contacted, tried to resolve family conflicts without violence, and sought outside assistance in circumstances where once they would have been alone and without resources.

Self-reliance empowered the men. Arron contacted the Department of Social Services to deal with his suspicions of child abuse instead of confronting his ex-girlfriend in anger and with violence. Kenny called the program to investigate how he should handle a potential new child in his life rather than simply ignore administrative obligations that could have resulted in complicated and long-term entanglements with CSE. Edmond made a personal commitment to building a relationship with his seventeen-year-old son, the two men creating their own "visitation" schedule to ensure that they would stick to their shared resolution. Fila-G, Big Joe, Bob, Mack, and Ventura at least contemplated giving up old ways of earning money in the drug game. The success of these efforts depended on many environmental, societal, and personal variables that peer support could neither control nor change. But the fact that these individuals took a first step encouraged facilitators and participants alike.

Not all participants viewed PFS as their "second family," however, nor did all view their group experiences as valuable. Discontent with peer support tended to build over time.

What I thought about peer support? Basically, most of the guys that was in the class with me, they basically was in there just because the nonsupport go down from $35 to $23.[15] I ain't seen but a couple people take the program for what it's worth, and I ain't find out what it's worth yet. I'm still searching. I'm doing my part. I even putting in an extra bit, you know . . . But all in all, if I don't get the proper job that I'm looking for, it was a waste of time. I should have carried my butt over to a temporary service and got a quick job. Really it was a waste of time for me to be without work for the whole three weeks in peer support, three weeks in job club, and now a week of job search. That's a month and three weeks! A month and three weeks! I'm sure JOBs Temporary Service would have found a job by now. So my time is my money because time is money and the time that was wasted in peer support and job club, therefore—that was a waste of time. If I end up having to go to a temporary service anyway, then that was really a waste of time.

[Jah, November 28, 1994]

Jah's disillusionment was not unique. One of the NCPs' biggest concerns was that despite their participation in peer support and the program as a whole, they would end up as they started out: poor. They were struggling financially when they entered PFS, and time spent in the program was time away from the sources of income that had helped them to survive. Attending peer support sessions could mean giving up being on call in the mornings for temporary jobs or could interfere with participants' opportunities to obtain unofficial work. Most NCPs were eager to move quickly into the job search/job club phase of the program and were frustrated that the program seemed to be getting off to a slow and dubious start:

Like I said, I'm hanging in there. Waiting for the program to get off, and what can become of it . . . I've been in [the facilitator's] office, and I've seen his little bulletin board where there's a lot of [peer support] graduates, keeping steadily on the phone, get those jobs and all this. He broken down and tell me I'm ready for it—I just wish it weren't so long. You know what I'm saying? . . . I wish it went for no month and a half and put me in the same boat again. I don't know, maybe I can cut a few [jobs] on the weekend. It all sounds, like, good, like it works, it promises to work. Stay off this minimum-wage system.

[Fila-G, August 26, 1994]

Disappointment ran deep when the program failed to deliver on its "promise" of employment.

Peer support encouraged participants to change their lives and to look ahead. They believed that the activities they had completed in peer support were moving them closer to their goals, when suddenly it seemed they that had arrived at nothing—there was little concrete satisfaction for their efforts, no employer's door open and awaiting them, no contract offering a solid salary—nothing but starting from scratch, nothing but more hard work and uncertainty. Those jobs that were offered presented little hope of future stability. The seeming lack of connection between peer support and job club/ job search often left NCPs bewildered and frustrated.

For others, peer support became a holding place. In lieu of a job, it was somewhere to go on a daily basis, where the community was accepting and the atmosphere familiar and comfortable. In most sites, participants could continue to attend peer support sessions even after they had completed their required cycle, while at the same time pursuing employment in job club or job search. But some NCPs spent months attending sessions or just "hanging out" at their PFS sites without making the transition into the labor force, "wading" in the program until presented with an opportunity that they were willing to take. For these men, moving out of PFS had the feel of leaving a friendly place, perhaps forever. Their reluctance to lose their "second family" was so strong that staying connected to the program seemingly became more important than immediately finding a job. This posed a challenge for facilitators and other staff whose objective was to move individuals through the program by helping them find employment.

CONCLUSIONS

In summary, the use of peer support groups within the context of the Parents' Fair Share program proved useful both for program staff and for participants. From the program's point of view, peer support was the first step in uncovering the participants' social, emotional, and personal strengths and weaknesses. When program staff actively participated in peer support, they got to know participants as individuals.[16] Sitting in these groups helped to dispel negative predispositions toward noncustodial fathers and to shed light on why these men might be unable to meet their roles and responsibilities. Having gained new insight into the lives of their client-participants, staff felt that they could speak more directly and honestly with the men, who often reciprocated with more openness—thus creating a positive environment for all involved.

For NCPs who had been unemployed for some time (more than two-thirds of the qualitative sample), peer support functioned as a transition to work. Peer support helped them to wrestle with big issues in their lives and to begin developing goals and strategies that would allow them to move forward. As Ray stated, "It helped me to be a better father, to get better perspective on what I'm suppose to do as a father, and I appreciated that." Some NCPs did not take to the group process and were more interested in finding work and freeing themselves from the grasp of child support enforcement than sitting in group sessions worrying about where they were going to get enough money to fulfill their obligations. In general, however, participants viewed peer support in a constructive and positive manner. The enthusiasm that peer support could generate was captured by an unsolicited comment from at least one group at every site: "The women should have something like this!" And in fact, one site ended up working with its human services department to create a support group for custodial parents, which consisted mainly of women who were receiving (what was then) AFDC.

Chapter 6

THE EMPLOYMENT AND TRAINING COMPONENT OF PFS: JOB CLUB/JOB SEARCH

NELSON: Job training! Now that's straight. If you have a lot of meaning to it, you gotta try to have you ready for interviews and stuff like that.

INTERVIEWER: And did you need that stuff?

NELSON: Well, I—everybody need to brush up on that stuff. You never know when you be challenged.

[December 14, 1995]

The men in this study entered PFS not only because they were under court order but also because the program offered opportunities to become employed in jobs that paid good money. The expectation and excitement of some NCPs was a mirror image of the discouragement and despair of men unable to obtain "good jobs."

WILLIE: Why should a human race, a race of people—why should there even be a doubt there to even try to help these people? I mean, we ain't talking about a bunch of goddamned birds. We're talking about a race of human beings who are declining because of ignorance, not because of your money or what you make, but because of ignorance, not money.

INTERVIEWER: What about opportunity?

WILLIE: What opportunity?

INTERVIEWER: Well, the lack of opportunity.

WILLIE: What, the opportunity to go to jail?

INTERVIEWER: You got that.

WILLIE: That's all you got! To work for a temporary service, to be treated like a dog? I'm going to get treated like a dog if I get a job, I'm going to get treated like a dog if I don't get a job. I mean, how many dogs can you be? It's all about money, so I'm going to do what I got to do to get some money. Now, I ain't got to deal with the white man and his shit, I ain't got to deal with the embarrassment and the frustration of a job, I just get me a ki[lo] and sell it. Give me an opportunity.

[April 19, 1995]

These men perceived that their communities, towns, and cities do not have any jobs available for them, and this perception posed a major challenge for the PFS program and staff seeking to prepare them for the local labor market.

After completing the formal peer support requirement, the participant was usually assessed for job readiness.[1] The assessment process could range from a formal conversation with a job club coach, job developer, and case manager about his personal work goals and objectives to a two-day test of skills and attitudes. During some of the conversations, with or without a formal assessment, an NCP would inquire about schooling or vocational training. Program staff would address these issues depending on whether or not the types of activities requested were available at their site and whether they thought that the candidate had the potential to complete the training or schooling. For the most part, the men were encouraged to become employed and to start paying child support, but in some sites, they were given the opportunity to pursue education and training opportunities.

Participants in the qualitative sample were somewhat more likely to participate in employment-oriented PFS services than were participants in the overall PFS demonstration. These men were more likely to be active in job clubs, job readiness workshops, on-the-job training, and occupational skills training. They also participated in more sessions in job clubs, job readiness, and skills training, but fewer sessions of on-the-job training.

JOB CLUB

For NCPs, looking to the future meant looking to the past to understand what went right and wrong in their prior work experiences.

They needed both to build on their positive work experiences and to reverse or discard habits that played a part in their losing jobs, quitting jobs, or not finding routes to promotions. The first step was to understand the employer-employee relationship, such as the need to get to work on time and to handle conflicts constructively. This is where the job club component of Parents' Fair Share commenced.

The basic goal of the job clubs was to help NCPs find confidence in their ability to enter work environments that many, like Willie, perceived as hostile and exclusive and to trust themselves to be as competent as any other applicant for the same job.

Job club was a group activity that, when conducted with expertise, was both interactive and informative. Participants shared experiences and ideas about the preparation required to get a job, the process of finding and keeping a job, in addition to other employment issues, such as communicating with higher-ups and coworkers, feeling safe to voice questions and needs, recognizing one's own desires, and setting goals. Participants usually began to accept job club activities as valuable after they learned something new or discovered a latent skill. Past members also gave testimonials and feedback on the program, the state of their job search, and their experiences with interviewing.

Job club offered participants concrete information, training in specific skills, and opportunities to practice these skills before venturing into the labor market. One useful skill was the creation of a résumé. Many men had never written one before, and they were offered instruction on what to include, how to use key words, and what to omit. See appendix E for an explanation of the "shield" exercise, a method of helping participants use positive language to promote their abilities. The exercise also coached NCPs in how to avoid language that brings attention to negative areas in their work histories.

NCPs were also assisted with the development of interviewing skills and techniques. Even those who had been in and out of the labor market, like Kenny and Hollywood, took these exercises seriously and found them to be beneficial.

KENNY: There wasn't really too much bad about [job club], I mean, 'cause it—it helped you. I mean, there was certain things that I knew, you know, as far as about obtaining employment and everything . . . But, I mean, for brothers who didn't know, it was a great help for 'em, you know what I'm saying? Teachin' 'em how, you know, [to] handle themselves in an interview, how to write they résumés up, references, how to present themselves . . . you know, to go out and get a job, so that they could start paying their, you know, thing—what type of fathers they wanted to be and things like that.

INTERVIEWER: You think that's helpful?

KENNY: Yes. Very helpful.

[September 25, 1995]

Hollywood's take on the component was equally positive:

INTERVIEWER: Tell me about job club. How was that? How did that help you? Or didn't it?

HOLLYWOOD: It did. You know, it give leads, good—great—leads . . . It's just up to people to follow up on it.

[October 18, 1995]

In the early spring of 1995, a group of about fourteen noncustodial parents who had been working together for two weeks, preparing to find jobs, were about to begin the formal job search component of PFS. Before seeking out employers and sending out their résumés, they practiced opening and closing an interview. The job club coach, who was also an experienced job developer, asked the group if they had any questions relating to the training video they had seen the day before; his words were received in silence. Looking around the room, he asked for a volunteer, while exhorting the men to "remember what you are applying for!" After a while, with great reluctance, a volunteer pushed himself forward, and the role play began. When the coach, as employer, greeted the applicant, he was again met with dead silence—the participant had frozen in his chair. Patiently, the coach offered the participant some information; in keeping with the role play process, the applicant was to answer one question and then close the interview. Fidgeting uncomfortably, the participant at last came up with a response, and they were able to move into the closing. Afterward, the group discussed his performance.

He needed to look the employer in the eye, while shaking his hand; he took a seat before being invited to do so; he forgot to thank the employer for the interview and the chance to work in his chosen field; he should have remembered the employer's name. This commentary came entirely from the participants themselves, who, though respectful, found much humor in the situation and were enjoying themselves thoroughly. Later in the session, the same participant asked to go again. Although he did not conduct a perfect interview, he had improved greatly since his first try, just an hour or so earlier.

The group setting helped participants feel comfortable about bringing up topics that the counselor had overlooked. As Arron explained, at almost all levels of employment, job applicants have to "dress for success."

ARRON: [T]o have a job, you have to be prepared for a job before you even get it, but then the way things are, how could you? Okay, so you get a damn job. You have to look just like slacks, nice shirt, and tie. I don't have any of that kind of stuff, though.

INTERVIEWER: You don't?

ARRON: Nothing like that, nothing. You know. Because—I buy my own clothes. When I buy clothes, I buy what I can afford. I pay $10 a pair of pants, they're khakis and T-shirts . . . that's all you can afford, khakis and T-shirts, and it's cheap, it's convenient for the price. That way we have more money to spend rather than spend it all on clothes. See, we can't afford to wear Guess jeans and all this stuff, suits and ties, and tailor made. We can't afford it yet. Give us a job! Just give me a month, give me a job, give me a good month to where I can get a nice paycheck, and I will buy that. Hold a job. Then you'll see me coming in, looking nice and clean-cut and what have you, but until then just bear with me. That's the thing. Sometimes people qualify for a job, but they don't want to bear with them on things, you understand? Transportation and stuff like that. You got to bear with a person for a minute. I'll come and work my ass off for you if you will bear with me.

[May 17, 1995]

In some sites, once participants had progressed to job club, they were expected to change their personal presentation and gradually move from casual clothing to work-appropriate dress; this could mean a switch from T-shirts and sweatpants to button-down shirts and jeans and eventually to shirts and ties. Program sites that tried to get participants to make these changes were attempting to implement a gradual process of resocialization, which was frequently more difficult than anticipated. As Arron and others pointed out, many participants did not have the money to purchase the basic items necessary for interviewing. When this problem came to light in the job club, coaches from all program locations took the initiative to provide participants with clothing or bus fare, while some sites set up clothing collections to serve their clients.[2]

Learning these types of skills made job club a useful endeavor for some NCPs.

INTERVIEWER: Tell me about the job club part, because I never get to see that, much. What do you guys do? Do you still go to that?

MACK: Uh-huh. They have résumés. We look in the paper, and people [follow] their leads, and sometime we like, some of the JOBs people, we get out in the car, and we go out for applications, everybody; that's that. We go out for applications in the same places. Stuff like that.

INTERVIEWER: The whole group of you do it, or do you . . . how was that?

MACK: Sometime it's all right.

INTERVIEWER: Tell me about the best part of this program for you.

MACK: For me? I finally found some people that, if they don't—they're doing an excellent job, they should all get Academy Awards! But I found lots of people, it seems they care about me. You know. They all government, you know what I'm saying; part of the fraction of the government that cares. Their job is to help me, and it seems they were.

INTERVIEWER: You think so?

MACK: I think so. If not, they got me fooled very well, and that's not easy to do.

INTERVIEWER: That's interesting. Do you think the other guys feel that way too, Mack?

MACK: Yeah, basically I think they do, you know. Because we all got a lot in common. We all basically alike, man, and I know, if we didn't want to be there, we wouldn't be there. I've heard many people say that a lot, you know. If they didn't like it, they wouldn't come at all.

[March 22, 1995]

Others, however, were less convinced of the component's utility. They believed they already possessed the job-seeking abilities and techniques that job club offered. In some groups, this created an element of "social distancing" between the men who needed to learn basic skills and those who wanted access to employment leads, trusting that they could do the rest.

ARRON: A part-time job outside of what I'm doing [participating in PFS] would be cool. I leave from there and go to work part-time. You know, that way I have money. I'd be prepared for the big job that they're training me for. I'd have the attire and everything to do whatever it is I have to do. Just like that, man.

INTERVIEWER: What does your girlfriend think about the program?

ARRON: She likes it because I told her I was guaranteed a job at the end—which I lied, because there's no guarantee. They didn't even say you were going to get a job. They just said we're going to be trained, and the EDD [Employment Development Department], then they send you on an interview. Well, shit! You can do that without having to go there. You know what I'm saying? I'm already registered [with] EDD, what the hell.

[May 17, 1995]

Arron did not think that he needed training but went along with the program for two reasons: because he wanted to help his children ("I do anything to be around my kids, and nobody [can] say I was a deadbeat, or anything like that") and because he dreamed of succeeding in the entertainment world ("I want to come up, like the blue in the sky").

JOB SEARCH

When a group of NCPs was asked, in an informal discussion in early 1995, "How did this program help you, or fail to help you?" a participant named Ray offered the following opinion:[3]

It helped me to be a better father, to get better perspective on what I'm suppose to do as a father, and I appreciated that. Some of the shortcomings that I've seen from the program—they said that it was supposed to help create jobs for these fathers so that they could pay child support. There was no jobs at all. All the way. I went through the whole program, and, personally, I don't know nobody who got a job from the program. And that's what they said it was about, to help us become better fathers and to get us on a work mode and to help us get a job, and there was no job.

[Ray, March 1995]

After Ray spoke, others recounted similar difficulties finding work and how they had labored at unskilled and semiskilled jobs like car washing, both before and after they entered the program. Finding a job remained the primary struggle for all participants in PFS, particularly for those in the qualitative research sample.

Some, like Viceroy, were successful in finding jobs on their own.

VICEROY: I mean, I think I can—as far as the job thing goes, it taught me a lot about unemployment, but I think I can do better on my own.

INTERVIEWER: You think you can find a better job on your own—than through the program?

VICEROY: That's how I did with my last job.

INTERVIEWER: You found it on your own?

VICEROY: I found it on my own. I went out and filled out applications on my own. [One of the program staff] knew the lady, but I did it on my own. I went out there, and I found me a job. I didn't sit up there and wait on Parents' Fair Share to help me. I mean, it's okay to do that, but it's just not me.

[March 26, 1996]

Job coaches and job developers were responsible for getting participants ready to work, for helping them find work, and for providing potential employers with dedicated, hard-working employees. The pressure was great to meet a broad range of expectations from employers, participants, and their respective program sites.[4] Staff had to be flexible when participants' expressions of their needs, skill levels, and talents differed from the perspectives of staff members. Even when the program did not think a participant was ready to progress with his employment objectives, if the participant *felt* ready, staff had to allow him to proceed. Likewise, when NCPs decided to seek low-paying jobs with no foreseeable future, staff had to accept their decision. However, the goal was to place men in employment situations that benefited both the participant and employer. Successful long-term job placement was rare, however, for men in this sample.

Inevitably the question arose, "Is any job a good job (or at least better than no job)?" Although some participants had never held a full-time job, all had worked at least part-time. Typically, they had worked for very little money and were looking for a way to move out of the low-wage world.

> So what's going to be left if you're making six bucks an hour? There won't be enough for me to live on. I'll be—just like to where I am now. Not, not able to afford a place to rent, or anything . . . I'd figure if I'm making about at least $3,000 a month, no matter what they do to me, I'll have, I'll have enough money left over to, to live on. To be able to rent my own place and do what I want to do.
>
> [Geraldo, June 15, 1995]

When Geraldo and others expressed their need and desire to make more money, they were also saying that they could not afford to work in dead-end jobs. On wages of $5 to $6 per hour, it was nearly impossible to pay child support in addition to paying rent, purchasing food, and meeting other essential personal needs. They no longer saw any growth potential or other benefit to be gained from taking these jobs, a realization that seemed to hold consistent for both older and younger NCPs in the sample.[5] Antonio, for example, held certificates of expertise in automobile and aerospace mechanics and was last employed full time in 1991 by a major company in the aerospace industry that paid him $16.50 an hour. Although willing to work for less, he insisted on earning a "reasonable wage," which he had been unable to obtain for nearly three years. His efforts included signing up for construction work funded by Los Angeles County because of the possibility that they would pay union wages.

INTERVIEWER: Now if you could get a job that pays almost $16 an hour, I'm sure you could get ahead.

ANTONIO: Hey, I'd be happy with a job that pays $10.50 an hour. The only thing is, I go out and I look all the time, but it's still real hard, like I said, financially—it costs me a lot of money to travel.

INTERVIEWER: Yeah, it costs you money to even look for a job.

[October 3, 1994]

The challenge, then, was to convince NCPs that the employment/training component was valuable and that their experiences could be transferred to viable work. Such work could stabilize their lives and allow them to expect gainful employment and independence. In reality, however, most NCPs could not afford to wait for a "good" job and so returned to the same types of low-paying, dead-end jobs—or to informal, off-the-books, or illegal work—they had pursued before entering the program.

A major obstacle to legitimate employment was transportation. Out of the thirty-two sample participants, only ten owned cars. Out of those who had cars, approximately half lost the use of their vehicle because they were caught for driving without registration or insurance or with a suspended license. One was in an accident that totaled his car. Public transportation to the PFS sites tended to be slow, unreliable, and for these men, expensive.[6] It was extremely frustrating for participants who, on the recommendation of their job developer and the prospect of a good forklift or warehousing job paying $8 to $10 an hour, made the long journey out of town, only to be denied the position. For their efforts, they ended up with no work, a long bus ride back (if the bus was still running), and fewer tokens in their possession. After several such trips, NCPs were less likely to jump at their job developer's every suggestion.[7] Sometimes job developers had a hard time convincing participants (and themselves) of the need to take a ninety-minute bus ride to the suburbs or across town.

As the job search dragged on, frustrations built on both sides, and communication between participants and staff tended to break down. For their part, participants felt that the effort they expended traveling back and forth to job interviews was seldom acknowledged and rarely worthwhile. Moreover, many complained that they were sent on interviews with the understanding that the program had some influence or relationship with their prospective employer, only to be received as if they had just walked off the street on a cold call, with nobody knowing who they were. They also talked about being "hustled" on job interviews through "bait and switch" techniques in which an advertised position at a certain level of pay was claimed to have been filled; in its place, they were offered similar employment at less pay.

Some participants felt that the staff did not recognize their personal needs and goals. Edmond hoped that the program would help him to find an internship or entry-level job in an aspect of computer imaging design, his chosen field.

Maybe I'm talking off the top of my head—well, I'm sure I am. But I would have—I don't know whose job it would be, but I would have made an effort to get me a job, even if it was just cleaning windows in an architectural drafting firm or something. Something related to what I'm doing, so I can find out early what I'm getting into, instead of—you know, I haven't got a clue what the environment will be. What kind of job I'll be doing. So that would have been an interesting thing I would have tried differently. I was disappointed at the community—or just the lack of appearance of what I thought—like the hand holding that should have went on between business and Parents' Fair Share.

[Edmond, May 6, 1996]

For their part, staff were frustrated when participants did not take advantage of the job opportunities offered them. The belief that a participant was not sufficiently grateful, motivated, or the right person for a job caused great tension when staff felt that the program had invested time and energy in preparing the person for a job placement that ultimately did not work out.

INTERVIEWER: Tell me about the follow-up [on job leads provided by job club], because I think that's really important. Why don't you follow up?

HOLLYWOOD: I don't know. I don't know. I don't even think about it, you know. Once I—

INTERVIEWER: You just don't do it.

HOLLYWOOD: Yeah. Once I leave, I know I gotta go take care of something, so, you know. I get on the bus, and I'm on my way. You know, it's startin', you know. Soon as I leave [job club], you know, it starts. You know, the real world.

[October 18, 1995]

As Hollywood implies, limited funds and time often forced NCPs to choose between taking care of immediate personal or family business and going on a job interview that might or might not pan out. Hollywood chose "real life" as he called it. Others dropped out of PFS, and generally out of sight, when they found that the jobs in which they had been placed were not geared for long-term employment and did not pay enough to enable them to meet their minimum child support obligations and their own personal needs.

LOST OPPORTUNITIES: THE DOOR SHUTS

Geraldo experienced much frustration with the CSE system and ultimately with PFS as well. His disappointment with the program cen-
tered around its failure to produce the jobs and educational training
he believed he had been promised. He also expressed concern that
he, like many of his peers, would be judged in an unfavorable light
if, after going through the program, he was still neither employed
nor paying his child support.

> They [CSE agency] want to put me to work now. Why didn't they leave
> me working, when I was working? They were trying to put me in jail.
> Why—because I'm three months late? Makes no sense. And then, [I'm]
> willing to pay off my debt, my balance, all $3,600 of it. Promised—I had
> a job. Making $1,000 a week—I could have been able to pay that and
> more . . . I would've provided more for my family. I knew me. I love my
> family. I love my children. But no. They want to be Mr. God, you know
> . . . And decide my fate and my career . . . [W]hen it's all said and done,
> they will be able to say, "This opportunity was given . . . and [these men]
> didn't take advantage of it. And it's too bad . . . They don't want it and
> don't want to comply, and . . . they are what we claim them to be." But
> you and I know that it's not because we didn't want it, but more because
> the people in charge of the program didn't make it available . . . [People
> will ask,] "What are we gonna have to pay for this . . . that we had noth-
> ing to do with?" I mean, the world is gonna look, 'cause eventually the
> DA will have it out on the news . . . "We gave them an opportunity, we
> put everything in their hands, but . . . they're still out there, not sup-
> porting their family, their responsibility. What should we do with
> them?" . . . What's going to happen to us? People will judge us unfairly.
> [Geraldo, September 28, 1995]

Geraldo left one job because of pressure from CSE, with the original
debt of $3,600. By the time he entered PFS it had grown to more than
$60,000. Program staff told participants that the PFS door was
always open. Perceptions of "open" and the degree of "openness"
with which participants were received varied, however. Just as staff
members differed in the degree to which they were willing to be up-
front, socially interactive, and familiar with participants, so too was
the door of return to PFS more open or closed depending on an
NCP's particular experiences, biases, and perceptions. Sometimes a
participant who had been out of contact with the program for more

than a month would return to find that staff who had helped him were no longer at the site. These individuals might seek a one-time consultation and then move on without reengaging with the program. Many times during this research, noncustodial parents spoke angrily about receiving letters regarding their lack of participation. In their view, the program had lost contract with *them*.

PFS did not anticipate that NCPs might need to maintain contact with the employment staff even after they found jobs and so did not have a plan or procedure for following up on program graduates.[8] In most cases, staff were unaware of the dismay, anger, and frustration that NCPs experienced "on their own." Nor did PFS anticipate that NCPs might be reluctant to return to the program when things did not work out.

Take the case of Lover, who quickly moved through the components of Parents' Fair Share: peer support, job club, and job training. In training, he worked diligently and finished first in his class. He budgeted his tokens in order to travel nearly two hours on public transportation in the morning and evening so that he could attend school. Lover often had to choose between going on interviews for part-time jobs or going to school, and 90 percent of the time he went to class. After finishing his training and passing the certification test, he started looking for work on his own. At this point, he had minimal contact with the PFS program.

Lover was used to checking in with his case manager during the beginning of his job search phase, but eventually changes in the lives of both the case manager and Lover made communication more infrequent. Within three weeks of completing his training, he landed a job in his field. Making it through the company's probation period, he was one of only three people to be asked to work full time. He worked for nearly two months, making and exceeding his weekly and monthly quotas. His managers knew who he was and spoke favorably of him. At the end of his second month, he was forced to take time off from his regular schedule and sometimes missed days (see chapter 7 for a description of his situation at this time). He tried to make the time up, but this became increasingly difficult. After about a month and a half of erratic attendance, the company, while sympathetic to his situation, let him go, and Lover became unemployed. He went back to the school to freshen up on some new technology but was received with less-than-open arms. He understood this treatment to be saying, "They aren't getting any money for me anymore, so they don't have to help me." When asked if he would go back to the Parents' Fair Share program for assistance, he usually avoided the question, instead showing anger and disappointment. His situation became so bad that he did not have the money, nor any prospect of money, to buy over-the-counter medicine for a case of the flu. Still, he did not ask PFS for help.

Eventually, staff officially designated him as terminated from the program. No one, not even his case manager or peer support facilitator, knew him well enough to understand what he had been going through, and his case was sent back to CSE, where it remained as of this writing. No one was at fault in this situation; Lover did what he had to do to survive, and program staff monitored him as they normally monitor participants. When they saw that he was neither making child support payments nor participating in activities, they probably sent him a letter asking him to see his case manager. Lover said he never received the letter, but he frequently did not receive mail due to his unstable living situation. Receiving no response, the program pulled the plug on his reprieve from his child support obligation.

Lover's case was unique in many ways, but it was not uncommon for NCPs to become involved in personal situations whose importance overrode their participation in PFS or their job. Nor was it unusual for NCPs in this sample to decide not to return to the program after an opportunity failed (perhaps because they were upset about losing a job and embarrassed about "letting the staff down"). As a result, a participant could be removed from the program and referred back to child support enforcement for failure to comply.

The challenge for programs like PFS is to find a host of jobs and opportunities for participants. The program often urged participants to take jobs that were a poor fit. Many of these men were tired of barely getting by and wanted to do more than survive. They did not need a lot of money to begin, just $7 or $8 per hour.

But the bottom line is that jobs that would enable these men to achieve stability and economic independence are not readily available. Many explanations have been offered as to why, given the steadily declining unemployment rates in counties and cities across the United States (with the exception of the city and county of Los Angeles during the period of this study), these NCPs were unable to capitalize on a growing economy. Job developers and some job coaches used terms like "unemployable," "without skills," and "lacking the right attitude." In a moment of indiscretion, one job developer complained that the NCPs with whom he was working were "hardly rocket scientists," which made his job of marketing them very difficult. Another job developer described how he had to be careful about whom he sent where, because some employers were only interested in certain types of employees or were afraid that bringing different types of people into the work environment would be disruptive. Excuses for not being able to place these men abounded.[9] Comments like these from employers are not unusual. Wilson (1996), Waldinger (1996), and Kirschenman and Neckerman (1991) find that employers exclude workers who do not fit subjective standards. Many of these standards are based on preconceived notions of how people of color work, which inevitably excludes them, African Americans primarily, from a profusion of jobs. According to Wilson (1996), the migration of jobs away from the central and inner cities of Chicago has affected African American workers more than other ethnic groups.

Of course, some of the obstacles to a successful job search were due to the NCPs' personal problems. In Trenton, for example, the job club coach and job developers tried hard to convince participants to give up smoking marijuana. At this site, early in the program, many men who were interviewing, getting called back, and receiving job offers were ultimately rejected because they could not pass drug tests. This compelled PFS staff to confront participants about their drug use. The message got through to Chris Adam, who was a frequent smoker before his job developer told him that many companies were performing drug tests.

Finally, Parents' Fair Share postponed but did not resolve the NCPs' problems with CSE. In an after-hours peer support session in Dayton, Billy Bob described how he thought the system should work.

> If a person is not paying child support and somebody said, "Well, I'll get you a job at $10 or whatever an hour," and you start making child support payments and you're gainfully employed—if I accept that, that's what I'm looking for, because I'm not working, I'm not making child support payments. Now, if I jump up and quit, once I get this job and start making ends meet, and I jump up and quit, then I'm open to anything that happens to me.
>
> [Billy Bob, March 1995]

Then Billy Bob described his own experience. When he started working, after completing PFS, support payments for his youngest child were deducted from his check, which he thought was as it should be. Billy Bob also had a grown son who had served in the armed forces, worked steadily after he left the service, and had a child of his own. Billy Bob said that he had stopped paying child support five years earlier when his son turned eighteen and graduated from high school. He assumed that he had met his obligations for this son. But as it turned out,

> After I got this job, then they called me in and said they found out that I was in the arrears of $2,800 [for his grown son] and they wanted me to start making payments on that, and they started taking it out of my check without me having a hearing or anything on it. Now that's something that would discourage a person to quit, because they start to make money, they're making child support payments, and now, all of a sudden, they pull up something way up in the back that's been dead for five years in my case, but I had heard nothing for five years . . . Why didn't they tell me about that earlier? Why did they wait until I started making decent money, and all of a sudden it come out? Now that would discourage a person and make them want to quit, because that's more money coming out.
>
> [Billy Bob, March 1995]

Participants had to negotiate many personal circumstances and choices in order to pursue a job, while job developers had to place men with histories of poverty, poor education, and uneven work experience. This put enormous pressure on both the PFS staff and on noncustodial parents. Because the jobs that would allow noncustodial parents to meet their basic needs were neither readily available nor easily accessible, many frustrated NCPs chose to leave the program, unofficially, to search for jobs and opportunities on their own.

Most NCPs in this study ended where they began. For the most part, the men in this sample ended up no better off, or in a few instances were worse off financially, than when they entered the program. Many were angry and discouraged as a result.

> You know, I've been seeing them [at the program] weekly, now, all this here; they ain't found me no job, you know. I got paperwork down there, where I been looking for jobs and stuff like that, you know . . . Like I say, I'm in the same old boat . . . that I was the day they picked me out of juvenile court. The only thing different, I ain't down in court right now . . . I was unemployed then, and I'm un-

employed now, so, you know. No cash flow—I was on stamps then and I'm on stamps now.

[Fila-G, February 1995]

However, the men who participated in this research were generally marked by a spirit of resiliency that allowed each, at some point, to put aside his anger and enjoy life, continuing to hold hope for the future. Overall, participants maintained their belief that there was a good job out there for them; they just needed some help in finding it—this was their expectation of and challenge to the program and to the employment and training component in particular.

MEDIATION

Mediation—a formal, conflict resolution process—was an underused component of Parents' Fair Share. None of this study's sample members accessed formal mediation services, although some felt that using services would have helped them work out relationship issues.

There are a number of reasons why mediation was not a bigger part of the PFS intervention. For one, the process was not binding, which meant that even if the parties reached an agreement, the mediator did not possess the authority to enforce an action or resolution if one parent later declined to follow through. Another reason lay in the nature of participants' relationships. Distrust of the process and of each other often prevented parents from considering mediation.

With too many unknowns, Parents' Fair Share could not encourage participants and their partners to engage in mediation, and thus neither party knew how to use or what to expect from the component. As a result, the mediation component of Parents' Fair Share did not materialize as a powerful tool for resolving conflict. Nor was it viewed as an integral part in improving the relationship between noncustodial parent and child.

CONCLUSION AND OVERVIEW

The employment side of Parents' Fair Share challenged all parties involved in finding work for low-income, frequently unemployed noncustodial parents. Participants found much of the job club activity useful—learning how to fill out a job application, how to use action words to strengthen a résumé, how to present themselves and be a more effective job applicant. But frustration set in when participants had to go and look for work. Staff members often complained that participants failed to seize opportunities, while participants lamented the lack of jobs, were disappointed with the positions they interviewed for, and had difficulty getting to job sites. Many NCPs had trouble finding gainful employment, despite the program's assistance. As a result, some limited their contact with the program to infrequent visits and an occasional check-in by telephone, continuing their job searches, and lives, on their own. Lover, who followed the prescribed path through PFS, was still struggling when this research concluded.

INTERVIEWER: So what are you doing to survive now, Lover?

LOVER: I'm not.

INTERVIEWER: You're just trying to get some GR [general relief].

LOVER: Uh-huh.

INTERVIEWER: Are they going to give it to you?

LOVER: That's what I'm up here for now.

INTERVIEWER: Okay. And then what? What are you doing today? Do you have enough gas and stuff for your car?

LOVER: No, no. I'm just going to sit—probably go somewhere and sit my little black self down.

INTERVIEWER: Where are you going?

LOVER: I have no idea. Believe me, it ain't far because I ain't got so much gas.

[May 1996]

The mediation process was the one component that did not flourish in the PFS structure. This is not to say that many people were not interested or willing to participate, but they never understood exactly how to engage the process. The underlying challenge for PFS was to make the components work for the participant in order to serve the program's goals.

The final chapter of this book looks at what the NCPs were able to accomplish after entering Parents' Fair Share. Chapter 7 also examines the policy implications of this research for welfare reform, child support enforcement, and macroeconomic employment issues.

Chapter 7

CONCLUSION

To wonder what the future will bring is a luxury. To fight to survive every day is reality.

[Willie, July 1997]

Inevitably, as noncustodial parents continued their efforts to make it in the world, Parents' Fair Share faded in importance. This is not to say that NCPs never thought about their experience in PFS or that the program's messages, lessons, and skills did not resonate with them. Rather, much of what the program offered takes time to translate into concrete, practical plans, strategies, and actions. In many ways, PFS challenged participants to reexamine their attitudes, beliefs, roles, and responsibilities. It is impossible to predict when these insights might take on concrete relevance in the men's everyday lives. Yet, these NCPs had to move on. Some left with the blessing and support of their program, while others slipped away to pursue their endeavors on their own. Where did Parents' Fair Share fit in the lives of these noncustodial parents? Why did some of these men believe it important to try to make the intervention work for them? For many of these men, the sole purpose of participating in PFS was to get a steady job and start paying their back child support. However, some of the men were looking for a friend or a safe place to relax away from the stress they experienced on the streets or at home. Finding work was important for these men, but achieving a degree of calm in their life was a higher priority.

Consider Jasper, who had a history of not working for long periods because of his heavy use of drugs and alcohol. He was fighting a constant battle to find stable housing or shelter. Jasper also felt the pain of separation from his young child, whose maternal grandparents forbade him to see her while the mother and child lived in their home. Jasper used PFS off and on to find the confidence and stability to handle his drug and alcohol use and to find work. Near the end of the study, Jasper had been missing for three or four months. The program was still active, and the staff was nearly the same as when he entered the program, a year or so earlier. One day in the fall, Jasper walked into the office and sought out the job developer with whom he had worked closely in the year prior to his absence. He wanted to discuss an important decision that he was about to make. After a candid and emotional conversation, Jasper departed. Shortly thereafter, with the understanding and support of both PFS staff and his family, Jasper signed himself into an intensive drug recovery and rehabilitation program. He had known for a long time that until he made this move, he would not be able to deal constructively with his living, work, and family situations. His relationship with the job developer allowed him to take this crucial first step.

This chapter seeks to understand what motivated Jasper and others to use PFS to attempt to change the direction of their lives and the degree to which the program and the participants succeeded. Three questions are considered: Did the lives of noncustodial parents change? How did they change? How did participating in PFS help noncustodial parents to make adjustments in their lives or develop the coping mechanisms that facilitated change?

The program and individual staff worked hard to help participants overcome hurdles in their lives, with varying degrees of success. As much as one might hope for clear, measurable results (employment, income, child support payments, involvement with children, relationships with the custodial parent), concrete changes in participants' lives proved elusive. Preliminary findings indicate that there were some impacts on child support, but few on employment and earnings (for more details on findings for PFS overall, see Doolittle et al. 1998). The obstacles facing these NCPs when they entered PFS did not necessarily disappear because they were recognized and addressed in the program. But this does not mean that PFS had no impact on the lives of participants. The first part of this chapter uses individual cases to illustrate the situation of some of the noncustodial parents when they left the program. The second part considers a series of policy and programmatic recommendations based on what we have learned from this qualitative study about the men who entered PFS and how the program did or did not meet its goals and serve their needs.

FOUR CATEGORIES OF NONCUSTODIAL PARENTS

Four categories of noncustodial parents entered and exited the doors of Parents' Fair Share: the survivor, the family-oriented non-custodial parent, those ready to change, and the outsider. These typologies were not mutually exclusive, nor were they static or fixed. A participant might move in and out of a particular category or fit into one category in some areas of his life but another category in other areas.

Survivors

In the more than two and a half years of this research, every member of this sample participated in PFS, spent some time in jail, and had a host of other experiences. When asked informally how they were doing, one of the more common responses was, "surviving," which is to say that they retained their spirit for life and sense of pride. Three such survivors were Lover, Willie, and Geraldo, each of whom struggled to preserve family, health, and self.

Lover   Lover was a survivor because of his positive outlook on life and his desire and determination to be with his children again. His wife died, leaving him with two children. While under the care of a friend, one of his children had an accident, for which Lover was charged with neglect. He spent a month in jail and two years in and out of court, with charges pending, and later lost custody of his children.

Despite being under the constant scrutiny of the law, the social welfare system, and the child support enforcement system, Lover trained for a career, gaining the skills and a certificate that qualified him to work in the travel and leisure industry. Eager to prove to the court that he was employable and a loving father, Lover found work on his own and was considered a valuable employee. But a year of deliberations in dependency court cost him the custody of his children, who were made wards of the state.[1]

His case was then tried in superior court, and after nearly ten continuances, the charges were dismissed. That same day, before he walked out of the courthouse, he was arrested and jailed on new charges brought by the district attorney's office. Although eventually released, Lover lost his job during this period. The final outcome of his superior court case was still undetermined at the time of this writing.

Lover's struggle to survive continued. He decided not to pursue full-time work because he feared he would lose such a job when his appearance was required in court, irrespective of his work schedule. He believed that the courts were waiting for him to "mess up" so that they could put him away and keep his children in foster care. In spite of the legal and financial obstacles, Lover continued to do something every day, with the goal of one day becoming a loving, responsible father to his children.

On the one hand, Lover still had unresolved issues with the judicial system, still cared for his children, and still was unemployed. Yet through his participation in PFS, he developed skills and found work in a potentially well-paid field that previously seemed inaccessible. The intervention gave him a chance to attend school and to prove that he had the talent and determination to succeed. His dreams grew as his success in the labor force continued. PFS was at the core of his success, because it provided him with the opportunities to make a positive change in his life.

On the other hand, Lover saw PFS as partly responsible for his inability to remain employed and to resolve his legal problems. According to Lover, he lost his job when his case required him to attend court on a regular basis. In building his defense, his lawyer asked him to request a letter from PFS certifying his participation in the peer support group, which included sessions devoted specifically to parenting skills. Both he and his lawyer believed that a letter from PFS would demonstrate to the court that Lover was working to become a better parent. Neither he nor the court received this letter. While under house arrest, he tried to contact the program, but got no response. In Lover's view, by not backing him in his fight to be an active parent, by leaving him alone to deal with the judicial and welfare systems, and by reintroducing the CSE system into his life, PFS let him down. Despite his initial progress and success with the various components and activities of PFS, Lover's primary success stemmed from his steadfast desire to be with his children again.

Willie   Willie was also a survivor. Willie lived with his wife of thirteen years and their two children (one her child and one her stepchild). For Willie, survival meant providing for his family.

Although both a high school and college graduate, Willie struggled to keep food on the table and a roof over their heads.

Willie came into Parents' Fair Share looking for work and a chance to succeed, but the program did not meet his expectations. Throughout the study, he was formally unemployed, earning small amounts of money through hustles: selling marijuana, fixing car stereos, and making dubs and musical remixes, which kept him and his family barely solvent. When his wife's temporary job ended, the family's telephone service was cut off, as was their electricity, several times; Willie depended on his pager to stay connected to the outside world. He applied for many jobs, but nearly a year and a half passed with no work and no prospects. The final blow came when the house he had inherited from his relatives, and in which he and his family were living, burned down. They were officially homeless, and for nearly two weeks they lived out of their car, followed by a stay in a local hotel.

Willie had just gotten a new job and was afraid to take time off, even for this emergency. But the company gave him time to get organized as well as a small advance to put down on a new apartment. Willie and his family had to start over, buying clothing, furniture, and everything else that was destroyed in the fire. Working harder than ever, Willie managed to keep the job and the apartment. Money was still tight, but Willie had the confidence and now the opportunity, given the possibility for advancement through his job, to see beyond just surviving day to day. Willie dreamed of moving with his company to another city and starting over. He believed that a black man, like himself, would have to leave Memphis if he wanted to succeed.

Willie's life changed not so much because of PFS but in many ways despite it. Willie had a strong sense of pride and resented the child support system and, to a lesser degree, the PFS program for its connection to that system. During his tenure with PFS, he took a stand against the system and stereotypes about African American men. He was outspoken about the program's failure to provide him and others with real opportunities (Willie was given only one lead to a part-time shipping job, which lasted two weeks). As a result of clashes with staff, he was sanctioned by the program for failing to participate even though he was participating; as a result, he was denied a reprieve on paying child support and had to settle the matter in court. With the help of a lawyer, he proved that he was in compliance with the program's requirements. The judge was lenient, and Willie avoided jail, although he later spent time in jail for legal problems not related to child support.

Willie's experience with PFS was anything but positive, yet he grew personally as a result of his time with the program. A large part of the caring and devotion that he demonstrated during this period of his life was due to his natural disposition. Informally, he stated that his interactions within the peer support component of PFS helped him to see that other men faced similar difficulties. Seeing and hearing other men discuss their struggles reminded him of his responsibility to himself and his family. His actions spoke for themselves. He stayed with his family, took jobs that were less than he wanted, and made personal sacrifices for the sake of his wife and children.

Willie left PFS, resenting that the program held the threat of jail over his head and believing that his choices were to pay child support to the system or to survive. More often than not, he chose survival over working with a system he abhorred.

Geraldo   Geraldo, raised as a migrant worker, broke away from his family and their lifestyle when he was a teenager. In spite of their ridicule for thinking he could escape poverty and their condemnation for abandoning his mother and siblings, he started his own business and eventually had a family of his own. Unreliable partnerships led to financial difficulties, which in turn caused stress and health problems. Unable to deal with the collapse of his business, Geraldo left his wife and three children to search for some breathing room, with the intention of one day returning. For a while he tried to support both himself and the family he had deserted. But the lack of steady work and income soon made that impossible. Geraldo had been evading the CSE system for nearly four years when he entered the Parents' Fair Share program. Optimistic that PFS would offer him an opportunity to get back on his feet and into a profession, Geraldo participated enthusiastically in the program.

Geraldo's participation came at a cost. During the time he was in the study, he never had a full-time job. He worked "off the books," putting most of his efforts into learning new skills. While attempting to pursue his education through PFS, Geraldo—often literally penniless—became homeless. He lived on the streets for about a week and also in a car because he did not have any money, did not want to impose on his adult son (from an earlier marriage), and did not have anyone else he could call on for help. His health deteriorated. He suffered from panic attacks and heart trouble, which frequently took him to one of Los Angeles's public health clinics, where he often waited from three to eight hours to see a physician. Geraldo worried about what would happen to him when the clinics were shut down because of budget cuts. When the clinic near his son's house was closed, he went for a number of days without his hypertension medicine. He became sick and shaky before he was able to get to the county hospital in downtown Los Angeles and obtain a prescription.

Geraldo never finished any of his training in part because of problems within the program and in part because of his own actions or inaction. In the course of his participation, he endured the growing pains of a program that itself was just getting started and often learning about its participants' real needs by failing to meet them. Although he sought to use the opportunities presented to him, most of the time he failed to complete an enterprise. He seemed unable to complete an advanced activity, such as schooling or job training. The many paths abandoned wore heavily on his well-being. Frustrated that his expectations of the program were never met, he eventually moved out of Los Angeles County, with hopes of leaving the state.

Despite disappointments, Geraldo's life changed as a result of his participation in PFS. He left PFS a more independent man than when he entered the program. Through his activities with PFS, he became a leader and advocate for some NCPs, speaking on their behalf and challenging the program to meet its mandate. In many ways, this cost him; he was labeled as difficult, and access to PFS resources was not forthcoming. He helped the program to understand some of the obstacles that participants faced as they navigated through PFS. Nevertheless, he still had difficulty committing himself to, and completing, an endeavor—whether staying by his mother's side in the fields, being a father to three of his children, completing school or job training program, or remaining connected to PFS.

Like many before and after him, Geraldo came to the program in search of opportunities, some more obvious than others. The more recognizable options were related to economics, health, and employment. In these areas, he appeared to go full circle or even backward: at the end of the study, he was again homeless, unemployed, and living from day to day. A more subtle goal for Geraldo and others involved personal decision-making. PFS helped Geraldo to make some serious personal choices. People outside of Geraldo's world might question whether some of his decisions, such as refusing to have anything further to do with PFS, were rational or smart. Yet in quitting PFS, Geraldo freed himself from the program and the mental and physical frustrations he came to associate with it. He accepted the responsibility of moving forward on his own and made peace with that reality. He developed a relationship with his oldest son from a previous marriage and, through this relationship, became closer to his grandchild as well. His decision to pursue work and to deal with his son and his family were choices that, in many ways, PFS would applaud and encourage.

Family-Oriented NCPs

From its conception, PFS had two goals: to help NCPs to become working fathers who pay child support and to help noncustodial parents become *involved* fathers or "daddies." Family-oriented NCPs are participants who created or renewed their ties with their family or child(ren). For young fathers, earning enough to afford a place of their own, rather than living with their own or their partner's parents, could be critical to establishing a new family. With older fathers, who had been separated from their children for a longer period of time, reestablishing paternal ties was more important and in some ways more difficult.

Viceroy   Viceroy, who started his own family during the course of this study, saw steady employment as the key to independence. He felt that he needed to be on his own and that to do so he had to get enough money together to rent an apartment. "I just wanted to have my own [apartment], you know what I'm saying? So I ain't got [to go at] 10:00 at night, leave, you know, because I can't stay, you know, whatever" [March 26, 1996]. An apartment would allow him to establish his autonomy from relatives and future in-laws. He felt that he was on a path to setting up an acceptable home environment for himself, his children, and his fiancée.

During the study, Viceroy also coped successfully with family demands. Under pressure from his own and his fiancée's family to get married, Viceroy did not rebel or run away; nor did he give in, resentfully.

INTERVIEWER: It seems that you are making a decision about when you get married. What's in that decision?

VICEROY: When am I going to get married?

INTERVIEWER: Yeah, why don't you just do it?

VICEROY: Why don't I?

INTERVIEWER: Yeah.

VICEROY: To tell you the truth, I ain't got no money to get married with. I mean, if I had the money, if I could use the $20 for a marriage license, or whatever, I would, but I don't have it like that. Sometimes I do get cold feet, and I'm like, I don't know if I want to get married. Then I'm like, I want to be with you. And my grandma tells me, she said, "If she's good enough to stay with, then she's good enough to marry." Which is true. I believe it is true. So I am going to marry her.

[March 26, 1996]

Eight months later, with his second child on the way, Viceroy and his fiancée were married in a quaint family wedding. Both of the couple's families were present and happy. Viceroy and his new wife tried to put their lives on a course that would be positive for both of them and for the children in his life.

In order to fulfill his dreams and provide for his family in a comfortable manner, Viceroy needed to find steady employment. As a teenager, he ran the streets with his friends but avoided serious trouble. After his first child was born, he worked off and on at a number of full- and part-time jobs that, combined with unemployment insurance, enabled him to make minimum child support payments most months and to qualify for a subsidized apartment. With some help from his father, he paid his rent and maintained his telephone and other utilities, including a cable bill. As the study drew to a close, he was working twenty hours a week through a temporary agency; even with his wife's contribution to the household income, Viceroy was struggling to meet his family's basic needs as well as his financial obligation to his previous child. At this juncture, his primary goal was to keep from falling back into his previous situation.

Viceroy changed in many ways after entering PFS. In addition to becoming more independent, he also became a more responsible and responsive father to his two children. Although he did not give PFS all the credit for his growing kinship with his children, Viceroy offered the program and staff as tangible proof of his progress in parenting. He brought his children, individually and together, to the program office to show them off and thus indirectly used PFS services to improve his relationship with his children.

PFS helped Viceroy to realize the significance of being engaged with his children as well as the importance of negotiating a relationship with his first child's mother and spending time with his son. He began to talk openly about his desire to bring his other child to live with him, his wife, and their child. PFS staff members encouraged his relationship with his son and reminded him to continue paying his child support, no matter how limited his resources. The program helped him to recognize that he could eventually gain by making an effort to meet his child support obligation. By taking major steps (obtaining his own apartment, getting married, being a dad to both his children) and keeping in contact with the program, Viceroy was a model of success, making the transition from father to dad with the help of PFS and others.

Edmond   In finding a job or repaying child support debts, Edmond was not very successful. Yet, through his participation in PFS he found the skills to forge new bonds with his son.

Edmond participated actively in PFS. He came into the program with serious issues concerning anger, fatherhood, and employment. He attended many peer support sessions to work through these difficulties and surpassed the average participant's attendance at fourteen sessions. He was one of the few men who took part in the program's education component to earn a degree beyond high school equivalency. (Pursuing an associate in arts in a computer-related field of architecture despite family problems, he earned a 3.5 grade point average in those courses he was able to complete.)

Edmond's biggest challenge, however, was dealing with his anger toward his child's mother and the distance this created between him and his son. For fifteen years, Edmond had little contact with his son, who had grown accustomed to having other men play the role of father. "I got two other dads to deal with" was how his son saw things; over time, Edmond had come to carry little significance for him.

Through the program's assistance and his own commitment to becoming more involved in his child's life, Edmond tried to reunite with his seventeen-year-old son with the persistence and strength of a pit bull. According to Edmond,

The opportunity to change, turn my life around through education and the motivation to make a real impact in my son's life for the better, it's just made all the difference in my life and I believe in [my son's] life too. We have our hard times, but I think we get along better. We understand each other a little bit more, a lot more, and Parents' Fair Share was if it weren't I don't know what it would have taken to improve our relationship that much if there wasn't a forum and a guiding hand and all of that. And the group, the group sections really helped me focus on my attitude and really showed me how my bad attitudes where I just felt like anything bad I did was water off a duck's back but in fact it sticks like glue. And I didn't want to accept it or believe it, and I didn't want to change my behavior and my attitude. And it helped me realize. And you know I didn't just boom convert. It took several—on each different point and each different principle that they tried to teach me, it took me several weeks to come around.

[Edmond, May 16, 1996]

He applied his insight directly to his relationship with his son, acknowledging that they had spent more time together after he attended Parents' Fair Share than they did in all the time before. Edmond hoped to continue this relationship in its current positive manner. Both father and son knew that the road ahead would be bumpy, but they formed a commitment and a bond to work through their past history, so they could continue to be friends in the future.

Ready to Change

A number of men in this sample entered PFS reluctantly. They did not want to go to jail for nonpayment of child support, but neither did they have much confidence that the program, the mainstream economy, or the system would treat them fairly or allow them to maintain a comfortable lifestyle.

For these men, recognizing that sooner or later they would have to change was, in itself, a success. Peer support facilitators and other staff emphasized responsible fatherhood and the near inevitability that NCPs would eventually have to pay child support. But PFS could not force participants to "go straight."

Big Joe and Mack   Big Joe and Mack, who eventually became good friends, faced many similar challenges as they negotiated their relationships with the child support enforcement world, with the

judicial system, and in their daily lives. Both men supported themselves by selling drugs and were involved in a lifestyle that, although demanding and dangerous, was difficult to give up because
of the money they made. Yet the program helped these two men to
see the need to disentangle the webs they had spun for themselves
(see chapter 2).

A staff person close to the two men made some straightforward
suggestions: they had to start making child support payments to the
court, and they needed to use their talents better if they wanted to
have something to show for their efforts. Big Joe and Mack recognized that they had to figure out a different way to support their
families, meet their formal child support obligations, and maintain
their comfortable lifestyle.

The trust and confidences shared between the staff and these participants led Big Joe and Mack to change the way they did business
and cared for their families. The result, still in its seminal stages, was
the creation of an industrial design business dedicated to refurbish-
ing homes and institutional housing within the African American
community. Big Joe and Mack were making a profit with this
endeavor. Still, with the business still in its infancy, they had not
completely given up their illegal activities.

Their other accomplishment was recognizing their responsibility
to pay formal child support. Accepting this fact, however reluctantly, they began making the minimum weekly payments required.
This was an important change in their child support payment history and one that helped them to avoid confrontations with the
police. Although they did not close the door on their former careers,
they made a tentative first step into the legitimate business world.
Certainly, their actions indicated a desire and willingness to proceed
down a different path than the one they had been traveling before
entering PFS.

Trane   Trane came into Parents' Fair Share in search of opportunity
and eventually realized that he would have to make change happen
for himself rather than wait for the program or others to turn things
around for him. Trane's success is evident on two fronts: his employment status and his sense of worth and ability to care for others.
Trane had been out of steady work since the Los Angeles riots that
followed the Rodney King incident. As explained in chapter 2, he

lost his job after the establishment where he worked as a manager was looted and robbed. Additionally, he had not been in contact with one of his three children for a number of years and was reluctant, despite appeals by his ex-girlfriend, to become responsible for the well-being of this child. The mother wanted the boy to live with Trane and to learn from his father. When he refused, she denied him access to their son.

Trane was more attached to and concerned for his two younger children, who lived with their mother and grandmother. The mother's drug problem caused him much anxiety. When he entered PFS, helping both the grandmother and the two girls as well as finding work were Trane's top priority. Part of his strategy for helping the girls was to find work that would allow him to start paying child support and to meet some of his other financial responsibilities. After going through peer support, Trane aggressively searched for work. He found not only one good job (thirty hours per week with benefits) but also a second job on a graveyard shift. The late-night job paid a good wage and helped him to assist his two younger children with their clothing and school needs and to give their grandmother some money to cover other expenses.

The two jobs gave Trane a feeling of financial independence, which in turn allowed him to consider, with more confidence, seeing his other child. Much to his surprise, Trane's ex-girlfriend welcomed and encouraged his participation in the child's life. They worked out an arrangement, and in the summer of 1996, Trane and his oldest child spent three consecutive weeks together. Thus Trane made some major changes during the two years he spent in PFS. Most important was his determination to become employed and be a connected and involved father to all of his children. There is no way to predict whether Trane's relationships with his children will continue on the same track, or whether he will keep both or either of his current jobs. Should he lose one, the question begs to be answered, will he continue to be an actively engaged parent of his children?

Clearly, the participants described so far varied in their degree of success at surviving, creating or renewing family ties, and taking steps toward major changes in their lifestyle. But success is a slippery notion in this context. If these NCPs had been steadily employed, earning a living wage, and making regular child support payments, they would not have been summoned by the CSE system and presented with the option of participating in PFS. At the same time, participants in this sample and the larger demonstration were moti-vated to change their lives. As discussed in chapter 1, these NCPs were a self-selected sample in that, for one reason or another, they actively participated in the PFS intervention. Most participated in a host of activities. Striving to meet the standards set by their program sites, as well as their own objectives, was in itself an accomplishment.

Outsiders

In some cases, however, the NCPs and the program did not connect. The outsiders were men who entered the program with the hope of finding a solution or an opportunity but left feeling disappointed and alienated. Many noncustodial parents fit into this typology at one time or another. Outsiders were neither ready nor willing to give the program a chance or attempted to participate but did not feel part of the process.

Outsiders were young men like Arron, Hollywood, Sly, and Bob who had the desire to "make it on their own." They came to the pro-gram with an understanding that they would receive help with eco-nomic and personal issues, with finding work, and with staying out of jail. Their hopes were never fully realized, and they were, or felt they were, excluded. There are two primary reasons why these men were not fully involved in the program. The first is that in their appearance and mannerisms, these men challenged the sensibilities and prejudices of the staff. As a result, some case managers, peer support facilitators, job-related staff, and administrators found it difficult to relate to and communicate with them. The second reason is that these men brought to the program reputations and attitudes that some staff felt were offensive, damaging, and dangerous to society. Whether the staff failed to give these participants a chance or these participants were detached and disinterested from the start, their interactions with the program were never fully grounded.

Arron   Arron confronted these problems during his tenure at PFS. Arron had had personal struggles since he was a young boy. When he was nine, one of his brothers was shot and killed. By eleven, according to his mother, he had a serious problem with ulcers; he was also a member of his brothers' gang. He eventually saw another brother shot and paralyzed. Arron also faced emotional stress. His mother reported that he was struggling in his relationship with his father, who wanted him to take one route toward getting straight while Arron had another vision of how he could become legitimate. They clashed regularly, and both were headstrong and unrelenting. Finally, Arron had serious problems with relationships. He had spent time in jail for domestic violence. On his release, he was instructed to participate in PFS and a domestic violence program. However, the domestic violence program was located in a rival gang's territory, and he could not go into that area without fear. He tried to convey this information to the program staff, but they did not understand the severity of his situation.

Arron's outsider status never changed despite his personal quest to change his life and get straight before he dies. (Aaron expected to be dead before he turned thirty: "You know what I mean? I'm look, I'm lookin' at, lookin' at the statistics and, the reality of things. I don't have no . . . no people in my neighborhood that's over thirty right now. And the ones that were twenty-eight, twenty-nine died, see?" [September 25, 1995])

Many of the staff and participants were apprehensive about approaching Arron or engaging him in conversation. Often he would sit in the peer support sessions and listen intently, but when he tried to add something, he was dismissed or his point was passed over. Yet, he stayed and took in information. One day, as he was driving around talking with the researcher, he produced some papers that had been presented that day. Others had left them on their chairs or had thrown them away after the session, but he kept his. When asked why he had kept them, he said that he was going to share them with his girlfriend. He thought that they would be helpful to their relationship. This shows how seriously he was taking both the peer support information and the messages from the peer support facilitator. Yet he was not getting interpersonal feedback from the program because there was no interaction between him and the staff.

As time passed, the distance grew, and eventually Arron stopped attending the program. He started to pursue work and music endeavors on his own. Unfortunately, Arron and the program became adversaries. The program reported him back to the CSE agency, and Arron ignored them. His position as an outsider was solidified.

I'm gambling, you know what I'm saying? My, my dice is like—I mean, my life is like rollin' dice, you know what I'm sayin'? Yeah, I take my chances, 'cause that's all I got, is a chance, a little chance I do have. The chance that I make for myself, you know? Not the chance that nobody gonna give me, 'cause ain't nobody gonna give me one. If you [find someone] givin' you a chance, they halfway your ass. And I don't like a halfway ass person. You know?

[Arron, September 25, 1995]

The others who distanced or removed themselves from the core of the program did so for reasons similar to Arron's: they did not feel a part of the process, or they did not feel that the process was working for them. They decided to stay outside and fend for themselves.

Hollywood and Sly   Hollywood and Sly made repeated efforts to use the program resources, but problems in other areas of their lives interfered. They were well aware that the program offered services and opportunities that they needed and wanted. Yet they were unable, for a host of reasons, to immerse themselves in the program. They could not set aside their other needs long enough to pursue the goals and objectives of the PFS program. This frustrated staff and at times frustrated Hollywood, Sly, and others. The staff's frustration sometimes manifested itself as indifference toward the participant. When the relationship between staff and the participant disintegrated, the participant usually felt that it was in his best interest to leave the program and disappear back into the community. Once again, he found himself on the outside of the public social support network.

Conclusions

These are just a few of the typologies that noncustodial parents can fall into as they move in and out of programs like PFS. Others could label and categorize these men differently. The men presented in this chapter illustrate a range of personal, social, and economic gains made by the NCPs in this sample overall and exemplify the levels of accomplishment that a program like PFS can attain. In most cases, these NCPs did try, and for the most part, they did more than try— they worked at the opportunities they were offered. Not all of their efforts were rewarded, yet few people who attempt new endeavors achieve the precise outcomes they anticipate or desire. Failures occurred when the program was unable to engage a participant in a way relevant to him. There would have been more outsiders if the participants in this study, and the staff from the seven program sites, had not been able to engage each other at different levels of inter-action (within the program itself, in the community, as friends). Neither party completely fulfilled the expectations of the other; however, people were moved from one point to another, and the program was moved from its infancy to becoming a functioning part of a community that was willing and able to serve noncustodial parents. In that movement, there was success.

These categories can also serve as guidelines for those interested in helping low-income noncustodial parents improve their own lives and hence their children's prospects. This inside view of PFS brings to life a complex and difficult process that takes a great deal of effort and commitment on the part of both the program and the participant. Change will not occur until both parties are committed to working toward positive change. The rest of this chapter outlines some pro-grammatic and policy recommendations that may help to move the futures of low-income noncustodial parents in a positive direction.

RECOMMENDATIONS

Throughout this book, the men have explained how poverty and the lack of, or limited access to, economic resources have shaped their lives, precluding choices that other Americans take for granted. One could argue that men who do not seize the opportunities available to them have only themselves to blame. But their experiences before and during participation in PFS illustrate the complex interplay of social and personal factors in their daily lives.

When they came into the program, the majority of these men were living from hustle to hustle. With hope and skepticism, they looked to PFS for help in getting prepared for, and connected to, regular employment. PFS attempted to meet these expectations on two lev-els. Overtly, PFS set up program models (discussed in chapters 5 and 6) designed to assist unemployed noncustodial parents to develop the skills they need to enter or reenter the world of legal work, including communication skills. More subtly, peer support helped these men to recognize and deal with personal, emotional, and atti-tudinal issues that might be barriers to work, involvement with their children, and relationships with employers, partners, and friends.

The stories of some individual NCPs are described in the first part of this chapter. In each case, their relationship to the program was tenuous, and maintaining or building on the relationship depended on finding regular employment. The PFS intervention, as designed, was not always able to meet its own or the participants' expectations of economic opportunity. These unmet expectations gave rise to the following policy recommendations.

Recommendations Concerning Program

Over the course of this research, many participants did find *some* work, and only a small number never worked at all. But the jobs they found did not translate into steady employment or greater stability in their lives. A frequent pattern was for participants to find a job before leaving the program (or to find one job, lose it, then find another), only to lose that job, fall further behind in their child support payments, and accumulate new problems and debts. Graduates could return to the program and use its resources to get work, yet this message was not always conveyed clearly to participants. After a brief tenure in the program, participants found themselves on their own, returning to the same battles they fought before entering PFS. This was a relief for some and a burden for others. Those who were relieved saw themselves as reclaiming their independence from the program, the child support system, and any other system that they felt was a nuisance in their lives. Others regretted that they no longer had an ally to help fight the system. They felt that once they had completed the program's components they were set adrift to "sink or swim," whether or not they had found a job, and this feeling was a source of frustration, anger, and disillusionment for the NCPs interviewed. Correctly or incorrectly, they believed that the fact they had been given a chance and failed would be held against them.

Therefore, *ongoing* communication should be improved between the participant and staff. Ideally, each NCP should have one staff member who is familiar with his personal situation and who maintains contact, at either the participant's or the staff member's initiative.[2] This contact should begin when a participant enters the program and continue until he has held a steady job for one year. The goal of PFS is not simply to help participants get a job, but to help them *keep* a job and meet their child support obligations after they have completed the program curriculum. Having a trusted staff member to help them work through employment or personal problems during this transitional period may help participants to stay employed, pay child support, and make the right choices in difficult times.

Second, programs should be set up with enough labor market connections and funding to provide long-term services. Programs should work closely with foundations and state agencies to secure long-term funding for the program's operation. To this end, they should devise ways to solidify their position in the community and in the minds of current and potential users. Low-income individuals have ongoing needs. Given the changes in welfare legislation and the decimation of public assistance services for single persons living at or near poverty levels, consistent and dependable social support is needed.

Program staff and administrators play an important role in making an intervention like PFS meaningful and significant to noncustodial parents. Yet program staff and administrators must realize that their reality at the moment of initial contact is different from that of the noncustodial parents they are about to serve. Staff and administrators should work hard to understand the life experiences and activities of these participants before rushing them into a designated activity. In order to bridge the gap in experience, administrators should engage participants in candid but respectful conversation. Through these conversations, where active and serious listening occurs, the staff and the participant will learn more about one another and develop trust. Trust then will become the linchpin that allows these two parties to work honestly with each other. Without trust and honesty, a staff person may never learn that the client has had a lifelong history of drug use that ebbs and flows with his erratic housing situation. Or that a client has had such traumatic experiences working with people from different ethnic backgrounds that he literally is unable to have conversations with them.

Similarly, program staff must understand that even after a conversation has taken place and suggestions, recommendations, and referrals have been presented, the participant may not act on those suggestions right away or at all. The challenge to the program is to leave the door open to these participants. Leaving the door open gives a recalcitrant the opportunity, at a later date, to act on the suggestions and begin a new path. Participants need to know that they are welcome to return to the program at any time, without judgment, and that the program is there to help them make beneficial decisions.

Third, programs should be flexible and consistent in both their message and their service provision strategy. Standardizing the process by which services and messages are delivered or trying to replicate more established programs may not be the best strategy. Rather a program's first priority should be to meet the needs of the participants who come in and out of it. What individual clients or participants need at different stages during the intervention will vary greatly. If a program is wedded to a particular process, strategy, or timetable for providing services, the potential for attrition or failure to participate increases. Individuals may not want what the program claims to offer. Programs must integrate group processes with specialized individual services.

Fourth, job developers and job-related staff need to conduct regular follow-up on participants who have been placed in or referred to a job. Regular check-ins and conferences with a participant can serve as an opportunity for a participant to tell the staff about his job and how he feels he is faring. The staff person can also use these meetings to determine whether the job is providing the worker with the resources that he needs to pay his child support obligation, cover his rent, and afford food. If there is a problem, these meetings allow the two to develop a strategy to improve his situation. Many times these men will endure a job for a time but then quit because it is not worthwhile to them financially, emotionally, or strategically. At these moments, unemployment seems more appealing than work. Job-related staff must try to prevent voluntary joblessness by articulating succinctly the pros and cons of quitting a job without having another one lined up. Regular, honest, and candid discussions may keep participants connected to work. Otherwise, they may continually drop in and out of the labor market, reducing their opportunities for longer-term employment.

A program like PFS depends on other agencies to meet participants' needs and to deliver on its promises. Participants in this study reported that in many instances PFS seemed unable to help them get the services they wanted or needed, that delays prevented them from pursuing opportunities (for example, tuition funds were released weeks after a training program had begun), and that PFS did not stand behind them in their dealings with other agencies. Some participants left the program because they thought they could manage as well or better on their own. Therefore, PFS staff should establish stronger working relationships with other agencies that have (or will have) contact with participants and engage active partnerships with other agencies. For example, in Los Angeles, general assistance recipients are required to work for the county. In partnership with PFS, the county could allow recipients to meet their work requirement through participation in PFS. Combining the two would increase the incentive to participate in the program (by tying participation to benefits), link the program with the larger social service community, and enhance the legitimacy of the program in the eyes of participants and their communities. This partnership would ultimately benefit all parties interested in investing in noncustodial parents for the betterment of the community and the family.

Along the same lines, PFS needs the wherewithal to lobby for its participants beyond the confines of the program. Acting as the participants' advocate is not part of PFS's current mandate, but the issue inevitably arises. PFS needs to be able to support participants who have worked hard in the program when they need a respected ally. For instance, if an NCP who has completed the peer support curriculum runs into difficulties with the CSE or another agency, PFS should be able to stand behind him, telling the questioning authority what the individual has achieved or might achieve as a result of participating in this program. Further, program administrators should seek to have the peer support curriculum certified as one of a number of options on which courts could draw in cases of custody and visitation disputes, child neglect, domestic violence, and other family matters. In dealing with the courts or public welfare system, NCPs would get credit and acknowledgment for their participation in PFS.

Finally, programs should try to work with county welfare and social service agencies to see how they can coordinate their activities with those offered to women in these public institutions. The coordination and integration of program services would promote cooperation and respect among women and men, as opposed to competition for slots and opportunity. The coordination of activities among the agencies and programs that serve both men and women would also help people to understand the need to facilitate open and constructive conversations between men and women. These programs should create a mandate—especially if they are dealing with issues of parenting and personal or societal responsibility—that any disagreement between parents should be limited to the parents and that the child should not be used as a foil by any party involved, including the agency. Programs, agencies, and service providers should reevaluate how they treat parents or biological mothers and fathers to see if their own structure has an inherent bias against one type of parent. Challenging the agency's structure for dealing with prejudice (based on gender, race, or age) would improve interventions and produce better child outcomes in the future.

Having service providers look honestly at themselves and the messages they promote, as they ask their participants to do, would help them to be more helpful in securing a better and more civil world for the mothers, fathers, and children who need their support and understanding.

Recommendations Concerning Employment

Another set of recommendations derives from examining the economic situations of participants when they come into the program; all the members of this sample were unemployed. The majority were surviving on irregular, unpredictable, odd jobs on, or more often off, the books and both legal or illegal. Often they had little or no money, and just getting to the program each day was a financial strain. Participation often forced them to give up an opportunity to earn a little income on a given day. This meant that participants had to weigh the usefulness and expectations they had for the program and for themselves against the economic cost of spending part or all of their day in it and having nothing tangible to show at day's end. The longer a participant stayed in PFS, the tighter his resources became. Parents, relatives, partners, or friends would sometimes pressure participants to leave the program because they were not making any money. To justify his participation in the program, Arron told his girlfriend that he was guaranteed a job; other participants used similar ruses to keep people off their backs as well as to keep their own hopes and expectations for the program alive. Arron, like many in this book, eventually left the program, in part because after four to six weeks, the cost of participation was more than he could afford.

Two recommendations arise from the cost of participation for low-income NCPs. The first is that PFS should create better work opportunities for these men—either part- or full-time (with program activities scheduled during evenings)—*while* they are participating in the program. A more costly and politically controversial option would be to provide short-term, paid community service jobs for participants who are unable to find unsubsidized employment. The second recommendation is to provide participants with a small stipend to cover or reduce the cost of attending the program. Reducing the cost of participation would help these men to stay connected to the program and to the goal of finding full-time work. Work experience and a stipend would be especially helpful to men trying to make the transition from illegal to legal work. Some men would have seen a stipend as an unprecedented signal of worth.

The experiences of the men in this study also suggest the importance of addressing their income needs once they find a job. Many of the men found relatively low-paying jobs that barely enabled them to meet their own daily needs and cover their child support obligations. A possible response would be to find ways to make noncustodial parents who work and meet their *current* child support obligations during a year eligible for the unclaimed portion of the full earned income tax credit, now available only to custodial parents who are working. Access to a higher level of tax credit would increase the financial payoff to work, helping them economically and providing a greater incentive to stay working even in low-wage jobs. Moreover, the interception of tax refunds for noncustodial parents who are currently paying but remain behind in their child support obligations should be reconsidered because doing so undercuts the income benefits of the earned income tax credit and weakens the incentives to stay with a job.

Recommendations Concerning Child Support Enforcement and Noncustodial Parents

The child support enforcement component of the PFS program also needs to be examined. As discussed in chapter 1, the history of child support enforcement reveals a long struggle with the special problems posed by low-income noncustodial parents. In today's political climate, the emphasis is on exacting strict compliance, based on standardized rules and regulations concerning child support enforcement. This position—or at least the current vision of the rules—does not serve either the low-income NCP or the CSE system.

From the perspective of the men in this study, the lack of flexibility in CSE enforcement has created a bifurcated system of justice for dealing with the rich and the poor. In their eyes, CSE is not interested in their financial situation or their children's well-being, but only in whether or not they make formal child support payments, which are used to offset the cost of public assistance. A system that has this look and feel is not one these men would feel comfortable using, should their situations change for the better.

The child support system should be more responsive to the non-custodial parent's economic position and the noncustodial parent as a person. The CSE system should take into account at least the minimal needs of the noncustodial parent and act in a way that does not unduly jeopardize his well-being or serve as a disincentive to seeking legitimate work and paying formal child support. For example, rules could be changed to make it more likely that judges will modify a child support order when an NCP has proof of unemployment or economic hardship. Child support guidelines could also be adjusted to allow very low-income NCPs to have a larger subsistence set-aside to prevent them from becoming unable to meet basic economic needs once a fixed percentage of their income is allocated to child support. In the case of ill health or incarceration, an NCP's debt to the state should not be held at the same level as it would if he were outside the walls of a hospital or jail, the rules for lowering an obligation should allow for the possibility of making retroactive adjustments in such circumstances. Small adjustments to the rules concerning child support arrearages owed to the state would make a big difference to men like those in this research. Such minor adjustments might improve the low-income NCP's perception of the CSE process and help to connect low-income men to their children financially.

Based on the data gathered, three final policy recommendations look to a future of improved implementation of child support enforcement. These are offered with the understanding that discovering methods for their effective application remains open for thoughtful, creative exploration:

- Child support itself, as collected and administered by the CSE agency, has to make sense to low-income noncustodial parents. For this to happen, programs like PFS and CSE agencies need to reconsider the implications of the often extreme states of poverty in which many of these men live.

- Making child support payments and complying with CSE should no longer be perceived as an adversarial matter, where noncustodial and custodial parents are kept divided from one another.

- In an effort to reach and unite families, CSE agencies themselves need to be based more positively in the community, developing into "community satellites" that ally staff with participants and offer information and assistance in all realms of child support, including visitation.

These recommendations are intended to improve the welfare of many poor children and their noncustodial parents. When we ignore the voices of these men and the insights that they have shared, we miss an opportunity to understand more about the origins and consequences of poverty, to learn which aspects of CSE programs are most effective and why, and to see how to make the best use of available resources given limited political and public support for assistance to the poor. In the end, we must ask ourselves if we believe that helping these men and others like them will ultimately improve the lives of the poor. The children who grow up in the state of economic deprivation for which we hold these men mostly accountable are the future fathers and mothers of the next generation of the poor. If we ignore these men's voices, we may be destined to hear the same stories, and worse, repeated again and again in the future. Instead, we can choose to improve our understanding and to reverse or repair policies that tend to distance poor noncustodial parents from poor custodial households and the children who live in them.

APPENDIX A

Sample, Data, and
Research Methodology

The qualitative research findings presented in this book came from a sample of thirty-two noncustodial parents randomly assigned to participate in the Parents' Fair Share program after April 1994. All those interviewed had at least three contacts with program services after their random assignment. This population provided a chance to learn more about why individuals would choose to use an intervention such as Parents' Fair Share and to understand what aspects of the intervention would induce participants to change their behavior.

This information was collected by Earl Johnson during a two-year period in seven cities. I met these noncustodial parents either at their initial intake or early during their participation in a PFS program activity. I sat in on and participated in their activities. In this setting, I made contacts and also learned how various components of the intervention worked. I initiated the contacts, or, after learning what I was doing in the group, individuals volunteered to meet with me. Not all volunteers became part of the core cohort of noncustodial parents presented in this book, but observations and conversations were noted and provided background information.

Sometimes individuals in the core cohort dropped out voluntarily. Disenchanted with the program and anything affiliated with the program, some wanted nothing to do with the research. Others did not think that cooperating with me was worth their time and effort and, after a few encounters, stopped participating.

Those who participated in this research did so on their own volition. They shared information and personal contacts with me and introduced me to their children, mothers, girlfriends, friends, and acquaintances, who shared their thoughts and opinions on issues of child support, politics, race, employment, and a host of other issues and topics. I had conversations with all types of noncustodial men. Access to white men was limited because so few were in the project.

All of the Latino participants were from Los Angeles and were bilingual. Our conversations were held in English, but participants would switch to Spanish when a friend or acquaintance addressed them in Spanish.

I gained access to these men, I believe, because of my ability to appear nonthreatening and to adjust to the environments that they shared with me. Some situations tested my sensibilities, perceptions, and expectations of what it meant to be a father, a participant in a national demonstration, and in near-constant search of work. There was little doubt about my role as researcher, but at times I became a friend, a role that was frequently guarded. The distinction between friend and researcher was made clear when various participants asked me to lend them money. Extreme economic distress and limited access to cash posed problems, especially during holidays, birthdays, anniversaries, and when rent and other bills became due, usually around the first of the month. My policy was not to lend money to participants, on the grounds that I did not have sufficient funds to lend and was uncomfortable putting people in a position where they would feel obligated to me as a result. In the course of employing this policy, a couple of men drifted from the study. Although they never discussed my failure to provide them with a loan, our contacts became fewer and sometimes ended abruptly after I denied their request.

In the course of this research, I was introduced to many men who were noncustodial parents. Most of these men were in the Parents' Fair Share program; those who were not were usually a friend or acquaintance of someone participating in PFS. The information gathered from those not involved in the Parents' Fair Share program was used to validate or challenge the stories, observations, and perceptions of the primary research subjects.

By spending time with participants in their own world, I began to understand how Parents' Fair Share fit into their lives. It also became clear that the program was unable to make all the changes in people's lives that it had originally intended, largely because program sites were not sufficiently involved in the day-to-day lives of participants. A few exceptional staff members went outside the physical confines of PFS to meet with participants and see what it would take to get them to participate in the program. Sometimes reaching out into the community and giving special attention to participants were questioned as a useful expenditure of time and energy. Other times these efforts were rewarded, but most outreach efforts were viewed with skepticism and animosity. It was not unusual for case managers, facilitators, or even lower-level administrators to be reproached for being too lenient, overly friendly, or too involved in the lives of the men with whom they worked. The irony of this finding is that participants attended peer support sessions because they viewed the facilitators as "real" individuals who understood and empathized with their situation.

Various techniques were used to collect data, including situational or activity-driven observations as well as participant-focused or socially interactive observations. Situational or activity-driven observations focus on the place and activity in which the research is based and seek to capture the tenor and feel of the event or activity. Participant-focused or socially interactive observations center on how the key informant or focus person interacts within a social or environmental context. Each of these types of observations delivers a different perspective on the research. Using these techniques, I had many opportunities to observe the lives of the men in this book. I would sit with participants in a peer support session or a job club activity and watch how they interacted with the group or facilitator. From these observations, questions arose that would fuel discussions with participants about their views of the utility of the activities in their everyday lives.

Some participants were more guarded than others, but most shared the parts of their lives that they wanted to share. Sometimes I got to see the seven apartments in which they had lived since childhood or the communities where they were not allowed to go because they were wanted by a rival gang. They showed me their names on walls, crossed out as a sign that they would soon be dead. They introduced me to the mother of their new baby. On various occasions, I had to share parts of myself in order to maintain the trust of key informants who served as informal "gate keepers" to their sons, boyfriends, fathers, or friends. Once I sang "Happy Birthday," however badly, over the telephone, a small price to pay—and probably more painful for those listening than for me—to maintain a relationship with a participant.

In other conversations, we talked about race, child support, anger, violence, love, and spirituality. If the participant did not want to discuss something, I would usually drop the subject, perhaps to broach it again later, at a more opportune time.

To gain the trust of and sustain contact with these men, much interaction took place in person, face to face. Yet, logistically, a substantial amount of contact had to be achieved through the telephone. I used phone calls to check on the men's status: whether they had been arrested, were working, were taking care of their own or someone else's children, and so forth. The telephone was an essential tool for accessing and measuring the availability of participants in the research; it helped me to understand issues of mobility and limited resources from their perspective. Many conversations were cut short or had to be rescheduled because someone else wanted to use the phone or decided that the participant had been on long enough. In order to maintain these participants' telephone privileges, we would try to set up another time to speak, or instead to meet, and get off the line as quickly as possible.

During the course of this research, twenty-four of the core thirty-two participants either lost access to a telephone, moved and changed telephone numbers, or had their phones disconnected. Some of the disconnected telephones were reconnected after two or three months, during which time I had little way of knowing whether a participant had obtained a new number under a different name or perhaps had moved. During these periods, I left messages with key informants (people to whom the participants themselves had introduced me), asking that the men contact me. These efforts helped me to maintain my relationships with these participants.

THE SAMPLE

This group of noncustodial parents of poor children was not a random sample of all such parents, and it is important to understand the steps that occurred prior to their selection for this research. Figure 1.1 presents the steps in the child support enforcement process that occurred prior to the point at which the sample was drawn (Doolittle and Lynn 1998 discuss in detail the steps in enforcement prior to referral to PFS).

The starting point was the pool of NCPs of children receiving AFDC in each PFS site who were not paying or were underpaying their child support. Paternity had been established, and a child support order was in place; many had substantial support arrearages. Typically, child support administrators found evidence of employment for some in this group (by matching automated records, following tips from individuals, and so forth), but for most, there was no evidence that they were working. For those with evidence of employment, CSE staff put an income deduction order in place.

When there was no evidence of employment, CSE staff sought to bring the NCP into court or the appropriate administrative agency for a hearing or review. The first step was locating and serving the NCP with legal notice; depending on the PFS site, up to half of the NCPs could be lost when child support staff were unable to achieve legal notice of the hearing. In some sites, personal service (that is, evidence that the NCP personally received the notice) was required for a hearing on nonpayment, while in others, mailed notice with return receipt could be used. In the latter group of sites, if the NCP failed to appear for the initial hearing, personal service was typically required for the next enforcement step. Experience in the early stages of the demonstration showed that the addresses for NCPs in official records were often outdated or the NCP was difficult to serve because he moved frequently or relatives and friends refused to provide information regarding his whereabouts. Not all those actually served for a hearing appeared or contacted CSE staff again with considerable variation in the appearance and contact rate among sites.

A substantial proportion of those who appeared or contacted the child support agency provided information on previously unreported employment, and staff put in place an income deduction order. A smaller percentage provided evidence that they were disabled, reunited with the other parent, or otherwise ineligible for PFS. For still others, however, there was no evidence of employment, and the individual was unable to produce a cash payment to reduce or eliminate his accumulated support arrearages. These NCPs were eligible for PFS and went through a lottery to be randomly assigned to a program group (almost all of whom were ordered by the court to participate in the PFS program) or to a control group subject to normal enforcement practices. Within the program group, some NCPs chose not to participate in program services (possibly because they had an unreported job and could not attend program services), but about two-thirds participated in some PFS activities. The sample for this book was drawn from these program participants.

The enforcement steps taken prior to selection of the sample meant that this group was likely to be more disadvantaged (and probably more interested in the program) than the average NCP seen at an earlier point in the process. Some NCPs who were working in jobs previously unknown to the child support enforcement system were identified earlier in the intake process (see Doolittle and Lynn 1998). Others continued to avoid the enforcement process, sometimes going further outside the mainstream economy. Thus, although it is interesting to compare the findings reported in this book with other writings on NCPs, it is important to keep in mind the purpose of this work and the specific way in which the sample was drawn.

In developing the sample, the interviewer contacted NCPs coming through the intake process during periodic site visits. Some of these initial contacts were made at either the various courts that handle PFS cases or at the PFS program sites. The second contact typically was made at the service center after the participant was admitted to the program. Other participants were referred to this study by past participants or staff members from the PFS program. As discussed in chapter 2, this qualitative research sample and the overall PFS sample had similar demographic characteristics, family history, and work experience (see table 2.1). Active interviewing and network sampling as well as theoretically grounded sampling were used to allow the research to develop, expand, and explore the themes being continuously uncovered (Holstein and Gubrium 1995; Johnson 1990; Glaser and Strauss 1967). To ensure that close attention was paid to issues of bias and validity of responses, methods offered by Miles and Huberman (1984), Holstein and Gubrium (1995), and Lofland and Lofland (1984) were employed. One of the methods used to enhance confidence in the data collected was careful expansion of the informant pool, using contrasting cases.

The characteristics of the thirty-two NCPs in the sample are summarized in table 2.1. Their median age was thirty-two. Almost two-thirds of the sample was African American, 24 percent were white, and the remainder were Latino. Nearly 90 percent had worked in a full-time job. Most reported being unemployed (that is, jobless but looking for work) for at least eight months within the past year. Although they said that they were unemployed, many had been doing odd jobs or some type of "hustle" on the side. A majority (81 percent) had not worked steadily or at all over the past two years. Their level of education ranged from completing eighth grade to some college, meaning that they went to a community college to get their GED or possibly an associate in arts degree. The average number of children was two. Many claimed to have at least some contact with their children, meaning that they had seen at least one of their children once during the previous month. A large portion of these men had been incarcerated.

Many of these NCPs had tenuous living arrangements. More than 40 percent were living with a relative (grandmother, mother, son, sister); 34 percent were living alone. About half of those who lived alone were homeless or sleeping on a couch or in a car. The other half lived in their own apartment or house in a relatively stable way, while others "bounced around" between living on their own and living with friends or a girlfriend and were currently living alone. Another 22 percent were living with their girlfriend, ex-spouse, or spouse.

DATA AND RESEARCH METHODS

Every participant in the qualitative research sample was interviewed at least twice. Most of the conversations and interviews were tape-recorded and transcribed verbatim. Formal interviews lasted nearly ninety minutes, and informal interviews and conversations lasted between five minutes and three hours. Participants were asked questions such as "Why did you go to court? What was your past relationship with your ex like? What is your relationship with your children right now?" The formal interview employed an open-ended approach that allowed the participant to relax, but the questions were prepared in advance (see appendix H for questions). Many times during less formal interactions with participants, formal questions were asked as a form of cross-reference and validation. Also, a number of questions were asked whenever a conversation or interview occurred, such as "Have you seen or spoken with your children lately? When? What have you been doing since we last spoke? Have you worked since we last spoke? How are you doing?" These questions related to interactions with the NCP's children, the custodial parent, and the NCP's current status in the program. Most of the data came from the conversations and program activities with the NCP, but the use of field notes from past observations and conversations with participants also supplied data on whether the intervention of PFS had any lasting effect on the program participants as well as on whether and how stories had changed since the previous interaction.

Conducting the conversations in a semistructured manner that gave the participants some control over the pace and depth of the conversation was an effective mechanism for maintaining contact with these men over a period of time. Their sense that they had ownership of the research helped me to follow them over time by making them more willing to open up and share their lives.

In addition, I offered the men disposable cameras to take pictures of their worlds (their families, girlfriends, jobs, buildings). Twelve NCPs had cameras and were taking photographs. Once the photographs were taken, I developed them, sent the NCPs copies, and later discussed them. The photographs were intended to get participants to think about their lives and community and to capture elements of interest or significance to them. The photos suggested future questions into the lives of these men.

To complement the qualitative data, baseline information on general characteristics of the PFS population was collected at random assignment from each person in the sample (see table 2.1). Also PFS program participation data were completed monthly by each program site for each person randomly assigned to the program group. These data, along with the interview and conversational data, helped in understanding the degree to which the program's socialization process was taking shape. The assumption was that the more contact the NCP had with the program, the more he could take from it.

The qualitative research passed through several phases, providing somewhat different insights. The project began with early focus groups with NCPs. These focus groups informed the program design of PFS and were integral in carrying out the current phase of more in-depth qualitative research. At the start of this project, there was a great deal of doubt that men—especially low- or no-income minority men—would participate on a regular basis in groups discussing issues about fatherhood, parenting, relationships, and societal views. Much of this doubt was based on preconceived notions (little of it based on research) of who these parents were. In an attempt to reduce the uncertainty about this group of men and lessen the dependence on stereotypes, focus groups were used to uncover the issues that these men identified as affecting their lives and to explore the feasibility of having low-income, minority men discuss issues concerning parenting and fatherhood. The use of focus groups is a standard method of capturing data or responses and is often useful in developing theoretically based, qualitative research (Kirk and

Miller 1986; Miles and Huberman 1984; Glaser and Strauss 1967; Johnson 1990; Daly 1995). These focus groups led to chapters published in Furstenburg, Sherwood, and Sullivan (1992).

These early focus groups led to some false starts in developing questions and an observational focus for later qualitative research. This was because more NCPs in the early groups were employed and earning income (albeit often unreported) than in later groups. Perhaps because of our focus on the child support system and unreported income, we initially underestimated the social and economic vulnerability of the noncustodial parent participating in PFS. Similarly, we misunderstood or overlooked the survival techniques that these individuals employed. Further, because some of the men in the early groups had not even had paternity established, they tended to have less of a relationship and interaction with their children than was the case for the sample reported in this book. In summary, the differences between participants in the earlier focus groups and those in the current sample highlighted the importance of understanding the point at which individuals are identified in the child support enforcement process.

APPENDIX B

Maps

Figure B.1 Location of PFS Participants by Poverty Status for Duval County, Florida (1990)

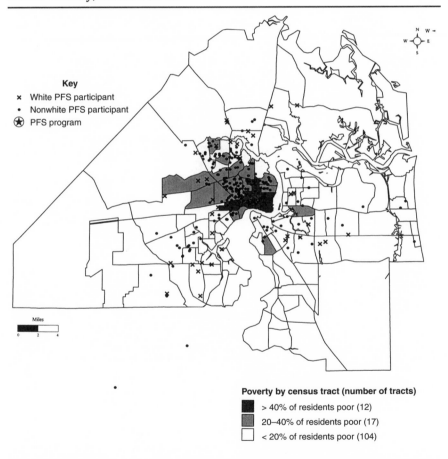

Key
- × White PFS participant
- • Nonwhite PFS participant
- ⊛ PFS program

Poverty by census tract (number of tracts)
- ■ > 40% of residents poor (12)
- ▨ 20–40% of residents poor (17)
- □ < 20% of residents poor (104)

Miles
0   2   4

Source: Manpower Demonstration Research Corporation analysis of 1990 census data and Parents' Fair Share administrative records.
Notes: Participants include NCPs randomly assigned prior to July 1995.

185

Figure B.2 Location of PFS Participants by Poverty Status for Hamden County, Massachusetts (1990)

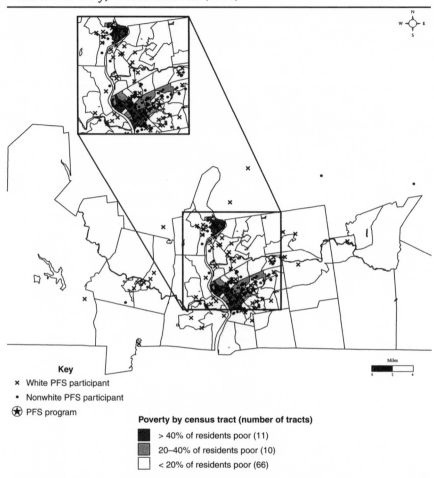

Key
- × White PFS participant
- • Nonwhite PFS participant
- ⊛ PFS program

Poverty by census tract (number of tracts)
- ■ > 40% of residents poor (11)
- ▨ 20–40% of residents poor (10)
- □ < 20% of residents poor (66)

Source: Manpower Demonstration Research Corporation analysis of 1990 census data and Parents' Fair Share administrative records.
Notes: Participants include NCPs randomly assigned prior to July 1995.

Figure B.3 Location of PFS Participants by Poverty Status for Kent County, Michigan (1990)

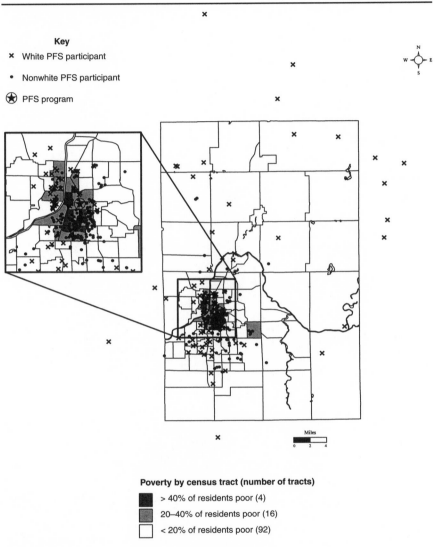

Key

× White PFS participant

• Nonwhite PFS participant

✪ PFS program

Poverty by census tract (number of tracts)

■ > 40% of residents poor (4)

▨ 20–40% of residents poor (16)

□ < 20% of residents poor (92)

Source: Manpower Demonstration Research Corporation analysis of 1990 census data and Parents' Fair Share administrative records.
Notes: Participants include NCPs randomly assigned prior to July 1995.

Figure B.4 Location of PFS Participants by Poverty Status for Los Angeles County, California (1990)

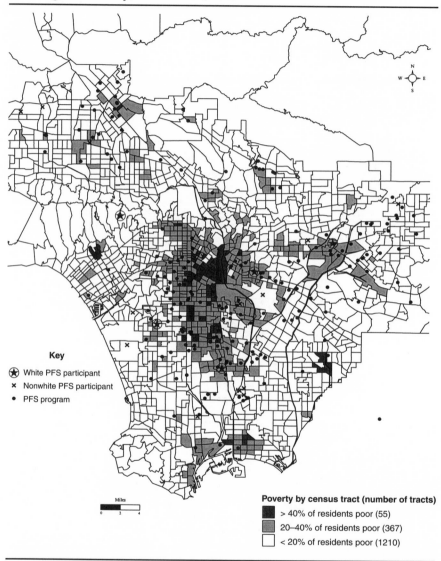

Key

⊛ White PFS participant
✕ Nonwhite PFS participant
• PFS program

Poverty by census tract (number of tracts)

■ > 40% of residents poor (55)
▨ 20–40% of residents poor (367)
☐ < 20% of residents poor (1210)

Miles
0   2   4

Source: Manpower Demonstration Research Corporation analysis of 1990 census data and Parents' Fair Share administrative records.
Notes: Participants include NCPs randomly assigned prior to July 1995.

Figure B.5 Location of PFS Participants by Poverty Status for Mercer County, New Jersey (1990)

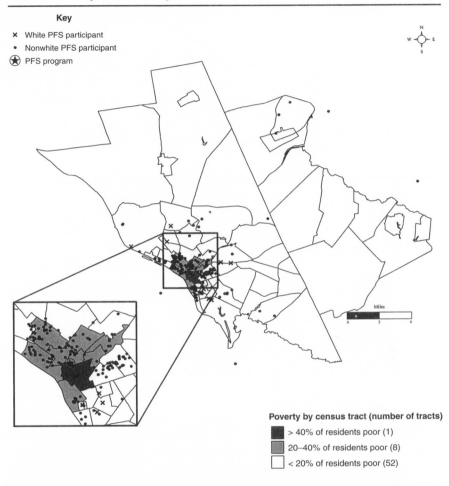

Key

× White PFS participant

• Nonwhite PFS participant

(★) PFS program

Poverty by census tract (number of tracts)

⬛ > 40% of residents poor (1)

▨ 20–40% of residents poor (8)

⬜ < 20% of residents poor (52)

Source: Manpower Demonstration Research Corporation analysis of 1990 census data and Parents' Fair Share administrative records.
Notes: Participants include NCPs randomly assigned prior to July 1995.

Figure B.6 Location of PFS Participants by Poverty Status for Montgomery County, Ohio (1990)

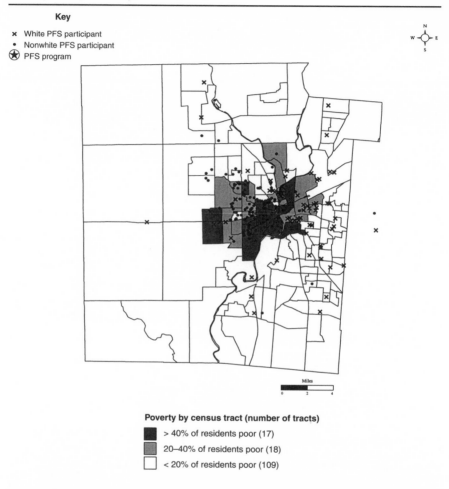

Key

× White PFS participant
• Nonwhite PFS participant
⊛ PFS program

Poverty by census tract (number of tracts)

■ > 40% of residents poor (17)

▨ 20–40% of residents poor (18)

□ < 20% of residents poor (109)

Source: Manpower Demonstration Research Corporation analysis of 1990 census data and Parents' Fair Share administrative records.
Notes: Participants include NCPs randomly assigned prior to July 1995.

Figure B.7 Location of PFS Participants by Poverty Status for Shelby County, Tennessee (1990)

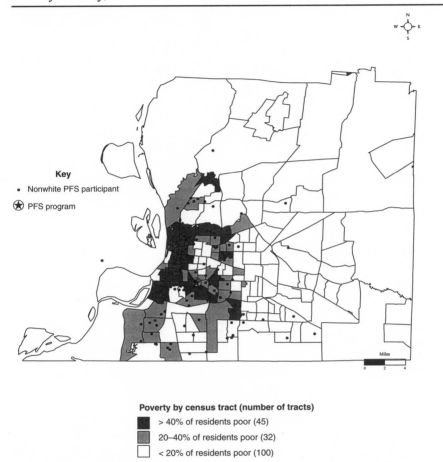

Key

- Nonwhite PFS participant
- ⊛ PFS program

Poverty by census tract (number of tracts)

- ■ > 40% of residents poor (45)
- ▨ 20–40% of residents poor (32)
- □ < 20% of residents poor (100)

Source: Manpower Demonstration Research Corporation analysis of 1990 census data and Parents' Fair Share administrative records.
Notes: Participants include NCPs randomly assigned prior to July 1995.

APPENDIX C

List and Description
of Peer Support Sessions

RESPONSIBLE FATHERHOOD CURRICULUM

Table of Contents

Introduction
How Does Peer Support Fit into Parents' Fair Share?
Using the Responsible Fatherhood Curriculum
Starting with the Peer Group
Confidentiality
What to Expect in a Group
Tips in Facilitating Peer Support Groups
Managing Behavior Problems in a Group
Concluding Comments

Curriculum Outline
    I. Introduction to Responsible Fatherhood
        Overview of the Program
        Icebreaker: What We Have in Common
        or
        Name Game
        or
        Name Yourself Mural
        What Can I Expect from Peer Support?
        What Can Peer Support Expect from Me?
        Feedback/Wrap-Up

    II. What Are My Values?
        What's New?
        Your Goals and Values
        or
        Family Tree
        Values Voting
        Feedback/Wrap-Up

III. Manhood
      What's New?
      What's It Been Like?
      or
      Manhood Collage
      The Stereotype Game
      or
      Debate: Is It Real or a Stereotype?
      Feedback/Wrap-Up

IV. The Art of Communication
     Part I:
         What's New?
         Warm-Up Activity: Telephone Game
         What Is Communication?
         One-Way/Two-Way Communication
         Active Listening

         Part II: Optional Activities
            Parent Communication Traps
            Listen to Understand
            Stating Your Needs
            Through a Child's Eyes
            Feedback/Wrap Up

 V. Fathers as Providers
     What's New?
     Father of the Year
     Being a Provider: What Gets in the Way?
     Feedback/Wrap-Up

VI. Noncustodial Parents: Rights and Responsibilities
     What's New?
     Paying Child Support
     Rights and Responsibilities
     Looking Ahead
     Feedback/Wrap-Up

VII. Developing Values in Children
      What's New?
      My Life as a Father
      The Values Auction
      Communicating Values
      Feedback/Wrap-Up

Strategies for Handling Conflict
Feedback/Wrap-Up

XIV. Surviving on the Job
What's New?
Employer-Worker Job Expectations
On-the-Job Negotiation
Feedback/Wrap-Up

XV. The Issue of Race
Part I: The Cost of Stereotyping and Discrimination
What's New?
The Stereotype Game
or
Debate: Is It Real or a Stereotype?
Looking In/Looking Out
Feedback/Wrap-Up

Part II
What's New?
Reflections from Past Sessions
My Personal Story: What It's Been Like

Part III
Where Do I Stand?
Quotations to Live By
Feedback/Wrap-Up

XVI. Taking Care of Business
What's New?
The Mirror
Optional Warm-Up: Self-Sufficiency Word Game
What Does It Mean to "Take Care of Business"?
My One-Year Plan
Feedback/Wrap-Up

XVII. Time and Money Management
What's New?
The Way It Was
Twenty-Four/Seven
Paying and Caring: Making Ends Meet
Feedback/Wrap-Up

XVIII. Building a Support Network: Who's on Your Side
What's New?
Getting Support

Who's in Your Support Network?
Negotiating for Support
Peer Support Group Closure
Feedback/Wrap-Up

Optional Session I: Alcohol and Drug Use and Abuse
What's New?
How Much Do You Know?
Do I Have a Problem?
Feedback/Wrap-Up

Optional Session II: Recovery
Circle of Recovery
or
A Gathering of Men in Recovery
Feedback/Wrap-Up

Optional Session III: Healthy Eating
What's New?
Food as Common Ground
Eating for Health
Cooking for Health
Feedback/Wrap-Up

DESCRIPTION OF THE SESSIONS

Cluster One: Taking Care of Myself

What are my values?   Have you ever wondered why it can be difficult to live by your values and accomplish your goals? Have you ever wondered where your values came from?

Boys to men—Experiencing manhood   How did you become a man? Do you remember any informal and formal transitions from boyhood to manhood?

Managing conflict/handling anger   Conflicts are a natural part of every relationship; when people have conflicts, they often become angry with one another. Anger is a natural, common emotion, and we all must find constructive, productive ways to express it without hurting other people.

Healthy living   Some helpful guides to living healthy are to eat right, exercise, watch out for common health threats, and develop healthy daily patterns.

Alcohol and drug use   Stresses in everyday life can lead to abuse of alcohol and drugs, but alcohol and drugs can lead to serious problems for family members and friends. Take stock of your life.

Cluster Two: Work-Related

Handling anger and conflict on-the-job   Try to maintain a positive work environment. Although conflict on-the-job is normal and, when resolved, can lead to stronger relationships, take a moment to reflect on your communication style at work.

Taking care of business   Oftentimes, if we transition in and out of the labor force, it can be a challenge to take care of our financial, social, and personal needs whether or not we are living with our children. Remember that self-sufficiency is a process, and it can involve establishing goals and developing plans for reaching those goals.

Time and money management   As parents, one of the first things we lose is time. We must plan every moment of our days because it involves our children. We are also responsible for financially providing for our children. Take a moment to reflect on how you spend your time and develop short- and long-term financial goals.

Thriving on the job   Work usually involves a contractual relationship between an employer and an employee. In this changing economy, workers are less likely to be connected to the workforce in a stable way and, oftentimes, will be freelance consultants or seasonal workers. Pay attention to your work and learn how to negotiate your needs.

Cluster Three: Parenting

Fathers as providers   Men who are successful as fathers work hard to care for their children. What qualities make a successful father and what can get in the way of being a successful father?

The noncustodial parent's rights and responsibilities   These days, many parents do not live with their children full time, and for many, this can involve constant negotiation with the custodial parent and with their child(ren). Noncustodial parents should reflect on their relationships with their children.

Developing values in children   Children begin to develop values from the moment they are born. You must try and identify the values that you want to pass on to your children. After you "name" these values, you can develop effective strategies for communicating them.

Being a single father   Single fathers with part-time custody of their children should know their children's physical, emotional, social, intellectual, and spiritual needs. Caring for children can be a challenging and satisfying experience, but remember that parenting does not come naturally for either men or women.

Building a father-child relationship   Sometimes, it can be difficult to teach children to learn and to help them grow up without becoming impatient, frustrated, tired, and confused. You may want your children to learn how to feed themselves, clothe themselves, talk, and generally be ready to take care of themselves well before they are really able to do so. Take some time to focus on different parenting methods.

Cluster Four: In Relationship to Other People

The art of communication   Communication involves sending and receiving messages. Because they have limited vocabulary, children often communicate their feelings and needs through their behavior and through nonverbal gestures. Take a moment to tune in to what your children are trying to communicate.

Relationships—Being a friend, partner, parent, and employee   Good relationships with adults and children require good communication, understanding, a sense of respect, and more. Take a moment to identify the basic qualities that must be part of successful relationships and set goals for improving some of your relationships.

Understanding relationships between women and men   A good male/ female relationship involves two people who feel good about themselves, care about each other, and are considerate of each other's feelings and needs. Be aware of how your relationship will affect your children's lives.

Race does matter   Believe that stereotypes can limit individuality; try not to judge people before you get to know them. In your relationships, pay attention to stereotypes; men and women should not be limited to certain roles and careers because of their gender, race, national origin, family background, or sexual orientation.

Cluster Five: Wrap-Up

Building a support network—Who is on your side?   Be willing to ask for help, all kinds of help. Learn how to develop a support network—people you can turn to.

APPENDIX D

Family Tree

ACTIVITY: FAMILY TREE

Purpose: To help fathers identify values that have been passed down by family members and to increase their awareness of family accomplishments and family ancestry. To help fathers clarify for themselves what they value in their lives.

Materials: Family Tree handout (enough for every participant), pencils (enough for every participant), colored markers (red, green, and orange), and newsprint.

Time: Thirty-five to forty-five minutes.

Procedure: In your own words, say something like, "Who we are as people, as parents, as friends, or as spouses is greatly influenced by the values held by the people in our family and by family friends and close neighbors. For some, this means that we adopted the qualities of our parents, grandparents, aunts, uncles, teachers, and so forth. For others, it means that we swore *not* to be like those people who were significant in our lives. In the Family Tree activity, we will be identifying *who* the important people were in our development and what *values* or *principles* these people lived their lives by. From this, we will develop a list of values that *we* want to live by as people and as parents. Our values will, in turn, influence how our children grow up and what *they* will be like as adults."

Give each man a copy of the Family Tree handout. The tree contains a number of circles, each of which holds a value or principle for which someone important to that person may have been known. Instruct the men to write down, under "People in My Life," the names of people who influenced their lives as they were growing up. (If they fill up the bubbles on the handout, they can use the back of the sheet to add additional names). Next, instruct the men to write in the circles the names of all the people who may have *strongly* held that value or principle listed in the circle.

Tell them that there are blank circles on the tree for them to fill in *additional* values that may have been important to their family and community.

When everyone has completed their circles, distribute three markers or crayons (red, green, and orange) to each of the men. Next, ask them to put a ring around the circle with a color that indicates how important that particular value is to their life, in the following sequence:

Red: Very important;

Green: A little important;

Orange: Not important.

Copy this guide on newsprint, using the colored markers, and post it in front of the room for reference. Make sure everyone understands the instructions before you get started. Allow approximately fifteen minutes. If you do not have enough markers to go around, instruct participants to use the following guide to complete their circles:

Star: Very important;

Check mark: A little important;

X mark: Not important.

DISCUSSION QUESTIONS

When most people are finished, reconvene the large group to discuss the following questions.

1. Who were the people you placed on your Family Tree? What were the values they lived their life by?

2. Which values on the Family Tree were easy to identify and connect with people in your life?

3. Which values were most important to the people in your life?

4. Which values are most important to you now? How much red is (or how many stars are) on your Family Tree? Why are these things most important?

5. Which values were not important to you? Why?

6. Who were the people with whose values you agreed?

7. Who were the people with whose values you did not agree?

8. Did this activity tell you anything about how you have come to value the things that you do? (Did you adopt as your own the values of people who were most significant in your life, or did you reject the values of people close to you?)

9. Are there "very important" values that you think will be hard to live your life by? If so, what gets in the way?

10. Which of these values do you want to pass on to your children, and how do you plan to accomplish this?

11. How much does the way you live your life reflect the values that you now have? What would have to change about your behavior to reflect these values?

Remind the group that there can be a great deal of diversity among families when it comes to defining values and that this diversity should be respected; knowing what our ancestors valued in their life, in addition to identifying the values that will shape ours, can give us a sense of direction and purpose.

OPTIONAL ACTIVITIES

1. After completing the Family Tree activity, ask each participant to draw his own Family Tree, filling in all of the values that reflect how he is currently living his life as well as changes he hopes to make in the future. You can do this by giving each participant a blank copy of the Family Tree, or you can reproduce the Family Tree on a large sheet of newsprint and create a group Family Tree. The group Family Tree can then become symbolic of the changes men are seeking to make in their lives, particularly related to their involvement in the program. This group tree should be hung in a place where you can all refer

to it throughout the duration of the fathers' participation in peer support.

2. After completing the Family Tree activity, tell participants to look at the Family Tree through the eyes of their children. Ask them to think about all of the people currently involved in their children's lives who have an influence over them. Who are these people? What kind of role models are they for your children? What values do they hold? What behaviors do they demonstrate to your children?

Give all participants a blank copy of the Family Tree and ask them to complete the handout with their children. Once they have completed the handout with their children, they should bring it back and discuss it with members of the group.

The goal of this activity is to get them thinking about the values and behaviors of the people who are shaping the lives of their children.

APPENDIX E

Personal Shields

PRINCIPLES:

1. Enable participants to answer employers' "Tell me something about yourself" question with enthusiasm and confidence,

2. Strengthen participants' relationships with each other,

3. Build self-esteem and communication skills,

4. Begin job consideration.

Transition:

"Tell me something about yourself" is a question most employers ask. That's a tough question, isn't it? We're supposed to condense our lives into brief comments. What does an employer want to know? All employers are not alike; each wants different information. We're different, too. Today we're going to create a tool that will help us answer this question. In early pioneer times, some Native Americans wore shields that described their roles in the tribe—hunter, warrior, chief. Today we are going to make shields that represent parts of what we are all about. (May substitute other examples for shields.)

RULES:

Instructions for shield should be given as you demonstrate your own first. Shields should be divided into fifths. (Keep your shield simple and fairly brief.)

#1 Five positive words that describe you.

#2 Your family.

204

#3 Your hobbies.

#4 Jobs you have had.

#5 Three accomplishments achieved during past jobs.

Emphasize that shields should be positive and remind participants that this is not an art competition and that stick figures and symbols are acceptable! Follow the following steps:

STEP 1. As each participant begins to share his shield in front of the group, ask the question: "Tell me something about yourself." Each should be followed with applause.

STEP 2. Before the participant returns to his chair, ask the group what specific points on the shield they think employers would be especially interested in and, as they respond, underline those specifics.

STEP 3. Explain: "When an employer asks 'Tell me something about yourself,' what they really want to know is, 'Who are you, really?' The interviewer has already noted if you arrived on time and are appropriately dressed. Now you have to be sure your first words impress the employer favorably. Using our shields, we are going to write a short personal profile that will help the interviewer know us *and* remember us." Ask participants to write on the back of their shields four to five brief, positive statements about themselves, using the positive relevant information from their shields.

"TELL ME SOMETHING ABOUT YOURSELF"
MY PERSONAL SALES PITCH

I am flexible, organized, and work well under stress. For five years I have been a single parent responsible for the care and nurturing of three children. I can sew and cook a variety of meals. I also enjoy entertaining friends. My children are in school now and excited about my working. I am eager for a career and a chance to put my skills to work for you.

STEP 4. When participants have completed their personal profiles, ask them to tell something about themselves and discuss the effectiveness of their responses.

STEP 5. When all are satisfied with their profiles, have them write theirs on their Tough Question page. Encourage them to begin learning the answer so that they will be able to respond to that important question with confidence. Then have everyone hang their shields up on the wall.

OBSERVE:

As participants are working on their shields, give suggestions to encourage them. When they write the personal profile, assist participants who may be having difficulty writing and understanding the concept.

EVALUATE:

Ask all of the participants to answer the question, "Tell me something about yourself?" appropriately.

"Your shield is a tool for helping you answer tough questions. When you hear, 'Tell me something about yourself' remember why the employer is asking and respond with your personal profile."

APPENDIX F

Profile of Two Participants Deciding How to Use Their Money

Viceroy had worked off and on since his first child was born nearly two years earlier. His child support debt, although not in the five-figure category, was in the thousands. The best job he had held to date paid him $8.50 per hour; after losing this job he collected unemployment insurance and kept current on his child support payments by having them deducted from his unemployment benefits. During this period, Viceroy, on his own, moved into a rent-subsidized housing unit where he was able to lower his rent, due to his unemployed status. With some financial assistance from his father, he consistently paid the bills for his telephone and other utilities, including cable, and for his rent.

Viceroy eventually found another part-time job that paid about $7 an hour. He made his minimum child support payments of $85 a week and had a little left over to meet his remaining obligations. (A child support obligation includes the amount specified in the child support guideline as well as any other public assistance debt affiliated with the child support order at issue. Therefore, an obligation may include medical costs, court fees, and any other public debt incurred relative to the child in question.) Ultimately, however, he lost this job as well. After entering PFS, he married and had another child, and even with his wife's contribution to the household income, their two salaries combined barely covered the basic needs of both his current family and his obligation to his previous child. Most recently, he took a job through a temporary service at $6.50 an hour for a twenty-hour work week. This job provided him with $100 a week in take-home pay, after taxes, further diminished by his child support obligation (itself reduced), leaving him with a weekly net income of $50. Yet despite his severely limited earnings, Viceroy continued to spend time with his son. For Viceroy, the economic sacrifices that he and his wife made together allowed him to be a connected and involved noncustodial parent.

Fila-G had seven children who had all, at one time or another, received public assistance. As a result, Fila-G carried a sizable child support debt. Fila-G was not sure how much he owed in child support or how much he owed for each child.

Despite Fila-G's lack of knowledge, or apparent concern, about the correct amount owed, his weekly obligation was $75 a week. Without dependable income, Fila-G was unable to pay many of his personal obligations and during the course of this study was arrested twice for not paying his child support. During the research period, he spent more than forty days in jail for this offense, and his telephone (which he shared with his grandmother and others with whom he occasionally lived) was shut off on three occasions. At the time of this writing, his telephone had been disconnected for three months. Fila-G's immediate expenses revolved around his need for cigarettes and alcohol. He used his food stamps as a source of cash income, trading them for the highest price he could get, which was generally about two-thirds of their market or face value. In June 1996, a lien was placed on his grandmother's house because they were approximately $3,000 behind in their mortgage payments.

Fila-G worked on and off but never made consistent money. When faced with the choice of spending his money on child support or on himself, he most often elected to fulfill his personal needs. Despite his economic woes and unmet obligations, Fila-G attempted, with some success, to establish an emotional relationship with a few of his children, one achievement that made him proud.

APPENDIX G

Profiles of Selected Participants

Antonio was a forty-year-old Latino father of three who had lived in East Los Angeles almost all of his life. He divorced his wife and had been living with his girlfriend for a number of years. Antonio saw his children as often as he could. His relationship with his oldest daughter had been very strained for a number of years. During the past year, they had started to talk and were working toward developing a friendship.

Antonio favored his boys. He liked the fact that both were budding athletes. Antonio tried to supply them with sporting goods (such as sneakers) when he could afford to purchase them. He liked to keep his children playing sports because it kept them out of trouble and he feared that his ex-wife would be unable to control them if they did not play sports.

Antonio used to work as a mechanic for an aerospace company before he entered the program. He had not worked steadily for the past three years. He had tried many would-be careers, but nothing had materialized. Through PFS, he was working on getting training for construction work and welding. Antonio came into the program to get work and training.

Bo was a thirty-two-year-old African American father of three. He had some contact with his children who lived in Trenton. He did not finish high school and had worked off and on since he was sixteen. Bo went through PFS to get a better job and ended up finding work at a medical supplier and pick-up company. He worked at this job for nearly a year before he lost it. Upon losing his job, Bo disappeared from the program and possibly from Trenton and his family.

Derrick was a twenty-six-year-old African American father of two from Springfield, Massachusetts. Born and raised in Springfield, Derrick graduated from high school and had hopes of playing basketball in college—a dream he continued to hold. Having children, however, limited his mobility, and he had left his family only once to go to North Carolina for a job he did not keep due to differences between himself and his employer.

His children were with him when they could be. Derrick had tried a number of jobs from removing asbestos to working construction on call in Connecticut to part-time cashiering and stocking for a local supermarket. Derrick knew his responsibilities and was making an effort to meet them; he simply did not earn enough money. Derrick came into the program to try to find work that he could rely on, so he could provide for himself and his family.

Junior was a forty-two-year-old black man from Jacksonville, Florida, who had four children. When he was staying at his mother's home, he lived with two of his children. Junior never finished ninth grade and for the most part was illiterate. Junior had little rapport with his children. They knew him, but he was in and out of their lives so frequently that they rarely depended on him.

Junior had a drinking and drug problem that got in the way of his keeping jobs and maintaining a constant living arrangement. Junior was described as a hard-working man when he was sober. However, he frequently slipped into a deep state of dependency. Junior had made many attempts to get straight (through religion, rehabilitation, and going cold turkey), but so far he had always fallen back into his old ways.

Junior came into the program to get help with his education and to find a job. When straight or only slightly intoxicated, he participated regularly in the public library's literacy program. This was the only task that Junior stuck with during his two years of contact with the interviewer.

Tyler was a white father of two children. He was a twenty-seven-year-old high school graduate who had spent most of his life working as a roofer in Southern California (Los Angeles and Orange counties). He had children by two different women. For a while, he had informal custody of his oldest child, which meant that he was keeping the child while the mother tried to get her life together. Tyler's mother helped to take care of the child, minimizing the burden on both parents. Tyler did not pay his child support because he thought he was doing his job by taking care of the child. Tyler was not interested in paying child support and did not believe that he needed to spend his money that way.

Tyler came into the Parents' Fair Share program to see if he could change careers. The roofing business was hard on his body, and the work was not consistent enough. He tried PFS to see if he could get into something different. He attempted to meet the program's demands and continued with his training, but his resources diminished, and he found himself back in the roofing business in another county.

Ventura was a twenty-three-year-old white father of Portuguese descent who had one child. Ventura had lived on the outskirts of Hampden County, Massachusetts, for all of his life. Ventura dropped out of school in the ninth grade to run the streets and become a "Mac Daddy" (in his own words), just like the rest of his friends. In order to make money, he worked as a carpenter and craftsman. At the age of twenty, his girlfriend had his baby. He and his girlfriend got along for a while before she grew tired of the situation and left him, taking the baby. She stayed in Springfield but had little contact with him. He got to see the baby, but he had a very poor relationship with the mother.

He came into the program to get work and possibly put his relationship back on course. In reality, he was not as concerned about employment as he was about his girlfriend and their relationship.

A young African American man who continued to strive for his independence, Viceroy nevertheless found himself frequently dependent on his family and girlfriends to get by. Twenty-two years old and a father of two children by two different mothers, his youth was divided between hanging out with some very tough people and helping his mother. Almost immediately after finishing high school, Viceroy became a father. He lived with his girlfriend and their baby while attending a local business school, but the struggle to provide for the family while attending classes proved too difficult. He quit school in search of a job. Soon afterward, he left his girlfriend for another woman.

Viceroy bounced around a great deal in his living situations. During the time of this research, he lived alternately with his mother and each of his two girlfriends. He was residing with the other woman and their one child in an apartment he rented on his own. Viceroy had been working through December of 1995 but lost his job at the beginning of the new year. He then began paying his child support through his unemployment benefits, until they were about to run out, pushing him to look for work again.

According to Viceroy, his new relationship was a change for the better. He and his new girlfriend stayed home more often, and he was not restless. They attended church regularly, which he viewed as a positive experience. He observed that when he was not working, his church attendance would drop. Viceroy came into the program as a young man who was thought to be rough and tough and only slightly interested in what the program had to offer. In fact, he was seriously looking for work to stabilize his life. Viceroy and his girlfriend eventually married with a large gathering of (mostly her) family in attendance.

APPENDIX H

Questions for Noncustodial Parents in PFS

EXPERIENCE IN PARENTS' FAIR SHARE

1. What do you think of PFS?

2. What activities have you participated in?

3. How long have you been in PFS?

4. When you were assigned to PFS in court, what did you think was going to happen?

5. What were you told would happen in court?

6. What do you think the purpose of PFS is?

7. What do you like and dislike about PFS? How could PFS be better?

8. What were the reasons that you did not pay child support in the past?

9. What is the most important reason for not paying child support?

10. Has PFS helped you feel more like paying, and why?

RELATIONSHIP WITH CUSTODIAL PARENT(S)

1. How do you and the mother of your child(ren) get along? What is your relationship like now?

2. With how many women have you fathered children?

3. What was your marital status when you had your child(ren)?

4. What was your relationship with the custodial parent(s) before the pregnancy? How did the relationship change after the pregnancy?

5. When did you establish paternity? What were the circumstances (were they voluntary or court established)?

6. What does (do) the custodial parent(s) think about PFS? Has her (their) behavior changed because of PFS? Explain.

7. What are the biggest issues regarding responsibilities and obligations for providing for your child(ren) that you have with the custodial parent(s)?

RELATIONSHIP WITH THEIR CHILD(REN)

1. How often do you see your child(ren)?

2. Do you have visitation rights? Are you pleased with them? Why? Why not?

3. Do you feel comfortable around your child(ren)?

4. How often does your family (mother, sisters, brothers) interact with your child(ren)?

5. Where do you visit with your child(ren)? At the mother's home or at your home?

6. Does the custodial parent(s) help or get in the way of your relationship with your child(ren)?

7. What activities do you do with your child(ren)? Has this changed since you began PFS?

8. How would you make the relationship between you and your child(ren) better?

9. Are there any problems raising children from two different relationships? What are they?

10. Has PFS helped improve interactions with your child(ren)?

11. Have you taken any steps to improve your interaction with your child(ren)? What were those steps?

12. How could the custodial parent(s) help make your relationship with your child(ren) better?

FAMILY PROVISIONS: SOCIALIZATION IN THE HOME

Has PFS affected your ability to manage your household and/or parent your child(ren)?

1. Is it more difficult now that you are in the Parents' Fair Share program?

2. Since you started PFS, have you noticed any changes in your child(ren)'s school attendance?

3. What kind of grades do your kids get? Have they always gotten these types of grades?

4. Would you say you are more involved with your child(ren)'s schooling since you entered into the PFS program? Why do you think this is?

Tell me how you feel about the following statements in regard to how you have changed or not changed since entering PFS:

5. I feel better about myself and my family since entering PFS.

6. I am more worried about the kids because I am not around as much.

7. PFS gets in the way of the things I want to do.

8. I have more control of my life since entering PFS.

9. PFS has helped me positively interact with the child(ren)'s mother or father.

10. Since entering PFS I am more helpful in managing my child(ren)'s custodial parent household.

PERSONAL DEMOGRAPHICS

1. How old are you?

2. How many kids do you have—ages, sex?

3. How old were you when you fathered your first child?

4. How many children live with you?

5. What is your current marital status?

6. What is your highest level of educational attainment?

7. Have you ever been homeless?

8. Are you currently supporting or helping to support another family?

9. What is the number one thing that would help you to be able to pay child support regularly?

PERSONAL ECONOMIC CONDITION

1. When was the last time you worked?

2. When was the last time you had a full-time position?

3. What is the longest period of time you ever held a job?

4. Have you ever worked "under the table" or for cash? What kind of job was that? (If no, then ask question number six.)

5. When you worked "off the books," did you share some of that income with the mother of your child(ren)? If yes, about how much would you give her and how often?

6. About how much did you make last year? What type(s) of jobs did you hold?

7. Do you buy your child(ren) things that are specifically for them? What types of stuff do you buy them?

8. Does your child(ren)'s mom ever call you or get in touch with you to ask you to purchase things for the child(ren)? What does she usually ask you to purchase? And how often does she make these requests of you?

Appendix I

PROFILE OF INTERVIEWEES

The following are aliases used for the thirty-two participants in this research:

Antonio
Arron
Ben
Big Joe
Bo
Bob
Chris Adam
Claudio
Derrick
Edmond
Fila-G
G Man
Geraldo
Hollywood
Jah
Jason

Jasper
Jonesy
Junior
Kenny
Lover
Mack
Marcus
Nelson
Ralph
Sly
Trane
Tyler
Tyrone
Ventura
Viceroy
Willie

The following men were included in this report, but not in the research group:

Billy Bob
Eric

Harry
Ray

Table I.1 Summary of Characteristics of Participants in the PFS Qualitative Sample

Participant	Site	Age	Race/ Ethnicity	Number of Children	Marital Status
Antonio	Los Angeles	40	Latino	2	Divorced
Arron	Los Angeles	20	Black	5	Single
Ben	Los Angeles	40	Black	7	Divorced
Big Joe	Grand Rapids	25	Black	7	Married
Bo	Trenton	32	Black	4	Single
Bob	Dayton	26	Black	5	Single
Chris Adam	Trenton	20	Black	2	Single
Claudio	Los Angeles	40	Latino	3	Divorced
Derrick	Springfield	26	Black	2	Single
Edmond	Jacksonville	36	White	1	Single
Fila-G	Memphis	36	Black	7	Divorced
G Man	Los Angeles	31	Black	5	Divorced
Geraldo	Los Angeles	43	Latino	3	Divorced
Hollywood	Grand Rapids	23	Black	1	Single
Jah	Trenton	29	Black	2*	Single
Jason	Dayton	32	White	2	Married

Living Situation	Past Employment	Education			Vocational Training
		Some HS	HS Grad	Beyond HS	
w/girlfriend	Mechanic	Yes			Mechanic
w/girlfriend and children	Part-time/ temp	Yes			
Alone	Electrical		Yes		
w/wife and children	Part-time/ temp/drugs	Yes			
w/girlfriend and children	Medical supply driver	Yes			Truck driving
w/mother	Part-time/ temp/drugs		Yes		
w/girlfriend	Service industry/ drugs	Yes			
w/girlfriend and her children	Physical ed.	Yes			Trainer/arts
w/girlfriend and children	Warehouse	Yes			
Alone	Computer			Yes	
Alone	Part-time/ temp/drugs		Yes		
w/girlfriend	Mechanic		Yes		Army
Alone and w/stepson	Entrepreneur		Yes	Yes	
w/mother and alone	Part-time/ temp	Yes			
w/girlfriend and children	Sanitation		Yes		
w/second wife and stepchild	Auto body repairman		Yes		

(*Table continues on p. 222.*)

Table I.1 *Continued*

Participant	Site	Age	Race/ Ethnicity	Number of Children	Marital Status
Jasper	Grand Rapids	37	Black	1	Single
Jonesy	Los Angeles	41	Black	3	Divorced
Junior	Jacksonville	42	Black	3	Single
Kenny	Trenton	25	Black	2*	Single
Lover	Los Angeles	28	Black	3	Widower
Mack	Grand Rapids	27	Black	4	Single
Marcus	Los Angeles	26	Black	1	Divorced
Nelson	Memphis	36	Black	3	Single
Ralph	Trenton	40	White	1	Divorced
Sly	Trenton	19	Black	1	Single
Trane	Los Angeles	36	Black	3	Divorced
Tyler	Los Angeles	27	White	2	Single
Tyrone	Jacksonville	51	Black	5	Divorced
Ventura	Springfield	23	White	1	Single
Viceroy	Grand Rapids	22	Black	2*	Married**
Willie	Memphis	37	Black	2	Married

*Participant's second child was born after entering PFS.
**Married his current wife at the time of the study.

Living Situation	Past Employment	Education			Vocational Training
		Some HS	HS Grad	Beyond HS	
Alone	Warehouse		Yes		
Alone	Entrepreneur		Yes	Yes	Army
w/mother and alone	Warehouse	Yes			
w/mother	Service industry	Yes			
w/relatives and alone	Fashion	Yes		Yes	Army
w/girlfriend and children	Service		Yes		Army
w/mother	(Jail)	Yes			
w/mother	Construction	Yes			
Alone	Transportation	Yes			Truck driving
w/mother	Service industry	Yes			
w/girlfriend	Food industry		Yes		
w/mother and alone	Construction	Yes			Carpentry
Alone	Mechanic	Yes			Mechanic
w/parents	Construction	Yes			Carpentry
w/wife and child	Warehouse		Yes		
w/wife and child	Mechanic/music		Yes	Yes	

NOTES

Chapter 1

1. The majority of participants in the PFS program were male. Accordingly, when the term "noncustodial parent" appears in the singular, we generally refer to "his" or "him."

2. PL 100-485, title II, section 201(b), codified as 42 U.S.C. 682 (d)(3).

3. Bloom and Sherwood 1994; Furstenberg, Sherwood, and Sullivan 1992. In addition, pilot programs also operated in Anoka and Dakota counties in Minnesota; Kansas City, Missouri; and Mobile, Alabama; these sites, however, were not part of the full demonstration.

4. The PFS program's success in achieving these goals was evaluated through four research methods: qualitative ethnographic research (of which this book is an example), implementation and process analysis, impact analysis using random assignment, and benefit-cost analysis (see Doolittle and others 1998).

5. Because PFS intake ended before the implementation of TANF, this section refers to AFDC. The term AFDC continued to be used in some PFS sites despite the change to TANF.

6. Under the 1996 federal legislation, federal financial support for this $50 "pass through" disappears, and states can continue the practice only if they finance it out of state or local funds.

7. See Temporary Assistance for Needy Families (TANF), the Personal Responsibility and Work Reconciliation Act of 1996 (P.L. 104-193), and U.S. House of Representatives, Committee on Ways and Means Greenbook (1998, 591).

8. In some PFS sites, personal service (that is, evidence that the NCP personally received the notice) is required for a hearing on nonpayment, while in others a mailed notice with a return receipt can be used for initial hearings. In these sites, if the NCP fails to appear for the initial hearing, personal service is typically required for the next step of enforcement.

9. Most of the noncustodial parents in this book were extremely poor. Yet, through friends, relatives, and other sources, some could obtain money to stay out of jail or reduce their time in jail.

Chapter 2

1. At the end of the data collection period, twenty men were sent a small monetary gift out of appreciation for their participation in the qualitative research. These men were never told that they were going to receive any type of compensation for their participation, and as a result, the gifts were unexpected and received with some surprise.

2. In an unpublished paper by Johnson (1992), similar behavior was noted among a group of homeless men living on the west side of Los Angeles. They preferred to spend the majority of their general relief money on a room in a low-end motel, at an average daily rate of $28.

3. On average black men earn only about 75 cents for every dollar earned by white men with the same degree. Moreover, a study of black/white wages that controlled for education, previous experience, years with current employer, and other factors found that racial differences in wages and promotions increased significantly in the 1980s, a decade during which the government cut back on enforcement of antidiscrimination laws (Cancio, Evans, and Maume 1996).

4. Although the term African American (and similarly, person of color) is part of the academic lexicon at this period in time, most participants used the term "black" to describe and identify race. Therefore, in acknowledgment of the diversity of usage, all three designations are used throughout this book.

5. Edin and Lein (1997) explore the caution and hesitancy that both African American women and men living in an economically depressed section show toward getting married.

6. In a recent study, Watson (1992) learned of the stress that young fathers face as they attempt to fulfill their roles as parents, providers, and partners. In this research, we hope to add to the base of knowledge regarding young, unwed, economically challenged fathers.

7. As John K. Galbraith (1996, 27) wrote, "Nothing is thought more sharply to define the middle class, normally referred to as the hard-working middle class, as its commitment to the work ethic and, in consequence, its unwillingness to support idleness in the class below. In the income structure leisure is not thought socially unacceptable if sought by those in the upper reaches. On the contrary; for the affluent and the rich it has a large measure of approval; it can be a personal and a social virtue. Thorstein Veblen, in his enduring classic, *The Theory of the Leisure Class* (1908), saw well-considered idleness as the prestigious

social hallmark of the rich, and so it remains. Intellectuals, not excluding college professors, are known to need recurrent and sometimes
extended relief from the pressures of mental toil. We must be tolerant
of this preference for leisure as it manifests itself at all levels of our economic system."

Chapter 3

1. The practice of providing participants with disposable cameras is discussed in appendix A on methodology.

2. This refers to the practice of pouring liquor onto the chalk outline of a
   victim of violence, out of respect for the deceased.

Chapter 4

1. Other research dealing with the CSE system suggests that the odds of
   going to jail for nonpayment of child support, as perceived by these
   men, are somewhat exaggerated. Doolittle and Lynn (1998) suggest
   that jail is an "infrequent" outcome for nonpayment of support in most
   of the PFS sites.

2. Many cities around the country have used such "sting" operations in
   the form of phony prize giveaways to lure unsuspecting parents who
   do not pay child support into environments where they can be
   arrested. These have been successful enough that people are becoming
   suspicious of a program that says it can help them find a job if they
   come to the courthouse.

3. With the passage of federal legislation—namely, TANF and the Personal
   Responsibility and Work Reconciliation Act of 1996 (P.L. 104-193)—the
   federal government no longer funds any "pass through" to the families,
   and states choosing to do so must fund it out of state resources.

4. Staff on the programmatic side of PFS reported that much of the confusion about child support and debt obligations results from many of
   the added obligations charged to noncustodial parents when their
   children use the services of the public social service system. These
   fees (which can, for example, include health care and court costs)
   complicate the child support obligation and confound some participants—as one administrator put it, "It all looks like child support
   to them."

5. Paraphrased; no tape recorders were permitted during these sessions,
   for purposes of confidentiality.

6. Both incidents were related during a conversation with a PFS administrator in August of 1996.

Chapter 5

1. Participation requirements varied from site to site. However, the standard requisite consisted of participation in one core activity at least three times a week. Some programs required a start-up participation period of five days a week and gradually reduced the days over time.

2. PFS was a mandatory program. To receive benefits, participants had to cooperate fully with its rules or be referred back to the child support enforcement agency. However, no amount of enforcement could compel people to participate.

3. In court, after being assigned to PFS, all noncustodial parents received a brief orientation, which was less thorough than the one they received later from the program itself. This is part of the reason why many NCPs initially did not understand the program's expectations, objectives, and services.

4. Other studies on PFS use different definitions of participation.

5. An "active participant" refers to the NCP who showed up at the program site on a regular basis; it does not reflect anything about his actions once in the confines of PFS.

6. According to implementers of group exercises, the practice of including past group members can inform a current group of its progress and sometimes offer methods of improvement. Therapists and other practitioners also feel that testimonials serve as a motivating and hope-inspiring process on which groups can build (Yalom 1995; Bion 1994).

7. This group consisted of both male and female noncustodial parents. In looking at PFS overall, 2.6 percent of the noncustodial parents assigned to the program were women.

8. For both ethical and legal reasons, we could not allow participants to reveal their identities.

9. Peer support sessions were structured to offer all participants a sense of safety and confidentiality within the confines of the group. However, facilitators were bound to report to authorities issues of domestic violence or child abuse.

10. Participants regularly helped one another when difficulties were expressed, and facilitators checked to see if participants needed assistance with their writing, because skill levels varied among NCPs.

11. A term used by Dean Curtis and Associates during one of their job club strategy sessions to indicate a potential obstacle to gaining employment.

12. Facilitators received continuous training and coaching throughout the duration of the demonstration. Additionally, participation in monthly teleconferences with other facilitators and outside consultants was required as a means of debriefing when complicated issues arose in sessions. These measures were taken both to reduce on-the-job stress as well as to maintain participants' confidentiality. Further explanation of peer support operations will be made available in an upcoming implementation report.

13. During the course of interactions with the NCPs of this sample and also others in PFS, peer support groups tended to vary in size. Sometimes only two or three individuals were present for scheduled meetings. At other times, fifteen to eighteen persons were in attendance. Facilitators had to be sensitive to the number of attendees and adjust their focus to meet the needs of those who were present.

14. This flexibility sometimes caused conflict between facilitators and PFS administrators, who were concerned with other program objectives.

15. The temporary reduction of an NCP's child support payments while he participated in PFS.

16. Program staff who participated were obligated to follow the rules and procedures of that group, including maintaining the confidentiality of all information shared within the group, in order to protect the level of safety set and held by group members.

Chapter 6

1. Although not all PFS sites required that a participant complete a specific number of peer support sessions before transitioning into the program's employment component, this was more often the rule than the exception. In some sites, satisfactory participation in peer support was a requirement for moving into the employment component.

2. "Help Us 'Dress for Success'" was the opening line of an announcement that ran in the December 1996 issue of the newsletter of the Trenton-based Union Industrial House. The article requested "suits, slacks, shirts, jackets, and shoes to wear to job interviews. (We are not in need of any ties.) Clothing should be in good condition." Donations were to be made to Trenton's PFS program office.

3. The particular group referred to here consisted of participants in Parents' Fair Share who had transitioned out of the program but were still attending peer support sessions when their schedules allowed.

4. In the PFS implementation study, the objectives of the various PFS sites will be explained in greater detail. On average, each site attempted to place 75 percent of its study sample in jobs that paid a minimum of $6

to $7 an hour. Minimum ranges were created because of the variation in labor market wages among PFS sites. See Doolittle et al. (1998).

5. This finding seemed to counter some of the findings of Newman and others regarding the utility and benefits of service jobs in the fast food industry. Although that study concentrated solely on young people in search of employment, many participants in this research implied that service industry jobs were more of a dead end than warehousing-type jobs. Moreover, the skills used in fast food service jobs did not translate into better employment in the future.

6. Transportation became a big issue in the job search component partly because of budget constraints on the program. PFS tried to provide tokens for noncustodial parents to travel back and forth to their respective program sites, but often there was little remaining to send them on interviews and jobs across the city or county.

7. Recall Trane's experience of following a lead on a warehouse job, only to be asked to sell radios on a busy Los Angeles street corner, as related in chapter 2.

8. After placement, technical assistance providers encouraged follow-up. However, economic and political barriers precluded many sites from fully implementing a comprehensive postplacement element within their employment/training component.

9. A PFS staff member who watched the Trenton labor market implied that some employers screened but then failed to hire African Americans who did not possess or have access to a vehicle.

Chapter 7

1. Ironically, the dependency court's decision was based partially on Lover's failure to make any attempt to see his children during his trial, even though he had been barred by his superior court case, under threat of jail, from making such contact. To stay out of jail, he chose to deny contact, although he unofficially saw his youngest daughter when he visited his sister.

2. If that staff person leaves the program, his or her replacement should take the initiative in contacting and attempting to establish rapport with the participant, rather than waiting for the participant to seek contact.

REFERENCES

Anderson, Elijah. 1992. "The Story of John Turner." In *Drugs, Crime, and Social Isolation,* edited by Adele V. Harell and George E. Peterson. Washington, D.C.: Urban Institute Press.

Bion, W.R. 1994. *Experiences in Groups and Other Papers.* 7th ed. New York: Routledge.

Blank, Rebecca M. 1997. *It Takes a Nation: A New Agenda for Fighting Poverty.* New York: Russell Sage Foundation.

Blankenhorn, David. 1995. *Fatherless America: Confronting Our Most Urgent Social Problem.* New York: Basic Books.

Bloom, Dan, and Kay Sherwood. 1994. *Matching Opportunities to Obligations: Lessons for Child Support Reform from Parents' Fair Share Pilot Phase.* New York: Manpower Demonstration Research Corporation.

Bloom and Dixon. 1993. *Child Support Enforcement: A Case Study.* New York: Manpower Demonstration Research Corporation.

Bourgois, Philippe. 1995. *In Search of Respect: Selling Crack in El Barrio.* Cambridge, U.K.: Cambridge University Press.

Cancio, A. S., T. D. Evans, and D. J. Maume, Jr. 1996. "Rediscovering the Declining Significance of Race: Racial Differences in the Early Career Wages." *American Sociological Review* 61(August): 541–56.

Coolio. 1996. *Gangsta Paradise.* Compact disk.

Daly, Kerry J. 1995. "Reshaping Fatherhood: Finding the Models." In *Fatherhood: Contemporary Theory, Research, and Social Policy,* edited by William Marsiglio. Thousand Oaks, Calif.: Sage Publications.

DeParle, Jason. 1998. "Shrinking Welfare Rolls Leave Record High Share of Minorities." *New York Times,* July 27, 1998, p. A2.

Doolittle, Fred, Virginia Knox, Cynthia Miller, and Sharon Rowser. 1998. *Building Opportunities, Enforcing Obligations: Parents' Fair Share.* New York: Manpower Demonstration Research Corporation.

Doolittle, Fred, and Suzanne Lynn. 1998. *Working With Low-Income Cases: Lessons for the Child Support Enforcement System from Parents' Fair Share.* New York: Manpower Demonstration Research Corporation.

Edin, Kathryn, and Laura Lein. 1997. *Making Ends Meet: How Single Mothers Survive Welfare and Low-Wage Work.* New York: Russell Sage Foundation.

Fagan, Jeffrey. 1992. "Drug Selling and Licit Income in Distressed Neighborhoods: The Economic Lives of Street-Level Drug Users and Dealers." In *Drugs, Crime, and Social Isolation,* edited by Adele V. Harrell and George E. Peterson. Washington, D.C.: Urban Institute Press.

Freeman, Richard B. 1987. "The Relation of Criminal Activity to Black Youth Employment." *Review of Black Political Economy* 16(1–2, summer–fall): 99–107.

———. 1996a. "The Supply of Youths to Crime." In *Exploring the Underground Economy: Studies of Illegal and Unreported Activity,* edited by Susan Pozo. Kalamazoo, Mich.: W. E. Upjohn Institute for Employment Research.

———. 1996b. "Why Do So Many Young American Men Commit Crimes and What Might We Do About it?" *Journal of Economic Perspectives* 10 (1, winter): 25–42.

Furstenberg, Frank F., Jr., and Kathleen Millan Harris. 1993. "When and Why Fathers Matter: Impacts of Father Involvement on Children of Adolescent Mothers." In *Young Unwed Fathers,* edited by Robert I. Lerman and Theodora J. Ooms. Philadelphia, Penn.: Temple University.

Furstenberg, Frank F., Jr., Kay Sherwood, and Mercer Sullivan. 1992. *Caring and Paying: What Fathers and Mothers Say about Child Support.* New York: Manpower Demonstration Research Corporation.

Galbraith, John Kenneth. 1996. *The Good Society: The Human Agenda.* Boston: Houghton Mifflin Company.

Glaser, Barney G., and Anselm L. Strauss. 1967. *The Discovery of Grounded Theory: Strategies for Qualitative Research.* New York: Aldine De Gruyter.

Harrell, Adele V., and George E. Peterson, eds. 1992. *Drugs, Crime, and Social Isolation—Barriers to Urban Opportunity.* Washington, D.C.: Urban Institute Press.

Harrington, P. E., and W. N. Fogg. 1994. *Education and Market Success.* Boston, Mass.: Northeastern University.

Holstein, James A., and Jaber F. Gubrium. 1995. *The Active Interview.* Thousand Oaks, Calif.: Sage Publications.

Holzer, Harry. 1996. *What Employers Want: Job Prosepects for Less-Educated Workers.* New York: Russell Sage Foundation.

Jencks, Christopher. 1994. *The Homeless*. Cambridge, Mass.: Harvard University Press.

Johnson, Earl. 1992. "The Other L.A. Story." Unpublished manuscript. Los Angeles: University of California, Los Angeles.

Johnson, Earl, and Fred Doolittle. 1996. Low-Income Parents and the Parents' Fair Share Demonstration; An Early Qualitative Look at Low-Income Noncustodial Parents (NCPs) and How One Policy Initiative Has Attempted to Improve Their Ability to Pay Child Support. New York: Manpower Demonstration Research Corporation.

Johnson, Earl, and Fred Doolittle. 1998. "Low-Income Parents and the Parents' Fair Share Program: An Early Qualitative Look at Improving the Ability and Desire of Low-Income Noncustodial Parents to Pay Child Support." In *Fathers Under Fire*, edited by Irwin Garfinkel, Sara S. McLanahan, Daniel R. Meyer, and Judith A. Seltzer. New York: Russell Sage Foundation.

Johnson, Jeffrey C. 1990. *Selecting Ethnographic Informants*. Newbury Park, Calif.: Sage Publications.

Kasarda, John D. 1992. "The Severely Distressed in Economically Transforming Cities: The Economic Lives of Street-Level Drug Users and Dealers." In *Drugs, Crime, and Social Isolation*, edited by Adele V. Harrell and George E. Peterson. Washington, D.C.: Urban Institute Press.

Kelley, Michelle L., and Christopher B. Colburn. "Economically Disadvantaged African American Fathers: Social Policy and Fathering." *Journal of African American Men* (1): 63–74.

Kirk, Jerome, and Marc L. Miller. 1986. *Reliability and Validity in Qualitative Research*. Newbury Park, Calif.: Sage Publications.

Kirschenman, Joleen, and Kathryn M. Neckerman. 1991. "'We'd Love to Hire Them, But . . .': The Meaning of Race for Employers." In *The Urban Underclass*, edited by Christopher Jencks and Paul E. Peterson. Washington, D.C.: Brookings Institution.

Lerman, Robert I., and Theodora Ooms, eds. 1993. *Young Unwed Fathers: Changing Roles and Emerging Policies*. Philadelphia: Temple University Press.

Levy, Frank., and Richard Murnane 1992. "U.S. Earnings Levels and Earnings Inequality: A Review of Recent Trends and Proposed Explanations." *Journal of Economic Literature* 30(3): 1332–81.

Liebow, Elliot. 1968. *Tally's Corner: A Study of Negro Streetcorner Men*. Boston: Little, Brown, and Company.

Lofland, John, and Lynn H. Lofland. 1984. *Analyzing Social Settings: A Guide to Qualitative Observations and Analysis*. 2d ed. Belmont, Calif.: Wadsworth Publishing Company.

Mason, Patrick L. 1996. *Joblessness and Unemployment: A Review of the Literature.* Philadelphia: National Centers on Fathers and Families. University of Pennsylvania.

Massey, Douglas S., and Nancy A. Denton. 1993. *American Apartheid: Segregation and the Making of the Underclass.* Cambridge, Mass.: Harvard University Press.

McLanahan, Sara, and Gary Sandefur. 1994. *Growing Up with a Single Parent: What Hurts, What Helps.* Cambridge, Mass.: Harvard University Press.

Miles, Matthew B., and Michael A. Huberman. 1984. *Qualitative Data Analysis: A Source Book of New Methods.* Newbury Park, Calif.: Sage Publications.

Murray, Charles. 1984. *Losing Ground: American Social Policy 1950–1980.* New York, N.Y.: Basic Books.

Newman, Katherine, and Chauncy Lennon. 1995. "Finding Work in the Inner City: How Hard Is It Now? How Hard Will It Be for the AFDC Recipients?" Unpublished manuscript. New York: Columbia University.

Seltzer, Judith A., and Yvonne Brandreth. 1995. "What Fathers Say about Involvement with Children after Separation." In *Fatherhood: Contemporary Theory, Research, and Social Policy*, edited by William Marsiglio. Thousand Oaks Calif.: Sage Publications.

Snow, David A., and Leon Anderson. 1993. *Down on Their Luck: A Study of Homeless Street People.* Berkeley: University of California Press.

Statistical Abstracts. 1996. *Statistical Abstracts of the United States. Austin, Texas:* The Reference Press.

Sullivan, Mercer L. 1993. "Young Fathers and Parenting in Two Inner-City Neighborhoods." In *Young Unwed Fathers: Changing Roles and Emerging Policies*, edited by Robert I. Lerman and Theodora J. Ooms. Philadelphia: Temple University Press.

U.S. Bureau of the Census. 1990. *1990 Census of Population and Housing.* Summary tape file 3A. Generated by Manpower Demonstration Research Corporation using http://venus.census.gov/cdrom/lookup.

U.S. House of Representatives, Committee on Ways and Means. 1994. *Overview of Entitlement Programs: 1994 Greenbook.* Washington, D.C.: U.S. Government Printing Office.

————. 1998. *Overview of Entitlement Programs: 1998 Greenbook.* Washington, D.C.: U.S. Government Printing Office.

U.S. Senate, Committee on Governmental Affairs. 1994. *Child Support Enforcement: Families Could Benefit from Stronger Enforcement Program.* Report to the chairman of the Subcommittee on Federal Services, Post Office and Civil Service. GAO/HEHS-95-24. Washington, D.C.: Government Accounting Office, December.

Veblen, Thorstein. 1908. *The Theory of the Leisure Class: An Economic Study of Institutions.* New York: MacMillan.

Waldinger, Roger. 1996. *Still the Promised City: African Americans and New Immigrants in Post-Industrial New York.* Cambridge, Mass.: Harvard University Press.

Waller, Maureen R. 1997. "Redefining Fatherhood: Paternal Involvement, Masculinity, and Responsibility in the 'Other America.'" Ph.D. diss., Princeton University.

Watson, Bernadine. 1992. *The Young Unwed Fathers Project.* Philadelphia: Public/Private Ventures.

Wilson, William Julius. 1987. *The Truly Disadvantaged: The Inner City, The Underclass, and Public Policy.* Chicago: University of Chicago Press.

——. 1996. *When Work Disappears: The World of the New Urban Poor.* New York: Alfred A. Knopf.

Yalom, Irvin D. 1995. *The Theory and Practice of Group Psychotherapy.* 4th ed. New York: Basic Books.

ABOUT THE AUTHORS

EARL S. JOHNSON is research associate at the Manpower Demonstration Research Corporation, New York and San Francisco.

ANN LEVINE is a freelance writer and editor.

FRED C. DOOLITTLE is vice president and associate director of research at the Manpower Demonstration Research Corporation, New York and San Francisco.

INDEX

Numbers in **boldface** refer to figures and tables.